Java!

Tim Ritchey

New
Riders

New Riders Publishing, Indianapolis, Indiana

Java!

By Tim Ritchey

Published by:
New Riders Publishing
201 W. 103rd Street
Indianapolis, IN 46290 USA

Copyright © 1995 by New Riders Publishing

Printed in the United States of America 1 2 3 4 5 6 7 8 9 0

CIP data available upon request

Warning and Disclaimer

Publisher
Don Fowley

Marketing Manager
Ray Robinson

Acquisitions Manager
Jim LeValley

Managing Editor
Tad Ringo

Product Development Specialist
Julie Fairweather

Development Editor
Suzanne Snyder

Production Editor
Laura Frey

Copy Editors
Cheri Clark, Cliff Shubs

Assistant Marketing Manager
Tamara Apple

Acquisitions Coordinator
Tracy Turgeson

Publisher's Assistant
Karen Opal

Cover Designer
Karen Ruggles

Book Designer
Sandra Schroeder

Production Team Supervisor
Laurie Casey

Illustrator
Jerry Blank

Production Analyst
Angela Bannan, Bobbi Satterfield

Graphic Conversionist
Jason Hand, Clint Lahnen, Laura Robbins

Production Team
Angela Calvert, Kim Cofer, Shawn
MacDonald, Joe Millay, Erika Millen,
Beth Rago, Gina Rexrode, Erich Richter,
Tim Taylor

Indexer
Bront Davis

About the Author

Tim Ritchey recieved his Honors B.S. from Ball State University in Physics and Anthropology and is currently working towards his Ph.D. in Archaeology from Cambridge University, England. He has worked on artificial intelligence, high-performance parallel architectures, and computer vision. His honors thesis was the development of an inexpensive 3D scanner using structured lighting. Present interests include aritificial intelligence, distributed computing, VRML, and, of course, Java. Besides computing and Archaeology, he enjoys scuba diving, flying, and riding his Harley Davidson motorcycle. His Ph.D. thesis includes adapting non-linear dynamics and artificial intelligence techniques to Archaeological theory.

Trademark Acknowledgments

All terms mentioned in this book that are known to be trademarks or service marks have been appropriately capitalized. New Riders Publishing cannot attest to the accuracy of this information. Use of a term in this book should not be regarded as affecting the validity of any trademark or service mark. NetWare is a registered trademark of Novell, Inc.

Dedication

This book is dedicated to Kristin Brannon, for her loving patience through all my crazy ventures.

Acknowledgments

Writing a book takes so much more than putting words to paper, and this book has especially benefited from many people's help. I would like to thank all of the New Riders Publishing staff for their help in getting this book off the ground and out the door. Laura, Suzanne, Julie, Cliff, Jim, Steve, and all of the other production, development, and editorial staff who worked hard on making this an excellent first book experience. Special thanks goes to Ian Sheeler for years of good friendship, and getting me the job. Additionally, I would like to thank Michael O'Connell for his help on the history of Java.

Of course, I wouldn't be where I am now without my family. Thanks to my dad, James, for keeping track of the chapters for me; my mother, Bonnie, for keeping the larder full; my sister, Michelle, for years of challenge; and my brother, Steve, for letting me use his bike as stress relief. Any writing skill I have is due to Mrs. Leslie Ballard, my high school writing teacher—a true mentor.

There are undoubtedly people I have forgotten to mention. To all of those who have helped me along the way so far, a heartfelt thanks. All the errors in this book are, of course, my own.

Contents at a Glance

Table of Contents

6 The Fundamentals—Types, Expressions, and Control Flow 125

7 Getting It Together—Classes, Interfaces, and Packages 163

8 Threads and Exceptions 189

9 The Java and HotJava Class Libraries 209

10 The I/O and Utility Class Libraries 237

11 Using the Browser and AWT Class Library   **261**

12 Java for the Internet   **283**

13 Interfacing with C and Using the Java Tools   **305**

14 Advanced Topics: The Java Virtual Machine   325

Further Information   345

Index   347

Introduction

The Internet has provided millions of people with total connectivity to the rest of the world. In the early computing days, to refer
to a computer meant a large mainframe in some basement that
you would time-share with others using terminals. Because
everyone was in fact using the same machine, sending a message
to a coworker meant that the information only needed to be
shifted *within* the computer to the new location so the recipient
could read it.

However, as computing progressed, individuals were able to have
all the computing power they needed right on their desk. Of
course, this meant that in order to communicate with coworkers,
all of these individual computers would have to be able to communicate with each other. The most popular solution was
Ethernet, developed at Xerox's PARC laboratory in the 1970s.
This form of interconnectedness was mostly between company
computers on a small scale. It was the Internet that made it
possible to link all of those individual computers with the rest of
the world.

The past several years have seen an explosion in the usage of the
Internet. This exponential growth has been mainly attributed to
the advent of the World Wide Web at the European particle

physics research laboratory CERN, and the graphical interface Mosaic, developed at the National Center for Supercomputing Applications in Illinois. Of course, the Internet had been around for some time before this, but it had always been the purview of the Unix guru. The World Wide Web changed all of that. It took arcane commands and plain text screens, and turned them into a graphical, formatted document where pointing and clicking was the main navigational tool. In many ways, it was the first revolution of the Internet, and it totally connected environments.

Welcome to Java!

Welcome to the second revolution of the Internet: Java! Java provides a completely new way to think about distributed computing. Just as when desktop computers freed individuals from depending upon a single mainframe for everyday work, Java frees client computers on the Internet from the dependence upon host computers for the execution of dynamic content. Up to now, everything presented in a Web page was completely static. It had all been developed beforehand. You were essentially bringing up the electronic version of a printed document. However, computers are about dynamic interaction, where the user receives immediate feedback, and the programs actually do things on their own. Java provides this functionality by allowing the execution of code that can be distributed across the Internet in a portable, robust, secure, high-performance environment.

The Purpose of This Book

This book covers three fundamental areas of Java:

➤ The Java layout and architecture

➤ The Java environment

➤ Programming in Java

The Java architecture provides an overview of how Java works, and the basics of the underlying design. It is important to gain a good understanding of how Java implements its features in order to place Java in the right perspective. While Java will be many things to many people, it is just as important to understand what it won't do. Understanding how Java works is important to implementing it effectively. You can do almost anything with Java, but remember that it has both strengths and weaknesses.

The Java environment refers to the programs you can use to run Java programs. For the vast majority of users, this is what they think of when they think of Java. Java is an interpreted language, and therefore needs a run-time system on every computer on which the applications are going to be run. This run-time system, or interpreter, can exist both inside other programs, such as HotJava or a WWW browser, or stand alone. By setting up and using these programs, individuals are able to execute Java programs that exist on Web pages, or are downloaded from an ftp site. Additionally, site administrators need to know how to serve Web content, along with how to set up the run-time environment on client computers.

Of course, Java *is* a programming language, and the majority of this book covers it in this respect. The Java language is similar to C or C++, but is completely new, and optimized for object-oriented, distributed, multithreaded computing. This book covers the basics of programming in the Java language, including classes, multithreading, and the class libraries. While the Java language is fairly fixed, the class libraries and other features can change as the Java environment evolves. For this reason, an emphasis is made on general programming strategies and techniques, rather than any specific programming tasks in Java. If you already know the Java language well and are needing to learn how to program a specific problem, then this book is not for you. However, if you are just learning how to program in Java from C, or you are learning Java as a first language, then this book provides you with the necessary instruction for getting up and running. Once the Java libraries and APIs have been finalized, you will be able to take the information in this book, and apply it to any application development you need.

The Organization of This Book

This book consists of fourteen chapters.

Chapter 1, "The Birth of Interactive Content," covers the history of the Internet itself, where Java fits in, and what Java will do for the Internet.

Chapter 2, "An Introduction to Java," covers the Java language and architecture.

Chapter 3, "Using the Java Environment," covers how to use HotJava and the Java interpreter as an end user.

Chapter 4, "Server Administration for HotJava and Java," covers how to set up Sun's Java release, including the HotJava browser, Java interpreter, Javac compiler, and documentation. Additionally, this chapter covers how to deliver Java content from a Web site.

Chapter 5, "Getting Started on Your Own Java Code," covers the very basics of programming in Java, and presents the infamous first program "Hello, World!"

Chapter 6, "The Fundamentals—Types, Expressions, and Control Flow," covers the grammar of the Java language, and shows the correct syntax for types, expressions, and control flow.

Chapter 7, "Getting It Together—Classes, Interfaces, and Packages," covers how Java implements object-oriented computing, and how to implement it in your own code.

Chapter 8, "Threads and Exceptions," covers how to implement multithreading in your applications, in addition to error detection and handling using exceptions.

Chapter 9, "The Java and HotJava Class Libraries," presents an overview of the class libraries that come with the language, and then covers the language library.

Chapter 10, "The I/O and Utility Class Libraries," covers more of the Java Class Libraries by presenting the input/output and utility packages.

Chapter 11, "Using the Browser and AWT Class Library," covers the graphical windowing classes provided with Java.

Chapter 12, "Java for the Internet," covers the networking classes, along with the different types of Java applications.

Chapter 13, "Interfacing with C and Using the Java Tools," covers how to use C code in a Java application, and presents a reference for all of the utilities provided with the Java release.

Chapter 14, "Advanced Topics: The Java Virtual Machine," covers advanced architecture features of the Java environment.

In addition, there is an appendix at the end with information about finding further information and resources on Java.

Conventions Used in This Book

Before you begin to read this book, you should be aware of several different kinds of print that are used.

➤ `Print that looks like this is program code.`

➤ Print that uses *italics* in programming code indicates that the italicized word is a variable—the actual word varies according to the situation.

➤ Italics are also used to indicate *new words* that are followed by a definition.

In addition to the different types of text used throughout the book, there are several different bullet types that indicate different aspects of Java.

➤ A regular bullet ➤ precedes any text lists that are non-specific.

✓ A method bullet ✓ precedes any text lists that are methods used in Java.

→ A constructor bullet → precedes any text lists that are constructors in Java.

✗ A variable bullet ✗ precedes any text lists that are variables in Java.

Also used in this book are icons that illustrate notes, tips, and warnings. The author made an effort to set these aside for your added information.

A note includes extra information that you will find useful. It complements the discussion rather than being a part of it.

A tip provides quick instructions for getting the most from Java.

A warning cautions you to be aware of certain situations that can arise during a particular step in a process. Make sure you read these carefully.

With these special fonts, bullets, and icons in mind, you will be able to read through this book with less trouble and more productivity.

Before You Begin

I hope you enjoy your tour of Java. I used to be a staunch C++ programmer, and for that matter still am. However, I believe that you will be as impressed as I was with the powerful, and feature-rich environment Java provides for distributed executables on the Internet. The aim of this book is to give you a head start in what looks to be the dominant technology of the Internet for some time to come.

At the same time, Java is a *very* new technology, and is still in its Alpha stage of release. This means that there will constantly be bug fixes, clarification, and updates in the works. By the time you read this, certain elements of the Java language might have changed. The areas that look to have the largest amount of improvement are in the I/O, Utility, Windowing Toolkit, and Networking class libraries. For this reason, an emphasis was placed on general programming, and not on the execution of any specific examples that might be obsolete in a few months. The main changes that might be seen in the Beta are

➤ More advanced windowing and graphical user interface classes for two-dimensional and three-dimensional graphics, including the Virtual Reality Modeling Language (VRML).

➤ Applets will be given the ability to communicate with each other.

➤ There will be classes that provide the ability to create a different look and feel for an object.

➤ There will be a host of new tools for programming in Java and Web authoring.

➤ There are possible ports of compilers for other languages such as Smalltalk, Sheme, and Ada underway, which would run on the Java Virtual Machine—essentially as if they were written and compiled in Java.

➤ There is work going on to define a Java applet API that will define what all browsers should be able to implement, such as the full windowing toolkit, networking, images, and audio. This means if you program to this set of features, all browsers should be able to run your applets.

While most of these changes won't affect the process of writing programs for Java, some of the particulars might change. However, the Java designers, wherever possible, are extending the language, rather than changing it.

The Java language is on the cutting edge of Internet technologies, and it has only just begun. It should be an exciting next couple of years for programmers and Web surfers alike.

Good luck, and smooth programming.

Timothy Ritchey

Chapter 1

The Birth of Interactive Content

The Internet as an information medium has exceeded all expectations. The number of users and Internet hosts increases exponentially, and there doesn't seem to be an end in sight. As telecommunications technology advances, so does our ability to connect electronically to the vast galaxy of information spinning around the Net. However, up to now all of the information stored on computers and shuffled around the Internet has been just that—information—a passive set of ones and zeros, each requiring its own protocol, support mechanisms, and applications for every platform to actually do anything. If you want to tap into all of this information, you are required to learn a complex set of commands, and have half a dozen different programs on your computer at once. E-mail, ftp, telnet, newsgroups, listserves, and HTTP have all grown out of a need to deliver information to the individuals who need or want it.

The World Wide Web and HTTP, the driving forces behind the recent explosion of the Internet, aim to solve many of the previous problems with the Internet by creating a single package that can handle many of the diverse protocols under one roof in a graphical and user friendly environment. Every time a new protocol, operating system, or platform becomes popular, however, developers of Web browsers must rush to make sure it is included in their package before their competitors get hold of it. If you want to look at where Web browsers could be heading, check out the growing number of mainstream applications that take up 20 MB or more of hard disk space due to feature-itis. Of course, software companies can't be blamed entirely—they are attempting to deal with a computer environment where, in order to stay on top, your software must do everything itself, because you certainly can't count on anyone else's being compatible.

There have been many attempts at solving this software crisis, and the solution is generally considered to be object-oriented computing. *Object-oriented computing* is the philosophy that software should act as individual agents, encapsulating a specific function that can be loaded dynamically when needed and otherwise taking care of themselves by either providing dynamic interaction or working in the background supporting the application that called them. There are in fact several different protocols on the market that attempt to provide this kind of service— Microsoft's Object Linking and Embedding (OLE), IBM's System Object Model (SOM), CI Lab's OpenDoc, Novell's AppWare Data Bus (ADB), Taligent's CommonPoint, and NeXT's Portable Distributed Objects (PDO). However, each of these models suffers from one or more deficiencies that make it difficult to implement in a heterogeneous networked environment where the object can exist on a Sun Sparcstation in California, and need to be run on a Pentium workstation in Maine.

Enter the Java language. The Java language provides a truly object-oriented, portable, robust, secure, high-performance, development environment for distributing dynamic content over the Internet. By allowing the same executable to run on any machine that includes the proper interpreter, Java has reduced the number of applications required to be ported to each platform to exactly one. After that, any application or object created in Java runs on any platform for which there exists an interpreter.

In addition, Java—a true programming language—provides the ability for the Internet to no longer be a static medium. Now when you go to your favorite web site, instead of clicking on the same screen of images and text, you can be greeted by running animations or an interactive menu. The information does not have to be passive anymore. Instead of making sure you have the right helper application for a movie file, the movie can have its own application, which can then run itself on your computer. Welcome to the birth of interactive content.

What This Chapter Covers

This chapter will cover the following:

➤ The history of the Internet

➤ Where Java fits into the Internet

➤ How Java will change the future of the Internet and pro-gramming in general.

The Internet is perhaps the most talked about technology at present. Everyone wants to get wired in. This importance has produced a mass of information available for use by those browsing the Internet. Java makes all of this information come alive. Not only does it make the end user's life more interesting, it creates a powerful programming environment for the software and content provider.

After You Finish This Chapter

Once you finish this chapter you should be ready to dive into the world of Java. The following chapters cover the Java architecture. Chapters 3 and 4 cover Java from the user and site administrator's perspective. The last half of the book concentrates on programming in the Java language itself. Once Java has been placed in perspective to the present and future of the Internet, you should be able to appreciate its possibilities as a portable and powerful tool.

History of the Internet

In 1957, the U.S.S.R launched Sputnik. In response, hoping to
catch up on the space race, the U.S. government created ARPA—
the Advanced Research Projects Agency. In 1969, the Department
of Defense commissioned the ARPAnet to be created for research
into networking protocols. Early on, it was realized that this
network of computers would need a standardized protocol, so the
TCP/IP protocol was created to fulfill this need. The TCP/IP
protocol, or Transmission Control Protocol/Internet Protocol was
proposed as a standard in 1973, but in fact was not adopted as a
standard until 1982.

The TCP/IP protocol is actually a collection of protocols that
allow divergent networking platforms to interchange information. In today's computing environment, the standard for routing
network data is ethernet; however, when TCP/IP was developed,
there was no standard for networked computers. The idea of
TCP/IP is a hardware-independent protocol, which is carried
along, on top of whatever hardware-based protocol is being used.

However, it wasn't the standardization of the protocol that
popularized TCP/IP. In 1983 the University of California at
Berkeley released a version of their Unix operating system, which
incorporated the TCP/IP protocol. Unix was running on many of
the computers connected to ARPAnet, and so the included
protocol became the de facto standard for connecting to the
ARPAnet. In 1983 there were 500 Internet hosts. In 1986, the
National Science Foundation entered the fray, by creating
NSFnet, a backbone spanning five supercomputing centers
around the country running at 56 Kbps. By the end of the year,
there were 5,000 Internet hosts. In 1989, with over 100,000 hosts
on the Internet, NSFnet was upgraded to a 1.5 Mbps T1 line. The
next year, ARPAnet ceased to exist. What was once a purely
academic research project was now suddenly the next big thing
on campuses and large corporations.

By 1992 there were over 1,000,000 hosts on the Internet, and it
was just beginning its meteoric rise. It took twenty years for the

original ARPAnet to reach the 1,000,000 mark, and within one year of reaching that mark it was doubled. By the end of 1994, the Internet had over 4,000,000 hosts connected and in 1995, the NSF decommissioned the NSFnet. The role of the government in starting this fledgling technology was over. In March of 1995, the official number of com, or business, addresses passed that of edu, or educational, addresses.

Development of the WWW

When the Internet began, it was widely perceived as an arcane and mysterious network useable only by Unix gurus and the strong willed. In many cases this was true. The protocols and commands were a dizzying array of cryptic codes for sending bits of information this way and that. However, there were attempts at making the Internet more useful, and applications such as e-mail and newsgroups increased the every day use of the Internet by non-technical users in the early eighties. of course, these applications were all passive. The e-mail file was just an electronic version of a letter, and newsgroups were simply electronic bulletin boards. As more and more users began to get onto the Internet, the demand for more and more useful programs grew.

In 1990, Tim Berners-Lee, from the European particle research laboratory CERN developed a protocol for delivering different kinds of files over the Internet using a common protocol. It was the beginning of the World Wide Web. Of course, at that time, the Web still had a text-based interface, and while popular, it didn't become the major force it is today until the National Center for Supercomputing Applications (NCSA) in Illinois, developed a graphical interface for the Web. This interface was known as Mosaic.

Overnight the Web was the golden child of the Internet. It was impossible for Net surfers not to be swept away by its formatted text and fancy graphics—a far cry from what the Internet was just a few years before. The text-based commands were gone, in fact, the command prompts themselves were gone! It was simply point, click, and poof, there it was—like magic. Of course, it wasn't magic. Pretty soon, people were including more than just the GIF images or audio sounds, and once you got away from the files that the browser could handle, you were searching the net for a program that could display the latest BIG THING on your computer platform, only to find out that your platform wasn't supported. Still, it was a world better than what it was before, and browser developers were constantly including more functionality. Even though it was just point and click, you were still the one doing all of the work. The content being provided was still as passive and static as ever—it was just getting easier to make it do what you wanted.

The Java Language

The Java language changes the passive nature of the Internet and World Wide Web by allowing architecturally neutral code to be dynamically loaded and run on a heterogeneous network of machines such as the Internet. Java provides this functionality by incorporating the following features into its architecture. These features make Java the most promising contender for being the major protocol for the Internet in the near future.

> **Portable.** This means that it can run on any machine that has the Java interpreter ported to it. This is an important feature for a language to be used on the Internet where any platform could be sitting at the business end of an ethernet card.

> **Robust.** The features of the language and runtime environment make sure that the code is well behaved. This comes primarily as a result of the push for portability, and the need for solid applications that won't bring down a system when a user stumbles across a home page with a small animation.

> **Secure.** In addition to protecting the client against unintentional attacks, the Java environment must protect it against intentional ones as well. The Internet is all too familiar with trojan horses, viruses, and worms to allow just any application to be downloaded and run.

➤ **Object-oriented.** The language is object-oriented at the foundations of the language, and allows the inheritance and reuse of code both in a static and dynamic fashion.

➤ **Dynamic.** The dynamic nature of Java, which is an extension of its object-oriented design, allows for run-time extensibility.

➤ **High-performance.** The Java language supports several high-performance features such as multithreading, just-in-time compiling, and native code usage.

➤ **Easy.** The language itself could be considered a derivative of C and C++, so it is familiar. At the same time, the environment takes over many of the error prone tasks from the programmer such as pointers and memory management.

The job of providing dynamic content for the Internet is daunting, but the protocol that succeeds will become as universal as e-mail or HTML is today.

Java is Portable

The Java programming language provides portability in several ways. Two of these ways are

➤ The Java language is interpreted. This means that every computer that wants to run it must have a program to convert the Java codes into native machine code.

➤ The Java language does not allow a particular machine to implement different sizes for fundamental types such as integers or bytes.

By executing in an interpreter environment, the Java code does not have to conform to any single hardware platform. The Java compiler that creates the executable programs from source code, compiles for a machine that doesn't exist—the Java Virtual Machine. The Java Virtual Machine is a specification for a hypothetical processor that can run Java code. You can find out more about the Java Virtual Machine in Chapter 14, "Advanced Topics: The Java Virtual Machine." The traditional problem with interpreters has always been their performance, or rather their lack of it. Java attempts to overcome this by compiling to an intermediate stage, converting the source code to bytecode, which can then be efficiently converted into native code for a particular processor.

In addition to specifying a virtual machine code specification to ensure portability, the Java language also make sure that data takes up the same amount of space in all implementations. C programming language types, on the other hand, change depending upon the underlying hardware and operating system. For example, an integer that occupied 16 bits under Windows 3.1, now takes up 32 bits on Windows 95. The same problem exists across processor platforms, where some computers, like the DEC Alpha are 64 bits, while others, such as Intel's 486 are only 32 bits. By creating a single standard for data sizes, Java makes sure that programs are hardware independent.

These features, plus others, make sure that Java is capable of running on any machine for which the interpreter is ported. This way, once a single application has been ported, the developer and user have the benefit of every program running on that platform.

Java is Robust

The Java environment is robust because it gets rid of the traditional problems programmers have with creating solid code. The Java inventors looked at extending C++ to include the functionality required by a distributed program, but soon realized that it would be too problematic. The major problems in making C++ a portable program are its use of pointers to directly address memory locations, and its lack of automatic memory management. These features allow the programmer to write code that is syntactically and semantically correct, and yet still proceeds to crash the system for one reason or another. Java, on the other hand, ensures a robust environment by eliminating pointers and providing automatic memory management.

Because the point of the Java programs is to be able to load and run automatically, it would be unacceptable for there to be a chance that one of those applications might have a bug that could bring down the system by, for example, writing over the operating system's memory space. For this reason, Java does not employ the use of pointers. Memory addresses cannot be dereferenced, and a programmer cannot employ pointer arithmetic to move through memory. Additionally, Java provides for array bounds checking so that a program cannot index address space not allocated to the array.

Java provides automatic memory management in the form of an automatic garbage collector. This garbage collector keeps track of all objects and references to those objects in a Java program. When an object has no more references, the garbage collector tags it for removal. The garbage collector runs as a low priority thread in the background, and clears the object, returning its memory back to the pool either when the program is not using many processor cycles, or there is an immediate need for more memory. By running as a separate thread, the garbage collector can provide the ease of use and robustness of automatic memory management without the overhead of a full-time memory management scheme.

Java is Secure

The necessities of distributed computing demand the highest levels of security for client operating systems. Java provides security through several features of the Java run-time environment.

➤ A bytecode verifier

➤ Run-time memory layout

➤ File access restrictions

When Java code first enters the interpreter, before it even gets a chance to run, it is checked for language compliance. Even though the compiler only generates correct code, the interpreter checks it again just to make sure, because the code could have been intentionally or unintentionally changed between compile time and run time.

The Java interpreter then determines the memory layout for the classes

Note

The *class* is Java's basic execution unit—equivalent to an object in OOP parlance.

This means that hackers cannot imply anything about what the structure of a class might be on the hardware itself and then use that information to forge accesses. Additionally, the class loader places each class loaded from the network in its own memory area.

Even then, the Java interpreter's security checks continue by making sure that classes loaded do not access the file system except in the specific manner they are permitted by the client or user. All together, this makes Java one of the most secure applications for any system. Site administrators are undoubtedly squirming in their seats at the idea of programs automatically loading and running, and the Java team has made every effort to assure administrators that their worst fears, such as an especially effective virus or trojan horse, will never become reality.

Java is Object-Oriented

Java's most important feature is that it is a truly object-oriented language. The Java designers decided to break from any existing language and create one from scratch. While Java has the look and feel of C++, it is in fact a wholly independent language, designed to be object-oriented from the start. This provides several benefits, including the following:

➤ Reusability of code

➤ Extensibility

➤ Dynamic applications

Java provides the fundamental element of object-oriented programming (OOP)—the object—in the class. The class is a collection of variables and methods that encapsulate functionality into a reusable, and dynamically loadable object. This means that once the class has been created it can be used as a template for creating additional classes that provide additional functionality. For example, a programmer might create a class for displaying rectangles on the screen, and then decide that it would be nice to have a filled rectangle. Instead of writing a whole new class, the programmer can simply direct Java to use the old class, with a few extra features. In fact, the programmer can do so without even having the original source code.

Once a class has been created, the Java run-time environment allows for the dynamic loading of classes. This means that existing applications can add functionality by linking in new classes that encapsulate the methods needed. For example, you might be surfing the net, and find a file for which you don't have a helper application. Traditionally, you would be stuck looking for an application that could deal with the file. The Java browser on the other hand, can ask the server with the file for a class that can handle the file, dynamically load it in along with the file, and display the file without ever losing a beat.

Java is High-Performance

Typically the cost of such portability, security, and robustness is the loss of performance. It is unreasonable to believe that interpreted code can run at the same speed as native code; however, Java has a few tricks that reduce the amount of overhead significantly.

➤ Built in multithreading

➤ Efficient bytecodes

➤ Just-in-time compilation

➤ The ability to link in native C methods

One way Java overcomes the performance problems of traditional interpreters is by including built in multithreading capability. It is rare for a program to constantly be using up CPU cycles. Instead, programs must wait for user input, file or network access. These actions leave the processor idle in single-threaded applications. Instead, Java uses this idle time to perform the necessary garbage cleanup and general system maintenance that causes interpreters to slow down many applications

Additionally, the compiled Java bytecodes are very close to machine code, so interpreting them on any specific platform can be very efficient. In cases where the interpreter isn't going to be enough, the programmer has two options: compiling the code at run-time to native code, or linking in native C code. Linking in native C code is the quicker of the two but places additional burden on the programmer, and reduces portability. Compiling at run-time means that code is still portable, but there is an initial delay while the code compiles.

Java is Easy

Finally, the Java language is easy. The Java language is simple and effective because of its well-thought-out design and implementation. The three most important elements that make it an easy language to use are

➤ It is familiar, being fashioned after C++.

➤ It eliminates problematic language elements.

➤ It provides powerful class libraries.

Java is consciously fashioned after the C++ language, providing a look and feel that most programmers are comfortable with. At the same time, Java eliminates difficult and problematic elements of C++ such as pointers and memory management. This means that programmers can spend less time worrying about whether code will run, and more time developing functionality. Java also has a powerful set of class libraries that provide much of the basic functionality needed to develop an application quickly and effectively.

The Future of the Internet

What does Java mean for the future of the Internet? Java is aimed at being the universal standard for the transfer of dynamic, executable content over the Web. This has benefits for the content developer, provider, and end user. Java is much more than a little animated image bobbing up and down on the screen when you link to a page. Its potential applications are quite diverse:

➤ Java could be used to provide stand-alone applications on an as-needed basis, or for upgrading existing applications.

➤ Java can be used as the principle engine for behaviors and interaction in the next version of VRML, the Virtual Reality Modeling Language.

➤ Java could be used to program intelligent agents to comb the Internet for interesting or necessary information.

For the programmer, the Java language provides a single development platform that can be used to construct applications that can be distributed safely and effectively to the entire Internet community. No longer will a project have to port an application to a dozen platforms in order to satisfy every user on the Internet. It is always amazing to see the number and kinds of systems users are clamoring for applications to be ported to. Only the major developers can invest the resources to porting programs to such a wide range of platforms. In this sense, Java will have the most impact on the individual, and small groups of developers who never had the resources before to port applications. Now, they can build for one machine—the Java Virtual Machine, and end up with an application that runs on any number of platforms.

For the provider, the Java language can be implemented on the traditional HTTP servers, allowing it to be served in Web pages like inline images or sound files. However, one of the greatest advantages to Java is the end of scripts for such mundane tasks as image maps or forms. Now all of that functionality can be subsumed by the Java applet. There is no need to link back to an executable on the server to figure out where the mouse was clicked in an image—the Java code can figure it out for itself. This means that site administrators can simply allocate the file space for the HTML files and Java executables. The directory system and CGI scripts will be a thing of the past, moving the interaction with the user where it should be—to the client machine.

For the end user, Java means a seamless integration of data, networking, and interaction. No longer will users need to make sure that they have the right helper file, or application for dealing with a specific protocol. The Java classes can provide the encapsulation of data into objects that can take care of themselves. Future Internet surfers will be able to load up their browsers, which simply consist of the Java interpreter, and a minimum class structure for getting onto the Internet; then automatically load the handlers they need as they cruise the Net. An out-of-date browser that doesn't support a protocol will be a thing of the past, because the browser will be able to update itself as needed.

Providing Applications

Java is more than just a programming language for the World Wide Web. It can create programs that behave in a stand-alone interpreter. These stand-alone programs work just like any other application, and can be used for more traditional computing uses, such as word-processing, spreadsheets, or any other typical application. Java's potential in this role is enormous. Perhaps the best example of how Java could be used would be in the metered use of an application.

There are many applications out there that you might like to have, but decide against because you would not use the program often enough to justify its high price. By using Java, you could connect to the software company over the Internet and download a copy of the program for temporary use. When you were finished with the program, it could connect back up with the software company, indicate how long it had been used, and then remove itself from the system. Instead of paying hundreds of dollars every other year to get the latest application, you could simply rent out the program for a few cents a minute. Additionally, if you already owned a copy of the program, you could download the latest updates and added features that Java could integrate seamlessly, regardless of your hardware platform.

Into the 3rd Dimension - VRML

Of course, Java's most powerful influence will surely be on the Internet. One of the areas it is already influencing is the development of VRML—the Virtual Reality Modeling Language. VRML is a file standard for building 3D worlds for the Internet. When HTML came along, its goal was to create a page metaphor where images, text, and other data were included as they would be in a book. However, this leaves something to be desired. More and more, the Web is being percieved not only as a conduit for information, but rather as a place where people go to interact with others; in other words, cyberspace. VRML is an attempt to extend this cyberspace metaphor all the way. With VRML, users can walk around virtual rooms, pick up virtual books, or flip through virtual card catalogs.

Of course, the goals of VRML demand that the user and environment be able to interact. In VRML's present incarnation (1.0) the resulting scene is a static space—the objects have no behavior. Cyberspace can't do anything for itself. Java is one protocol being considered for providing that interaction. As people download the virtual room into their computers, the Java applets associated with objects in that room would be downloaded. The applets could then start to execute, and give the virtual room a life of its own.

Intelligent Agents

One of the most interesting uses that Java might have in the future is as an intelligent agent. The use of intelligent agents has already begun to infuse software. Applications such as Microsoft's Bob, and MagicCap's Telescript software already attempt to place more and more decision-making and chore-handling features on the shoulders of software. The Internet is the perfect medium for intelligent agents.

Perhaps one of the biggest problems with the Internet is difficulty in finding information. You could use intelligent agents to cruise through the Internet, gathering data that you either sent them out specifically to get, or as a routine service. These intelligent agents would need to leave the confines of your computer, and venture out. They would actually run on diverse systems, moving from database to database attempting to gather the information you need.

Java provides the perfect language for implementing such a system. Because it is dynamically extensible and portable, a Java agent could move from system to system—no matter what underlying hardware platform was being used—link in with a running database, collect data and move on. However, being able to do this is only half the battle. Convincing server administrators to allow wandering agents on their computers is another matter. Java is able to provide a secure environment within which such intelligent agents can run, without risking the security of the host system itself.

Object-Oriented Development

In addition to allowing for the development of many challenging technologies for the Internet, Java has the possibility of making the most challenging aspect of program development much easier—writing the code itself. There are many products out on the market today that implement a "visual" programming environment where the programmer can take objects and manipulate them to create a program. Visual C++, Visual Basic, and NextStep's development environments are good examples of this kind of tool. Java is a programming language easily modified to this purpose. Tools for development are already underway, and should be out shortly that provide the programmer with an easy to use interface for developing Java code by simply pulling in whatever objects they might need. Of course, it will still be necessary to learn how to program in Java, but it will just be much easier.

Summary

As you can see, the possibilities for using Java are endless, and only the future will tell what it will eventually be used for. However, one thing is certain, Java is already gaining widespread acceptance throughout the Internet community. Netscape's plans for supporting Java in its browser is a clear indication that Java can be expected to quickly become widely used and supported. Today many pages on the Internet include Java applets, and Sun's decision to release the Java development tools has spawned the creation of many new applets already. Java is well on its way to becoming the most important technology of the Internet for the next decade. Hopefully this book will provide you with the fundamentals necessary to put you in the driver's seat of this new and exciting technology.

Chapter 2

An Introduction to Java

The Java environment provides the means for distributing dynamic content through applets in hypertext documents, platform independent stand-alone applications, and protocol handlers. With this functionality comes the means to develop the future of the Internet such as intelligent agents, interactive 3D worlds, and self-updating software and multimedia titles.

Java provides this functionality through its object-oriented structure, robust environment, multithreading capability, and ease of use. Because of these features, Java can be employed for creating demanding applications, such as VRML engines and intelligent agents, which will be required for providing the imagined future of the Internet. An understanding of the architecture of the Java environment is the first step in realizing the potential of Java in this future and the wider world of distributed computing.

Quick Review

Up to now, this book has covered Java from a philosophical viewpoint. It has looked at the wider stage of the Internet and distributed computing, and where Java fits into this paradigm. You have seen how the Internet and online services fostered the development of networked applications in both the academic, corporate, and home atmospheres. The culmination of this development has been the distribution of hypertext and 3D documents written in HTML and VRML over the World Wide Web. The introduction of Java brings with it the next stage in the evolution of the Internet.

What This Chapter Covers

This chapter will cover the architecture of the Java environment—providing the basis for understanding how it fits into the wider realm of the Internet, and distributed computing in general. What is presented here is not necessary for using Java, just as understanding HTML isn't necessary for using the Web; however, if you are just curious about Java, or wanting to develop Java content, this chapter provides you with the general structure and terminology needed to make your way around the system. Because the direction in which Java is moving is the same direction the entire industry is taking, what is presented here will also provide you with an idea of the general movements in advanced computing. The following topics are covered in detail in this chapter.

➤ **History.** Java's history pre-dates the World Wide Web itself, Java's most accepted medium.

➤ **Environment.** Java provides the developer with a wide range of tools to help the development process. These include class libraries for browser and stand-alone applications, along with a compiler, interpreter, and browser all developed for the Java Virtual Machine.

➤ **Language.** Java's language, an evolution of the C++ programming language, provides a familiar, object-oriented, feature-rich environment within which stable, robust, high-performance code can be produced.

➤ **Architecture.** Java provides portable, dynamic, multi-threading, secure applications over heterogeneous hardware.

This chapter should give you a good idea of what Java is and isn't, what you can do with Java, and where Java fits in relation to other development and operating environments. Java is in its early stages as a development tool, and like all of computing, is bound to change over its lifetime; however, even as specifics of implementation evolve over time, the fundamental architecture and philosophy of design will remain intact. It makes learning the present and future releases of the Java environment much easier if you begin with a basic understanding of the framework underneath.

After You Finish This Chapter

Once you have completed this chapter you should have a good idea of what Java is, how it works, and what advantages it has over competing technologies. Use this chapter to gain an understanding of how *you* will use the Java technology. You can then approach the later chapters from the standpoint of how they fit into your implementation goals for Java. In the next chapter you will be looking at Java from the point of view of the end user mostly interested in viewing content, and perhaps including a few applets in his or her home page. Following that, the next chapter will discuss Java for the systems administrator and how it will change the role of those providing Web content. The last chapters in the book are for programmers and non-programmers interested in writing their own Java applications. Having gained an understanding of the Java environment and architecture will help guide you through these chapters and on your way to getting the most out of Java.

History of the Java Language

In April, 1991, a small group of Sun employees moved off campus to Sand Hill Road, breaking direct LAN connection and most communication with the parent company. Settling on the name Green for their project, work began on what they considered a move into commercial electronics. In May, 1995, Sun officially announced Java and HotJava at SunWorld '95. Over this four year period, the Green group moved through consumer electronics, PDAs, set-top boxes, and CD-ROMs to emerge as the most likely contender for becoming the ubiquitous language of the Internet in the next decade. What follows is a history of how the Java language came to be.

When the Green group was first envisioned as a foray into selling modern software technology to consumer electronics companies, it was realized early on that a platform-independent development environment would be needed. The public was not interested in what processor was inside their machines, as long as they worked well—developing for a single platform would be suicide. James Gosling began work by attempting to extend the C++ compiler, but soon realized that C++ would need too much work for it to succeed. Gosling proceeded to develop a new language for the Green project—Oak. The name came to Gosling when he saw a tree outside his window as he was entering the directory structure for the new language; however, after failing a trademark search, it would later come to be known as Java.

Originally four elements—Oak, an operating system known as the GreenOS, User Interface, and hardware were put together into a PDA-like device known as *7 (star seven), named for the telephone sequence used to answer any ringing phone from any other in the Sand Hill offices. The small hand-held device was good enough to impress Sun executives, but they were uncertain what the next step should be.

The technology in *7 was at first envisioned by the Green team as a marketable product that could be sold to consumer electronics manufacturers who would place the company logo on the front of boxes, similar to what Dolby Labs had been doing for years. However, in early 1993 the Green team, now incorporated as FirstPerson, Inc., heard that Time-Warner was asking for proposals for set-top box operating systems and video-on-demand technology. These boxes would be used to decode the data stream that entertainment companies would be sending to consumers all over the country for display on television sets.

Ironically, at the same time FirstPerson heard about and began to focus on the set-top box market of interactive television, NCSA Mosaic 1.0, the first graphical Web Browser, was released. Even as the Green technology was being developed for one market—set-top boxes, the field in which it would gain the most acceptance was just getting started itself. The Web had, of course, been around for several years by this time, developed at CERN by Tim Berners-Lee in 1990. However, up to this point it had still retained the text-based interface which reminded people too much of Unix and lingering DOS—a text-based interface that was quickly becoming obsolete in the new graphical user interface environment of software development. NCSA's Mosaic changed the face of the Internet by allowing graphics and text to be merged into a seamless interface from what had been a cryptic and confusing system of protocols and commands.

Java and the Web were both developed at the beginning of the decade, an ocean apart. It would take another three years for the potential of the Web to be realized in Mosaic, and another two years before Java was made available to the wider Internet community.

At the time of Mosaic's release, FirstPerson was bidding on the Time-Warner TV-trial, where hundreds of homes would be fitted out with experimental video-on-demand hardware for testing. In June, 1993 Time-Warner chose Silicon Graphics, Inc. over Sun. By early 1994, after a near deal with 3DO fell through, and no new partners or marketing strategy was forthcoming, First-Person's public launch was canceled. Half of the staff left for Sun Interactive to work on digital video servers, and FirstPerson was dissolved. However, with the remaining staff, work continued at Sun on applying FirstPerson's technology to CD-ROM, online multimedia, and network-based computing.

At the same time that FirstPerson was losing the race for interactive television, the World Wide Web was winning the bandwidth race on the Internet. There was no doubt about it—the Web was big and getting bigger. In September of 1994 after realizing the potential of Oak and the World Wide Web, Naughton and Jonathan Payne finished WebRunner, later to be renamed HotJava. Soon, Arthur Van Hoff, who had joined the Sun team a year before, implemented the Java compiler in Java itself, where Gosling's original compiler had been implemented in C. This showed that Java was a full-featured language, and not merely an oversimplified toy.

On May 23, 1995 the Java Environment was formally announced by Sun at SunWorld '95.

Java took four years, and an evolution of purpose, to make it into the Internet mainstream. With Netscape Communications, maker of the popular Web browser Netscape Navigator, incorporating Java into its software, and 3D standards such as VRML possibly using Java for interactive behavior, along with its potential in future applications such as intelligent agents, it is almost certain that Java is destined to be the most overreaching technology of the Internet in the next decade.

Of course, Java's infusion on the Internet is not the end of the Java mission. Sun sees Java's success on the Internet to be the first step in employing Java in interactive television set-top boxes, hand-held devices, and other consumer electronics products— exactly where Java began four years ago. Its portable nature and robust design allow it to be used for cross platform development, in stringent environments such as consumer electronics.

Main Features of the Java Environment

The Java technology is actually a group of technologies:

➤   The language for developing the code necessary for applications

➤ The architecture for running the applications that have been developed

➤ The tools necessary to build, compile, and run those applications, in combination, which make up Java

The Java language is meant to be object-oriented, familiar, and simple. The Java architecture provides a portable, high-performance, robust run-time environment within which the Java language can be used. In addition, the Java tools give the programmer and end user the programs they need to develop the Java code and classes necessary for providing advanced, dynamic content over heterogeneous networked environments. To understand Java is to understand each of these components and how they fit in relation to all the others.

The Java language is familiar, being derived from C++, simple in using automatic garbage collection and thread synchronization, and object-oriented from the beginning—not a hack of procedural programs to provide object-oriented behavior. As will be discussed presently, Java is an evolution of, but not a direct extension of, C++. It was found early on that extending C++ would not be enough to provide the necessary development environment for distributed computing, therefore Java is a new language in its own right. Even though it is familiar, the new features of the language add simplification to the programmer's job by adding advanced features such as automatic garbage collection and thread synchronization. Also, Java is, from the beginning, object-oriented. This means that the language has thrown away the vestiges of procedural programming in order to create true object-oriented behavior from the foundation. The Java language provides the features necessary for rapid, powerful programming on today's advanced systems.

The Java architecture, or the run-time environment that the language and Java Virtual Machine provide, is portable and architecturally neutral, high-performance with its dynamic, threaded capabilities, and robust with its compile time checking and secure interactions. Java provides an interpreted environment in which architecturally neutral code can be run across a heterogeneous network of machines. This, however, does not preclude Java from being a high-performance environment. On the contrary, Java provides near native code speed, with the added benefit of dynamic linking and threaded execution. In addition, Java provides a robust atmosphere with stringent security features and code verification. The Java architecture provides the framework for high-performance distributed computing across divergent platforms such as the Internet.

The Java tools incorporate the HotJava browser, Java interpreter, and Java compiler along with class libraries to support programming for these environments. The HotJava browser provides the run-time system necessary for running Java code distributed over the World Wide Web. In addition, it provides the necessary framework for additional protocol and content handlers that content developers can build using Java. The Java interpreter is the stand-alone run-time system for Java applications. It can be used for running platform independent code on a variety of machines in a robust, high-performance manner. The Java compiler allows programmers to develop the machine-independent Java byte code necessary for running under the browser and interpreter environments. Java also comes with a substantial list of class libraries for both the browser and interpreter environments, providing the programmer with a host of useful routines from the outset. The Java tools allow content developers to get under way quickly and easily by providing all of the necessary tools for programming quality code.

Features of the Java Language

Gosler realized early on that C++ was not going to be able to take on the role of a truly object-oriented, networked, development language. C++ was developed as an object-oriented patch of C by Bjarne Stroustrup at AT&T Bell Labs in the early 1980s; and, while C++ is perhaps the most powerful language in the modern programmer's tool chest, it undoubtedly has its faults, the least of which is that many popular compilers still don't even support the full functionality of the language. In any event, extending the extension of an extension, as it were, was not going to produce the language that the Green group was looking for in its distributed systems. It was decided that Java, which was then called Oak, would have to be an entirely new language.

To say that Java is a completely new language, however, is somewhat of a misnomer. In fact, Java still retains much of the look and feel of C++. C++ is the dominant programming language today, and making Java much different was going to cost programmers time and headaches in conversion. Maintaining as much of the C++ style as possible was important, but in fact the language is a rewrite from the ground up.

Java is first and foremost an object-oriented language. Although C++ is considered object-oriented, it still allows programmers to write the same way as they have always done—procedurally. Java forces the programmer to accept object orientation from the beginning, eliminating the problem of combining two dissimilar programming philosophies. Of course, in maintaining the look and feel of C++, it is easy to look at Java in terms of what it does and does not have from C++. In many cases, Java eliminates redundancies from C to C++, and any features that smell of procedural programming. What Java added was automatic boundary checking by eliminating the use of pointers and encapsulating arrays in a class structure, and automatic garbage collection, in addition to many other features that made developing in C++ so difficult.

It is in fact the built-in memory management, in addition to the built-in multithreading features, that make Java an ideal language to program in. The C++ language allows programmers to write code at a very low level. This means that they are able to access hardware more efficiently and deal with memory addresses and individual bits efficiently. While this creates very efficient programs, it is at the cost of portability, because each program has to be developed for an individual platform. Java eschewed this philosophy by ensuring that portability could be maintained by providing for all of the bounds checking and memory management. At the same time, Java maintained its respectable performance by adding built-in threading functionality that could perform much of the garbage collection in a background process. In this way, the resulting Java code was assured to be robust and high-performance.

In rewriting Java as a new language, the Green group was able to produce a feature-rich, yet functionally compact specification. Extending C++ would have left much procedural residuals that would only increase the size of an interpreter, and slow down the overall performance, not to mention making portability and robustness nearly impossible. Consider Java a reformed old friend who, after years of dragging along the old procedural habit, awoke clean and fresh as a wholly object-oriented person, devoid of the vestiges of the old ways.

Java's Object-Oriented Features

Java is to the very core an object-oriented program. There is no way of writing a procedural program in Java unless all of your procedural code is carefully hidden behind class encapsulation. It would be difficult to speak of packaged, message passing, dynamic paradigms, and know if advanced Internet protocols or object-oriented computers is meant. Referring to Java this way is a simple way of showing how the two technologies are well suited to each other. By developing Java as an object-oriented language, it automatically becomes a model of the underlying hardware architecture it is supposed to work with. You shall see how encapsulation, inheritance, and dynamic binding are the key elements of object-oriented technology and how Java provides for them.

The fundamental unit in object-oriented computing is, of course, the object—in Java it is called a *class*. A class is a grouping of code that models in software the behavior of objects. The class is that which provides the encapsulation of what was traditionally all of the trappings of procedural programming. The theory behind object-oriented computing is that you live in a world of objects— you are accustomed to dealing with them. When you turn on a light bulb for example, you don't worry about telling the electrons where to go, or how to emit photons from a heated tungsten filament. You simply flip the light switch. In addition, as long as you have paid your electricity bill, you don't worry about the light going out when you leave the room—it takes care of itself (see fig. 2.1). In object-oriented computing, all of these behaviors are modeled in the object.

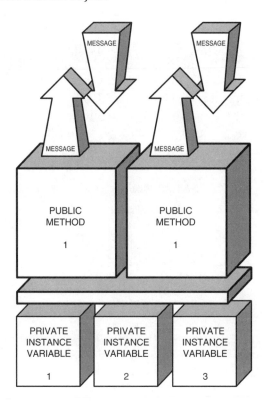

Figure 2.1

A graphical representation of an object.

All objects have a state. In this case, it could be whether the light was on, how much current was flowing through it, perhaps its wattage, and how old it was. All of these values would describe the state of the light bulb. A class has a state also, represented by *instance variables.* These variables are controlled by the class and are inaccessible to any other classes except in special circumstances. You would not be able to change the wattage of a light bulb, so you shouldn't be able to change it in our class. So, how do you use the light bulb? In the parlance of Java, you would use a *method*. Methods are equivalent to functions in procedural programs, except that they belong to the class of which they are members. The method is a small group of code that performs a function you might need more than once. For example, computing the sine of a number. You interact with the class by calling these methods. With the light bulb, you control its state by using the light switch to turn it on and off. In fact, besides removing the bulb from the switch, this is the only way you have of controlling the light bulb—through its method. This is also how object-oriented computing works. You are limited in what you can do to a class by what its methods allow you to do. Table 2.1 compares a real world light bulb with a software equivalent.

Table 2.1 A Java Object Compared with a Real-World Object

Java Class	Light Bulb
Instance Variables	Is light on or off?
	Wattage
	Age
Methods	Light switch

Of course, there are rare situations where programmers will allow direct access to instance variables; however, this is not a recommended practice—it defeats the whole purpose of object-oriented computing.

Exactly what *is* the advantage to writing programs in this way? Imagine your house. How many light bulbs do you have? Was each light bulb made specifically for each socket? No, of course not; however, in procedural programming that is exactly what programmers had to do! Object-oriented programming allows you to use the same code over and over without rewriting. You simply create another *instance* of the object, and use it for what you need. You only have to design it once. The reason you can do this is that you don't need to know *how* it was created or works.

All you need to know is that you use the light switch method to turn it on and off. The object's class does all the rest. In Java, programmers can write classes to do whatever they want, distribute the compiled code, and only tell the users what to do to control the object.

In addition to this reusability feature, the next most important aspect of object-oriented computing is inheritance. Say you are happy with your light bulb, but you wanted to have a red one also, or perhaps you would like to be able to clap your hands to turn it on instead of using the switch. Would you have to rewrite the code from scratch? Not in object-oriented computing. Instead, you would create a new object that *inherited* the properties of your old light bulb. You could then change only those aspects of the light bulb you needed to make it red, or turn on when you clapped your hands. The new class is called a *subclass* of the old class and the old class a *superclass* of the new (see fig. 2.2).

Java implements the object with classes and provides several features for their use. The class can be seen as a template for each instance of an object. In order to create a new instance of a class, you would call its constructor, which is a particular method invoked whenever a new copy of the object is created. When the program is finished with the class, or Java determines that it is no longer being used (if your program ends for example), its finalize method is called in case any cleanup is needed. Of course, a finalize method is not required as in C++ because Java will perform automatic garbage cleanup.

Controlling access to variables and methods is accomplished in Java through access modifiers. Java defines four levels: public, protected, private, and friendly. *Public* methods and variables are accessible by anyone. *Protected* variables are accessible only by methods in that class and any subclasses. *Private* methods are only accessible by that class alone. If none of these are explicitly stated, the *friendly* state is assumed, where any classes in the same package have access to it. The package in Java is a single compilation unit which is a collection of similar classes. This has the advantage of allowing the related objects access to each other, while keeping them private to any classes outside the package.

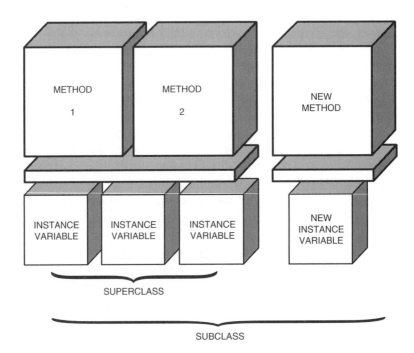

Figure 2.2

Inheritance—Subclass and Superclass.

Much time has been spent discussing the object-oriented structure because it is important to Java. It *is* Java. There is no method
for creating a program without creating a new class. What is
more, any class you create—no matter how rudimentary—is
automatically a subclass of the superclass *Object*. Java runs your
program, whether in the browser or interpreter, by creating an
instance of your class and letting it run. With the programming
burden of object-oriented computing also comes the functionality provided by the superclasses available, such as the Object,
Applet, and Thread classes. The Java class is discussed in more
detail in Chapter 7, "Getting It Together—Classes, Interfaces, and
Packages," but you should be prepared to hear about them
throughout the book.

Changes from C++

As was mentioned previously, Java can be considered a derivative of C++. It was deliberately designed to look and feel like C++. Although this means that C++ programmers will have an easier time converting to the new language, they will also have to drop some old habits. In learning Java, it is the differences that will present the most challenge for programmers. These differences include:

➤ no structures or unions

➤ no #defines

➤ no pointers

➤ no multiple inheritance

➤ no individual functions

➤ no goto

➤ no operator overloading

➤ no automatic coercion

Java has eliminated structures and unions. There are no more #defines or typedefs. In addition, Java uses *interfaces* instead of header files. The role of #define has been subsumed by constants and typedefs. Structures and unions are now the purview of Java's classes. The argument for dropping these features is that C++ was riddled with redundancy—the class subsumes the role of the structure and union, so they are not needed separately. Its attempt to maintain compatibility with C meant that many features were being duplicated throughout the language specification. The use of #define was also considered by the Java development group to encourage difficult-to-read code, despite the fact that is was implemented as a way of clarifying code letter in the development cycle.

Individual functions have been dropped from Java. Instead, any functions you need must now be encapsulated in a class. In the same vein, Java drops multiple inheritance and replaces it with interfaces. The problems with fragile superclasses—a term used to refer to the unstable way in which multiple inherited classes are used in C++—was considered too great. The *interface* in Java is the way in which other classes see what methods a class can implement. Instead of letting out the whole structure of a class in header files, interfaces will only show the methods and final, or constant, variables.

Finally, goto, operator overloading, automatic coercion, and pointers are all gone. The goto statement has been decried in programming for years now, but it somehow hung around for some poor programmer stuck in a bind to fall in love with. Automatic coercions, which were allowed in C++, must now be explicitly called with a *cast* statement. An automatic coercion would allow you to place an incompatible variable into another without explicitly saying you wanted the change. Unwanted loss of precision through automatic coercion is a common error in C++, and Java's creators saw this as a liability. For example, placing a signed 32-bit number into an unsigned number would make all numbers positive.

And, of course, C and C++'s beloved pointer is gone. According to the Java group, pointers are one of the primary features which introduce bugs into programs, and few programmers would disagree. By getting rid of structures and encapsulating arrays as objects, Java has attempted to get rid of the original reasoning behind pointers. Some hard core C/C++ programmers will have a hard time swallowing the lack of pointers. In some ways, learning about pointers was considered a rite of passage for programmers, and if you use them correctly, they are very powerful. If you use them incorrectly, however, you can ensure yourself long nights of debugging code. It is obvious that pointers are a massively weak link in a portable environment, and the Java group made the right decision in eliminating them. By encapsulating the use of pointers into objects, they have made sure that writing for Java will produce robust, efficient code much less prone to difficult bugs, memory leaks, and corruption. Especially in a secure environment, hanging pointers are a disaster waiting to happen.

By building Java from the ground up as an object-oriented language, programmers deal with only one thing—the class. After they have learned how to handle one class, they can handle all classes. In addition, the many features of the Java environment can be encapsulated within classes, providing a rich set of pre-defined classes for use by programmers. With only a few lines of code, programmers can use advanced features of the Java architecture with a greater understanding of the process than many visual programming environments evoke by hiding complex APIs and code generation behind automated tools.

Memory Management and Threads

Perhaps the greatest benefit of the Java language is its automatic memory management and thread controls. In C and C++, memory must be explicitly managed using free, malloc, and a host of other memory management standard libraries. Knowing when to allocate, free, and generally keep track of all your memory usage was difficult. Using threads in C and C++ meant using a class library for all thread control. Although threads still require the use of classes, Java also includes thread synchronization at the language level.

Java has taken over the role of the memory manager. Once an object is created, the Java run-time system keeps track of the object until it is no longer needed by keeping track of all *references* to an object. When Java sees there are no more references to an object, it places it on the stack for garbage collection. To keep performance loss at a minimum but still provide the benefits of automatic garbage collection, Java runs this garbage collection utility as a background process (or low priority thread). In this way, it stays out of the way until there is either a sufficient pause in the execution of foreground threads to run, or the system explicitly requires the use of memory which might be available but is taken up by defunct classes.

The background memory manager is a good example of how multithreading can increase the relative performance in the Java environment. Because of its importance, multithreading has been incorporated at the language level by allowing for thread synchronization. The Java language supports the synchronized modifier for methods, indicating the order in which threads should be run. In addition, threadsafe gives the environment clues about how methods interact with instance variables to make sure that no two threads conflict in trying to modify data.

Java's memory management and thread support are examples of how both a reduction of and a minor addition to the syntax produce a simpler language for the programmer to use. By getting rid of pointers, the use of malloc and free, and incorporating these tasks into the Java environment, the programmer is free to work on the actual programming job, not mundane housekeeping chores which typically occupy the most time in fixing bugs. At the same time, Java can still boast impressive performance for a portable, interpreted system. By balancing the addition of thread synchronization between the language and class level, Java takes advantage of modern operating systems to further boost application performance without overburdening the language or environment with unnecessary elements.

The Java language is fine-tuned for its environment—high-performance distributed computing on heterogeneous systems—essentially the Internet. Although you might not consider desktop systems high-performance, what you now have sitting on your desks is quite an advance compared to even four years ago when Java was conceived. In addition, all of today's modern operating systems include advanced features such as built-in networking, a true multitasking, multithreading capability that was found only in expensive Unix workstations even a few years ago. By providing a familiar, simple, object-oriented language, Java enables the programmer to concentrate on the work at hand, developing advanced content for distribution over a variety of hardware and software platforms.

The Java Architecture

The Java architecture, as was discussed before, provides a portable, robust, high performance environment for development. Java provides portability by compiling bytecodes for the Java Virtual Machine, which are then interpreted on each platform by the run-time environment. Java also provides stringent compile and run-time checking, and automatic memory management in order to ensure solid code. Additionally, strong security features protect systems against ill-behaved programs (whether unintentional or intentional). Java also is a highly dynamic system, able to load code when needed from a machine on a desk across the room or across the continent.

Java's Interpreted Features

When you compile your Java code, the compiler outputs what is known as Java Bytecode. This bytecode is an executable for a specific machine—the Java Virtual Machine—which just happens not to exist, at least in silicon. The Java Virtual Machine executable is then run through an interpreter on the actual hardware which converts the code to the target hardware and executes it. By compiling for the virtual machine, all code is guaranteed to run on any computer that has the interpreter ported to it. In doing so, Java solves many of the portability issues; however, interpreters have never had the tradition of performance thoroughbreds that is needed to survive in today's marketplace. Java had to overcome a large obstacle in making an interpreted architecture endure.

The solution was to compile to an intermediate stage where the file was still portable across different platforms, but close enough to machine code that interpretation would not produce excessive overhead. In addition, by taking advantage of advanced operating system features such as multithreading, much of the interpreter overhead could be pushed into background processes.

The advantage of compiling to bytecodes is that the resulting executable would be machine neutral, but close enough to native code that it could run efficiently on any hardware. In Chapter 14, "Advanced Topics: The Java Virtual Machine," you will look at the virtual machine specification in more detail. For now, imagine the Java interpreter as tricking the Java bytecode file into thinking that it is running on a Java Virtual Machine. In reality, this could be a Sun SPARCstation 20 running Solaris, an Apple/IBM/ Motorola PowerPC running Windows NT, or an Intel P6 running

Windows 95, all of which could be sending Java applets or receiving code through the Internet to any other kind of computer imaginable.

Java's Dynamic Loading Features

By connecting to the Internet, thousands of computers and programs become available to a user. Java is a dynamically extensible system which can incorporate files from the computer's hard drive, a computer on the local area network, or a system across the continent over the Internet. Object-oriented programming and encapsulation mean that a program can bring in the classes it needs to run in a dynamic fashion. As mentioned previously, multiple inheritance in C++, however, can create a situation in which subclasses must be recompiled if their super-class has a method or variable changed.

This recompiling problem arises from the fact that C++ compilers reduce references of class members to numeric values and pre-compute the storage layout of the class. When a superclass has a member variable or function changed, this changes the numeric reference and storage allocation for the class. The only way to allow subclasses to be capable of calling the methods of the superclass is to recompile. Recompilation is a passable solution if you are a developer distributing your program wrapped as a single executable. However, this defeats the idea of object-oriented programming. If you are dynamically linking classes for use in your code (classes which may reside on any computer on the Internet) at run-time, it becomes impossible to ensure that those classes will not change. When they do, your program would no longer function.

Java solves the memory layout problem by deferring symbolic reference resolution to the interpreter at run-time. Instead of creating numeric values for references, the compiler delivers symbolic references to the interpreter. At the same time, determining the memory layout of a class is left until run-time. When the interpreter receives a program, it resolves the symbolic reference and determines the storage scheme for the class. The performance hit is that every time a new name is referenced, the interpreter must perform a lookup at run-time. With the C++ style of compilation, the executable does not have any lookup overhead and can run the code at full speed. However, Java only needs to perform this resolution one time. The interpreter reduces the symbolic reference to a numeric one, allowing the system to run at near native code speed.

The benefit of run-time reference resolution is that it allows updated classes to be used without the concern that they will affect your code. If you are linking in a class from a different system, the owner of the original class can freely update the old class without the worry of it crashing every Java program which referred to it. The designers of Java knew this would be a fundamental requirement if the language were to survive in a distributed systems environment.

Java's Robust Features

The fragile superclass problem is a perfect example of the problems faced in attempting to develop a robust development and run-time environment and the solution which Java implements. In addition to the fragile superclass problem, Java has many other features that provide a reliable environment for running distributed applications, including automatic memory management and strict compile-time and run-time checking. Java attempts to reduce application failure by both stringent checking and the reduction of crash-prone elements of a language.

In addition to solving the problem of the fragile superclass, automatic memory management and the elimination of pointers and unbound arrays create an environment where the programmer is less likely to write bad code in the first place. Most destructive errors occur when a program writes to an incorrect memory address. When a programmer must address memory in C++, he does so by the use of pointers—essentially variables which hold the address of the memory range in use. To address memory, a programmer takes the pointer value, and, using pointer arithmetic (essentially adding or subtracting the number of memory blocks to move), calculates where to move next. Of course, if there are any mistakes in the pointer arithmetic, the pointer can go anywhere, even into essential areas of memory such as the operating system.

Today's modern operating systems are typically protected against such occurrences; programs with runaway pointers, however, are like small children with guns—they are sure to harm themselves and likely anyone around them who hasn't taken cover. Java eliminates the pointer from the programmer's repertoire and encapsulates memory usage into finely tuned, robust classes that provide all the necessary functionality without the difficulty in managing and dangers in using pointers.

Besides eliminating language elements that are dangerous and difficult to use, Java adheres to strict compile time and run-time checking to ensure that all programs adhere to correct syntax and procedure. C++ is also considered a strong type checking language, but its compatibility with C brings along with it situations in which such stringent requirements are not possible. Because Java is a new language, the compiler can check all syntax for errors strictly. This way, a programmer will know about errors before they get a chance to make it into running code.

However, the checking does not stop there. After the program has compiled correctly, the interpreter performs its own type checking to ensure that distribution, dynamic linking, or file corruption has not introduced errors into the code. Instead of assuming the code is correct, the linker makes sure that everything is consistent with the language and each other before execution. This is an important step because an application might pull in fragments from anywhere in the distributed environment. If they were not checked at run-time, there would be no way to ensure that the program would run.

Multithreading

A major element to the Java architecture is its inclusion of multithreading at every level. Multithreading begins at the syntactical level with synchronization modifiers included in the language. At the object level, the class libraries allow the creation of threaded applications by inheriting classes developed for this purpose. Finally, the Java run-time environment uses multithreading in areas such as background garbage collection to speed performance while retaining usability.

Multitasking is when an operating system can run more than one program at a time. Multithreading is when those applications can have more than one thread of execution each at a time. Multitasking would be having both Word and Excel running simultaneously, while multithreading would be having Word spell checking one document and printing another at the same time. The majority of PC systems (both Windows and MacOS), however, are cooperative multitasking, multithreading. Each program or thread must give up control for the others to have a chance—many times the software didn't want to do this. However, preemptive methods allocate each program a certain amount of time with the system, and then pass it on. This ensures that each task or thread gets an equal share of time on the system. Multithreading works because the majority of programs require some amount of input from the user. Because humans are frequently slower than computers, while one task is stalled waiting for some input, other threads can have time to carry out what they need to.

Multitasking and multithreading are probably considered two of the primary benefits in the new wave of operating systems being developed at the time of writing. While preemptive multitasking, multithreading has been around for some time at the workstation level, until recently desktop systems provided little more than cooperative multitasking, and no multithreading solutions.

New PC (and many old workstation) Operating Systems are preemptive—they control programs and give them each a slice of processing time according to their priority. Java takes advantage of this and allows applications written for it to be preemptive multithreading. In fact, programs running in the Java interpreter are automatically multithreading. The background garbage collector runs as a low priority thread, collecting unused memory from finished objects. By providing a multithreading system, Java overcomes many of the inherent difficulties in interpreted environments and provides the developer with the most advanced features available in today's operating systems.

Secure

In addition to these performance, extensibility, and robust features, Java also provides a secure environment in which programs run on distributed systems. Java provides security in three main ways:

➤ By removing pointers and memory allocation at compile time as in C or C++, programmers would be unable to "jump out" of their own area into restricted segments of the system to wreak havoc.

➤ The first stage in the interpreter is a bytecode verifier that tests to make sure that incoming code is proper Java code.

➤ The interpreter provides separate name spaces for each class which is uploaded, ensuring that accidental name references do not occur.

The Java language makes every attempt to assure that violation of security does not occur. Viruses, Trojan Horses, and worms have added many headaches to a network administrator's job. It is tough enough keeping out destructive programs when you can limit executables to deliberately stored files. The thought of automatically executing programs in HTML pages is an administrator's nightmare and a system breaker's dream. Java provides a multilevel system for ensuring that both intentional and unintentional errant programs are caught.

The first line of defense is always prevention. Java prevents many of the security problems in executables by removing the tools necessary—pointers. By providing all memory management, Java ensures that many of the tricks used to gain access to system resources are unavailable. Deferring allocation of memory layout until run-time prevents a programmer from implying how memory will be used and forging pointers to restricted spaces.

However, just because the actual Java compiler checks for these problems doesn't mean someone can't create a compiler that won't. Java overcomes this problem by checking the bytecodes at run-time also. To ensure correctness, Java puts the code through a theorem prover to ensure that the code does not do the following:

➤ Forge pointers

➤ Violate access restrictions

➤ Incorrectly accessed classes

➤ Overflow or underflow operand stack

➤ Use incorrect parameters of bytecode instructions

➤ Use illegal data conversions

After the code has left the bytecode verifier, the interpreter can operate at near-native speeds, ensuring the program will execute in a secure manner without compromising the system.

Java provides a host of security features to ensure that distributed programs to be executed on the system will behave. The idea of dynamic and extensible applications which may come from anywhere on the Internet is a breeding ground for attempts to break systems. If there is a system to break, someone will try. Protecting against this eventuality is of paramount importance, and the Java environment provides just the tools for doing so. The administrator always has the ultimate line of defense in restricting access to his machines from certain protocols—protocols which Java adheres to—but this also defeats the purpose of the Internet to be a completely connected system where information flows freely in all directions.

The Java Tools

Not only does Java provide a feature-rich language and run-time environment, but it provides tools for developing and using Java content for the programmer and end user. For the programmer and end user there are a host of tools available for developing and using Java content.

➤ Java provides extensive class libraries that programmers can use to get their applications up and running quickly.

➤ Java provides the browser environment which can be utilized by the end user to execute dynamic content on their own machines.

➤ Java provides a stand-alone interpreter for running applications outside the Java environment.

➤ The Javac compiler enables programmers to write their own code, linking in predeveloped classes to create applets and handlers for the Internet, along with stand-alone applications for primary development.

By providing these powerful tools to developers and end users, Java comes as a complete package for dynamic content.

The Java Class Libraries are a package of predeveloped code which can be linked in with individual applications. They provide the programmer with a set of robust classes that have been thoroughly tested. Some of the libraries are detailed in table 2.2.

Table 2.2   The Java Class Libraries

Library	Description
Language Foundation	Provides the rudimentary classes for strings and arrays which are part of the basic language structure of Java
Utility	Provides useful utilities such as encoding/decoding, hash tables, vectors, and stacks
I/O	Provides standard input/output, along with file utilities
Browser	Provides utilities for dealing with the HotJava browser
Another Window Toolkit	AWT provides graphical interface tools such as fonts, controls, buttons, and scrollbars
Network	Provides utilities for accessing network utilities by protocols, such as telnet, ftp, and WWW

By using these libraries, users have their own readily accessible copy if an applet or application needs to link in a class, and programmers are able to get started right away on developing useful programs without reinventing the wheel. These classes represent the great potential of object-oriented computing.

The Java browser enables the end user and programmer timely access to the Java applets and handlers being developed. HotJava is the only browser available at the time of writing, but several could be out by the time you read this. The browser environment is a minimalist system where Java handlers dynamically provide the ability to deal with diverse data streams, freeing the users from the burden of providing a helper application for every file they want to get off the Internet.

The Java interpreter provides the environment needed to run stand-alone applications on different systems. It enables developers to produce applications which have nothing to do with the Internet, and yet which prosper in a portable environment. Today's users demand portability. They expect the same programs to work no matter what platform they use. Java provides this portability while maintaining ease-of-use and high-performance.

Finally, the Javac compiler enables developers to compile for the Java Virtual Machine, providing applications which will run on any system for which the browser or interpreter have been ported. This frees the developer from worrying about portability issues at all, and lets him or her concentrate on creating the best application possible.

Summary

The Java environment is a threefold set of specifications and tools that allow developers to produce dynamic, portable, and high-performance programs as easily as possible, while giving the end user and administrator a secure, robust run-time environment in which these applications can be run. Java provides an object-oriented, familiar, easy-to-use language within which applications can be developed. The Java architecture incorporates modern features and is tuned to distributed, heterogeneous platforms. The Java tools enable programmers and end users the flexibility to produce and use the content which will shape the Internet in the next decade.

The next chapters expand upon the user side of Java. Exploring the uses of the interpreter and browser programs will be the first step. You will be able to look at how programs are run, and how they perform on your system. Next, you will look at Java from the site administrator's viewpoint. Ensuring that both the client and server side are ready for Java is important in making sure that a transition to these new technologies is as smooth as possible. After looking at the user side, you will begin looking at developing for Java. You will begin slowly, looking at the language element, then object-orientation, and finally class libraries and the virtual machine.

You should by now have a grasp of how Java works and fits into today's computing environment. Java is a powerful and feature-rich specification that attempts to overcome the many hurdles in the way of distributed, object-oriented computing. Java has attained the portability, security, and robustness necessary, while keeping the language easy-to-use and at a high-performance level. Java, from its beginning more than four years ago in consumer electronics, is a powerful tool which foresaw many of the advancements of computing in recent years. Object-oriented, dynamically extensible, multithreading, and robust—Java fits in well with the emerging realities of the Internet and personal computing systems.

Chapter 3

Using the Java Environment

To an end user, the Java environment provides the functionality, diversity, and performance which is necessary for creating portable, executable content. These features are furnished by the Java interpreter, the HotJava browser, and the dynamic content delivered by the Java applets themselves. The Java interpreter provides the stand-alone run-time environment needed for Java applications to run on a host of diverse platforms, allowing developers to create a single product and focus less on porting and more on creative issues. The HotJava browser is another implementation of the Java run-time environment, executing portable, extensible content for the Internet. Java gives the World Wide Web the capability to include active content in the form of applets and the distribution of new data types through protocol and content handlers.

Quick Review

Up to now, Java has been covered from a philosophical and architectural viewpoint. The first chapter covered the philosophy of Java and distributed computing in general. It was particularly focused on how the Java environment fits into the panoply of the

Internet. Although discussions of what might be possible in the future stimulate growth, the future cannot happen without concrete technology to support it. The second chapter looked at how Java attempts to provide the technology needed for this future in its design. It is the convergence of imagination and technology that pushes the highly networked world envisioned for tomorrow into today.

The Internet and the wider world of distributed computing is promising powerful tools with complete connectivity. This promise of networked computers, pagers, PDAs, set-top boxes, telephones, and so on is that such connectivity will give us the freedom to explore and gather information as never before. Whether this connectivity, touted by Bill Gates of Microsoft as "information at your fingertips" will become a reality is based solely on the capability of these divergent technologies to come together under a single standard.

Java has the capability to become that standard. Certainly its adoption on the Internet—a conflagration of divergent protocols and hardware—is a perfect example of how it can cut across these heterogeneous platforms to provide dynamic and powerful distributed computing. It is propitious that at the same time that Java is being picked up by the World Wide Web, almost all online services are rushing to connect to the Internet. Originally, the Internet was the domain of educational and government research institutions. In March, 1995, the number of Internet sites with COM extensions officially surpassed the number with EDU extensions. The COM extension is given to companies, while the EDU extension is given to educational institutions. The final stages in the explosive takeover by commercialization of what was once the purview of academics is almost complete. At the same time, Java makes its grand entrance at SunWorld '95.

Java provides the capability to distribute the dynamic content that the emerging users of the Internet will want by allowing portable code to be loaded and executed on any machine. People will soon tire of the static Home Pages of the Web, demanding what they can get through TV and interactive multimedia. At the same time, the public doesn't care about what hardware they happen to be using, as long as it works, and works all the time. There are several dozen different hardware platforms used on the Internet itself. Providing robust, dynamic content for each of these different platforms not only demands extensibility, but portability, both of which Java can provide.

What This Chapter Covers

Java's immediate presence in distributed computing will not occur in commercial electronics for some time, but it will quickly be seen as the end-user technology for viewing new media being distributed over the Web, primarily through browsers and, to a lesser extent, the stand-alone interpreter. The purpose of this chapter is to familiarize the reader with the end user tools of Java.

This chapter also covers the following:

➤ How to obtain the latest Java release, set it up on a system, and run the different executables used in this chapter.

➤ The Java stand-alone interpreter, and how it can be utilized by the end user. Although stand-alone execution will not be the primary use for Java in the beginning, as developers begin to appreciate the portable nature of the Java language, more and more utilities, shareware, and more substantial applications will be written and distributed over the Internet.

➤ Fundamentals of using the HotJava browser, both as a web server and Java interpreter, are covered because they are integrated into the same package. The HotJava browser will be the first point of contact for most people with Java. In fact, most won't even know the difference because it will become integrated into the major browsers, including the next major release of Netscape.

➤ The rudiments of including Java content on a personal home page for others to see is covered last. This section is mostly for the use of those wanting to include other's applets which have already been written. A more in-depth look at providing Java content is covered in Chapter 4, and the ultimate, writing your own Java programs, is the focus of the majority of this book.

After You Finish This Chapter

After you finish this chapter, you should be familiar with using the Java interpreter and HotJava browser, and with the process of including Java applets in your home pages. This familiarity will provide you with a springboard for using the Java programs on a regular basis, both as you explore the Internet and begin to work through the more advanced chapters in this book. Don't be too worried about memorizing all of the methods presented here because they're raised in the subsequent chapters, as well. None of the material is too complicated, and if you have any experience with Web Browsers and creating HTML pages, this chapter will already be very familiar.

In the next chapter, we will cover Java from the point of view of a systems administrator, looking at how to set up the system and software. You will explore methods of setting up Java for both client and server side distribution and see how to include Java content in Web pages. After Chapter 4, you will move straight into programming in the Java language. You will first learn the fundamentals of the language, then move on to classes, threads, exceptions, class libraries, and the differences between applets, stand-alone applications, and handlers. The last chapter covers more advanced topics about the run-time environment and Java Virtual Machine.

But first, we must get the Java environment running on a system.

Getting the Software and Setting It Up On Your System

To run Java programs, you must have the Java Run-time systems installed on your platform. These include the Java interpreter and

HotJava browser. See Chapter 4, "Server Administration for HotJava and Java," for how to install Java on a client system.

In addition to the Java programs, you will need to have a TCP/IP connection to the Internet in order to take advantage of some of Java's features, specifically the Web browsing features of HotJava. You can still use the interpreter and browser for viewing Java programs you have on your system, but you won't be able to bring up other Web pages from the Internet. Most likely, you already have Internet connectivity, but if you don't you should note the following: Windows NT and Sun SparcStations have built in TCP/IP connectivity, but setting up a connection will be different for each situation. If you are on a network, check with your system administrator about gaining Internet Access. If you are wanting to use it from home over a modem, check with your local service provider for how to get connected.

Using Stand-Alone Applications with the Interpreter

After you have completed installing the Java components onto your system, you should be ready to run the Java interpreter. The Java interpreter is used to execute stand-alone Java applications. By compiling applications for Java, programmers know that their programs will be able to run on any system for which the Java interpreter has been ported. This gives them the flexibility to worry about the content of their applications, rather than specific implementations for all the different platforms they want for it to run on.

You have undoubtedly experienced the problem of trying to find a specific utility or application on the Internet. You can usually find a program to do what you want, but it often might be for the wrong system. With Java, a developer can write a single program and automatically gain the full compatibility for all platforms that Java provides. As long as there is an interpreter for the platform, you can use it.

The command for running the interpreter is as follows:

```
C:\> java classname
```

When the Java compiler produces the bytecode file, it appends the extension CLASS to the original file name. When you run the Java interpreter, you only need to provide it with the class name, not the whole file name. In other words, drop the class extension when running a program.

On the disk are several stand-alone applications which can be used with the Java interpreter. Change to the /applications/HelloWorldApp directory on the disk and run the HelloWorldApp class. You do so by entering:

```
C:\> java HelloWorldApp
```

You should see the output of the HelloWorld class just under the command line (see fig. 3.1).

Figure 3.1

Running the stand-alone HelloWorld application.

There are several other stand-alone applications on the disk, which are covered in the programming sections in later chapters. You can run any of the classes if you want to get a better handle on using the Java interpreter. Otherwise, you have run your very first Java application—that is all there is to it!

Note that the command is not `C:\> java HelloWorldApp.class`. Simply drop the extension from the file name. You should also see file names with a JAVA extension. These are the source code files for the compiler and are to be covered in the sections on programming in Java.

The Java interpreter also accepts a host of command line options, which are covered in the "Tools" section of Chapter 13, "Interfacing With C and Using the Java Tools." For now, the following list suffices to allow you to run programs. A formal presentation of the java command line is

```
java [ options ] classname <args>
```

Some of the options are listed in table 3.1. The arguments (args) are passed onto the class when it executes.

Table 3.1   Java Command Line Options

Command	Purpose
-cs, -checksource	Looks at the Java source file to ensure it hasn't been modified since the last compile. If the source is newer, the interpreter recompiles the code and loads the renewed class. It only works if the source code is available.
-classpath	Tells the interpreter where to look for the class file. The format is -classpath .:path[:optional paths]. Each new path is separated by a colon. This option overrides the CLASSPATH environment variable.
-v, -verbose	Causes Java to print a message every time a class is loaded.
-verbosegc	Prints a message anytime the automatic garbage collection feature of the Java interpreter frees memory.
-verify	Runs the verifier on all code, regardless of where it came from.
-verifyremote (default)	This option runs the verifier on all code that is loaded into the system by the class loader.

continues

Table 3.1 Continued

Command	Purpose
-noverify	Causes the interpreter to ignore verification of any code. This could be used if you were only running code that you knew was safe.
CLASSPATH	This is not a command line option, but rather an environment variable which you can set to tell Java where your classes are. It uses the same parameter as the -classpath option: `.:path[:optional paths]` If this variable is not set correctly and you try to import a class from outside the default settings, Java gives an error, saying the class has violated access restrictions.

Note

If you are using options regularly, you can save time typing by creating a batch file for Java. To do so, open your favorite editor and type in the command options you want to use following Java. Where you would normally enter the class name and command line arguments, place %1, %2, and up to %9. For example:

```
java -verbose -verbosegc -verify %1 %2 %3 %4 %5 %6 %7 %8 %9
```

Save the file under a name which would identify it to you, with the BAT extension (that is, javav.bat). Place the file in your /hotjava/bin directory. To run the batch file, enter your new name plus the class name and any arguments you want sent to the class. In order to run a class *classname* with *arguments* you could enter:

```
javav classname arguments
```

The %n's will enable you to enter up to eight command line arguments to be sent to the class, in addition to the class name itself.

You can now use the Java interpreter to run any program that you find on the Internet in Java, knowing that it will be running in a secure, robust environment. When developers begin to use Java regularly, you can expect new utilities and shareware programs to automatically work on your system. It will save you time in finding, and peace of mind in using, new programs from the Internet.

Using HotJava

Of course, where Java aims to become entrenched first is in the World Wide Web browser arena. Soon after Sun announced Java, Netscape, the most popular developer of WWW browsers, announced an agreement with Sun to license the Java run-time system for their own browser, Netscape Navigator. By the end of 1995, there should be at least two, if not more, browsers with built-in Java functionality, one of them, by some reports, with more than 70 percent of the browser market.

At the time of writing however, there is only a single browser available—HotJava. The version of HotJava that is discussed is the Alpha 2 Release. An Alpha 3 Release for Sun workstations exists, but because there are only minor differences, the least common denominator, Release 2, is covered.

By the time you read this, the Beta version of Java might have already been released. Check out the section on Further Information at the back of the book for where you can find out about the most recent release.

Note

The HotJava Architecture

As users became more and more accustomed to advanced features in their programs, software makers were forced to add more and more functionality, many times repeating each others' work for the sake of a spelling checker or inline Jpeg display. Several platform-specific solutions are being tried, including Microsoft's OLE and Apple/IBM's OpenDoc. However, Java provides a much more portable and easier to use programming interface for distributed objects. Before Java, a Web browser had to include all the networking and display functions it would need or assume that the user had helper applications needed to view content the browser couldn't. This meant supplying functionality for HTML, SMTP, GIF, JPEG, FTP, GOPHER, NNTP, URL, and a host of other content and protocol types if you wanted to be able to provide a decent browser (see fig 3.2).

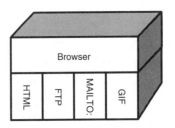

Figure 3.2

The traditional browser architecture.

The HotJava browser breaks from traditional browsers and, in fact, from the general movement of applications in the last few years. Java can provide the functionality needed dynamically, allowing the actual browser to be much smaller. This means that you no longer have to worry about your browser supporting the next great feature on the Web, or trying to find and link in a helper application for the specific file you want to view. It can automatically download the handler necessary and deal with it inside the browser as the new file type is called from the Web. More importantly, developers of browsers no longer have to repeat each others' work by including all the functionality themselves. They can take advantage of Java's extensibility to expand the capabilities of their program (see fig 3.3).

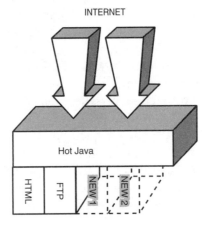

Figure 3.3

The Java architecture for browser functionality.

The HotJava browser is the first browser to incorporate the Java Run-Time system in its design. Although other browsers that include Java functionality will soon be on the market, through the incorporation of the Java technology in a World Wide Web browser, it is important to look at this first attempt at bringing to fruition the promise of object-oriented technology on the Web.

Getting Started

Of course, the first step in using the HotJava functionality is using the program, so you will first look at running the browser, bringing up URLs, and viewing Java applets. In the last section, how to include an existing Java applet in your own Web pages is briefly covered.

You can run the HotJava browser in two ways. From the command line, you can issue:

```
C:\> hotjava
```

Or, if you have created a program item, click on the HotJava icon. You are greeted by the screen shown in figure 3.4.

The Welcome page is an HTML document which presents you with several options for getting more information. All of these links, except for *Latest Info*, are local documents on your hard drive.

If this is the first time you have run HotJava, you are presented with a dialog box about security. See the section on the menu bar, under options, for information about this dialog box. After you complete the questions, you proceed to the Welcome page.

You should start with the README file, which provides you with information on your specific release of the HotJava browser. Make sure to read it to find out about your version, since there will constantly be updates and added features as Java develops, and the release you have may be later than those mentioned in this book.

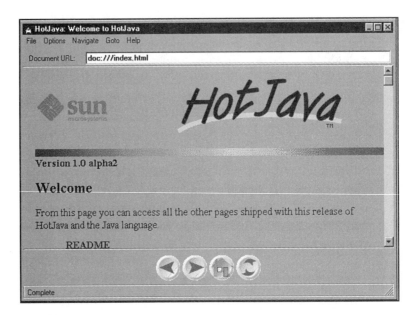

Figure 3.4
Welcome to HotJava.

The next link, *HotJava: A White Paper,* is a document on the HotJava browser itself, giving you an overview of the Java technology and how it is implemented in HotJava. In addition, *The Java Language: A White Paper* provides information on the Java language itself and how it can be used by developers to begin rapid production on disparate platforms.

Cool HotJava Demos is next. This link takes you to a page of included HTML pages which have examples of what you can do with the Java programming language and HotJava. Take time to run through the different demos. They are self explanatory and run automatically. This is the main advantage of Java—you don't actually have to do anything to benefit from Java's technology. As long as your browser supports Java, the pages and applets take care of themselves.

The *Documentation* link provides all kinds of information on using HotJava and the Java language. It includes release information, overviews of the technology, a guide to writing applets, man pages (Unix help files), and reference material to the language, run-time environment, and APIs.

The next link, *Latest Info*, is the only link on this page that requires a TCP/IP connection. Latest Info takes you to the HotJava homepage at java.sun.com. You should be sure to use this link for checking out the absolutely latest information, especially if you received your release from anywhere other than the java.sun.com server itself. You will also find here links to more cool applets, both on their server and across the web. This is the perfect place to start browsing the Web for Java enabled pages and to see what people have been doing with it.

The rest of the selections, *Copyrights and Licensing* and *Meet the People*, include information on the legal uses of the binary and source code for the Java environment. Be sure to read this section to ensure that you are complying with the software license agreement. Finally, you can meet the individuals on the team who brought you Java.

Although HotJava is like any other WWW browser, this book still covers the controls and menus it includes. A note of caution here: Your version may be later and undoubtedly will include more functionality that the Alpha release 2. Be sure to read the README and Documentation for your specific version.

A First Look at HotJava

There are five areas of the HotJava program that should be noted. First, is the menu bar. This provides the basic controls of the HotJava environment. Under the Menu bar is the Document URL entry, which displays the current location and enables you to enter a new URL. Next, the display area occupies the largest area, which is where the documents are displayed and applets run. Anything in this window it a product of the HTML pages you are visiting. Under the display window is the toolbar. The toolbar provides buttons for navigation and URL reload. The last portion of the application is the status line which provides information on what HotJava is doing.

The Menu Bar

The Menu bar consists of the following five options:

➤ File

➤ Options

➤ Navigate

➤ Goto

➤ Help

The following sections describe each of these options and their menu selections in detail.

File

➤ **Open.** This command enables you to enter a URL for loading. You can also type this information into the Document URL field and press Enter.

➤ Reload. This command reloads the current page from the source. It's useful if the original file has changed for some reason.

➤ **Print.** Invokes the standard Print dialog box. This command is disabled in the Alpha2 release.

➤ **View Source.** This allows you to view and save the raw HTML file of the current document.

➤ **Quit.** Exits HotJava.

The New, Save, Save As, and Close commands are disabled in the Alpha2 release.

Options

➤ **Security.** Presents the dialog box shown in figure 3.5.

The HotJava Security dialog box enables the user to set the desired level of security. If you click on Apply when the dialog box first appears, you will have a safe environment within which to run applets. Read the Security section in Chapter 4 for configuring the security of your browser and talk with your system administrator about how he or she wants Java used on the network.

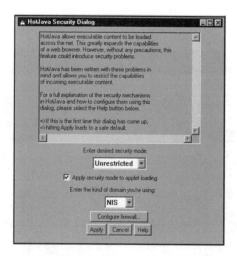

Figure 3.5
The HotJava Security dialog box.

> ➤ **Properties.** Brings up the HotJava Preferences dialog box (see fig. 3.6).

The Firewall, FTP, and Caching Proxies are used as buffers between your computer and the Internet. The purpose of the Firewall proxy is to restrict access to the computers behind the firewall. The FTP and Caching Proxies are for grabbing recently used sites. When you send a command to the Internet, the proxy issues it for you and sends the result to you, while at the same time caching the result. Say you want to view the java.sun.com Web page, for example. If you have a proxy set up, the browser would send the command to the proxy, which would then attempt to retrieve the document. After it has received the document, it sends it to you for viewing, and caches it. Then, next time someone wants to view the same document, the proxy will be able to send it from its own cache, instead of having to download it from the Internet again.

Check with your system administrator about Proxies in your area and whether your site is using a firewall.

The Read and Write paths tell HotJava where to look for its configuration files and where to send its output. Be sure the read and write paths point to valid paths.

Underline anchors, Delay image loading, and Delay applet loading tell HotJava how to display the documents. Simply mark or unmark the boxes with your preference.

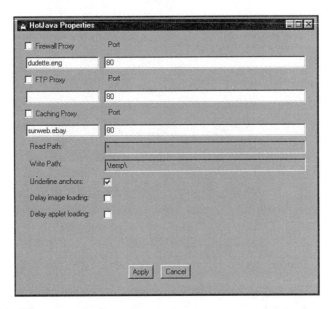

Figure 3.6
The HotJava Preferences dialog box.

➤ **Flush Cache.** Enables you to clear HotJava's personal cache. HotJava keeps recently downloaded files much like other browsers to speed drawing when you return to them. If you flush the cache, HotJava empties the cache, causing it to reload the pages from their source when you return to them.

➤ **Progress Monitor.** In the Alpha3 release for Solaris, there is an experimental progress monitor that tracks how far along the loading of documents is.

Navigate

➤ **Forward.** Moves you forward one URL in your current session if you have moved back.

➤ **Back.** Moves you back one URL in your current session, moving to links you previously visited. If you get somewhere, and you can't remember how, using the Back command will take you through your steps.

➤ **Home.** Takes you to the HotJava Welcome screen, or whatever HOMEpage you have set for Hot Java. You can change the homepage by setting the WWW_HOME environment variable to the URL you wish to use.

➤ **History.** shows you a list of all the Web pages you have visited.

➤ **Add Current to Hotlist.** Adds the present page to the Hotlist.

➤ **Show Hotlist.** Shows you a list of all pages you have included in your Hotlist for easy retrieval of URLs.

Goto

➤ **Add Current.** The same command as Add Current to Hotlist, except it adds the URL under the Goto menu item.

➤ **Hotlist.** The rest of the menu items under Goto are URLs selected with the Add Current command.

Help

➤ **HotJava Help Topics.** The list of help topics will take you to the respective documentation.

➤ **Search HotJava Documentation.** This command displays a dialog box to search through the HotJava documents for a particular topic.

The Display Window

The display window is where HotJava presents the HTML documents and runs the Java applets. HotJava works just like any other Web browser, so there is nothing new to using it this way. There are several new icons which appear that have to do with Java applets. These are defined in table 3.2.

Table 3.2   Applet Icons and What They Mean

Icon	Meaning
Raised Gray Box	The Image or Applet is still loading.
Yellow Box	Delayed Image Loading has been selected. Click on the box to load the image.
Yellow Box With Arrow	Delayed Image Loading has been selected, and the Image is a link to another page. Click on the arrow to load the link, or the rest of the box to load the image.
Orange Box	Delayed Applet Loading. Click on the box to load the Applet.
Red Box	An Error occurred when trying to load an image or applet. Make sure the file requested is available to the browser.
Red Box With Arrow	A delayed image with a link has failed to load. Make sure the browser has the capability to load the file.

In addition to the new applet icons, HotJava supports many of the newer Netscape extensions, including all IMG tags, except for LEFT and RIGHT justification. HotJava also handles URLs, such as the following:

➤ **News:** The news protocol enables you to read newsgroup articles with HotJava. Make sure your NNTPSERVER environment variable is set to your news server.

➤ **ftp:** This command enables you to browse FTP URLs.

➤ **Mailto:** The mailto protocol enables you to send mail with HotJava. You can either simply use the mailto command to bring up the mail dialog box or include the mailto:subject/

name.address option. The Composing Mail Message dialog box appears (see fig. 3.7).

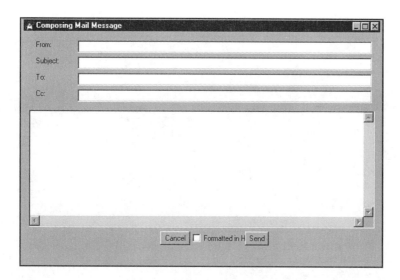

Figure 3.7

The Composing Mail Message dialog box.

The To and Subject fields will be entered if you specify them in the Document URL line; otherwise, fill in your e-mail address in To, the subject, the recipient's e-mail address, and, in Cc, the addresses of people to whom carbon copies should be sent. The Formatted in HTML check box at the bottom automatically formats the document into proper HTML.

HotJava can natively handle several protocols, in addition to its capability to extensibly add protocols by importing new handler classes. In essence, HotJava as a browser would never become obsolete.

The Toolbar

The toolbar below the display window (see fig. 3.8) enables you to select certain HotJava navigation commands. The arrows move you forward and back one link in the current session. The house takes you to the homepage, and the dual arrow button reloads the present page. The Solaris Alpha3 release also includes a stop button to halt the loading of a URL in progress.

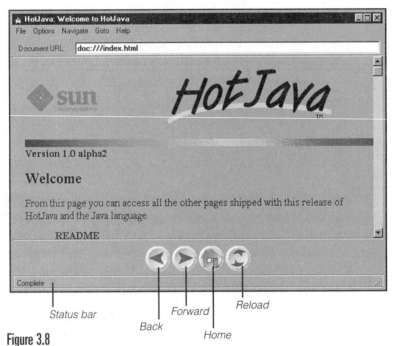

Figure 3.8

The HotJava toolbar.

The Status Bar

Along the bottom of the application is the status bar. When you run your mouse button over links in a document, HotJava displays in the status bar where the link is pointing. In addition, any errors which come up are reported here.

HotJava, whether the Sun or NT version, follows the standard user interface specifications for their respective platforms. The command bars at the top of the application behave like any other Solaris or Windows NT program. You should check out the documentation with the release you have for additional features.

Providing Applets

There is one last topic to cover—providing your own content. If you want to include Java applets in your own HTML documents, there are a few simple steps you should follow.

First, in whatever directory you are placing your HTML file, create a subdirectory called classes. Figure 3.9 gives an example directory structure for an HTML document.

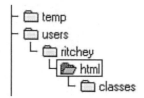

Figure 3.9
The HTML directory structure.

Make sure that the directory structure is available to those browsing your web site. Talk with your system administrator to find out where to place these directories.

Next, you must create your HTML file and include the Java <APP> directive. The <APP> directive works like any other HTML directive, and tells the browser to format the included information in a specific way. The <APP> directive tells a Java equiped browser to load the executable designated by the CLASS attribute and run it. Whatever Java applet you want to include, the bytecode file ends with the extension .class. Place this file into the class' subdirectory. Wherever you want the Applet to appear, place the following command:

```
<APP CLASS="classname">
```

As with the Java interpreter, be sure to leave off the .class extension. That is all there is to it! You will now have a Java applet in your Web Page. The HelloWorld applet document in the applets/ HelloWorld directory on the book's disk looks like the following:

```
<HTML>
<HEAD>
<TITLE>Hello, World!</TITLE>
</HEAD>
<BODY>
Say Hi to Everyone:

<APP CLASS="HelloWorld">
</BODY>
</HTML>
```

Try using some of the applets included on the disk under the /applets directory. Move them into your own classes directory and see how they look in your pages, or bring up the HTML files directly on the disk.

The <APP> directive has several options which configure how HotJava and other browsers will display the applet.

```
<APP CLASS="classname"
     SRC="URL"
     ALIGN=alignment
     WIDTH=width
     HEIGHT=height
     //optional applet values
>
```

CLASS is the only necessary attribute for the <APP> tag; the others are all optional.

The CLASS attribute holds the name of the class you wish to load. Note that it does not include the class extension. The SRC attribute tells HotJava where to look for the class file to load. If there is no path given, HotJava looks in the /classes/ subdirectory of the directory the HTML file was read from. If you are specifying a path, make sure it is in the CLASSPATH directory or available for downloading by the HTTP server. The align attribute tells HotJava how to place text on the same line as the applet. The options are TOP, MIDDLE, and BOTTOM.

TOP aligns the text with the top of the applet. MIDDLE centers the text, and BOTTOM aligns the text with the lower edge of the applet. The WIDTH and HEIGHT specifiers tell HotJava how much space to give the applet. HotJava can use these to layout the page before an applet is finished loading. If these attributes are not given, the loading of the applet can alter the layout of the page. In addition, the applet programmer may have additional attributes they want to use. Read the documentation that should come with every applet to find out exactly what attributes they require. Generally, these are placed in quotation marks.

Summary

This chapter covered the basics of using the Java environment as an end user, getting the files, setting them up on a system, running the interpreter, browser, and including applets in your own HTML pages. Hopefully this gets you started in using the Java environment.

You have undoubtedly noticed by now the early nature of the Java programs. For the end user, there is still much development to be done to provide the top class tools Internet users are accustomed to. With the entrance of Netscape and the continued work of Sun toward the development of Web browsers, Java content will be seamlessly integrated into the present Web system. Sun's purpose for the Alpha releases is to provide the developer and user time to begin creating content for these forthcoming browsers. If content is to be provided, however, then site administrators will have to prepare their system for serving such content. The next chapter deals with this topic in detail, especially in terms of site security for the client and server.

After you have looked at the administration of Java content, you will begin looking at Java as a development environment. The rest of the book focuses on this topic by covering not only the language specification, but the class libraries and environment with which feature-rich Java programs can be developed. By the end, you should be able to create your own Java programs, including stand-alone applications, applets, and handlers.

Chapter 4

Server Administration for HotJava and Java

Serving Java content adds a new challenge to site administrators' jobs. Not only do they have to come to grips with getting new software up and running on their client machines, they have to be ready to serve Java programs that World Wide Web page builders will soon want to incorporate into their HTML pages. On top of all this is the looming specter of new security risks. It might seem as if Java is just one more protocol in a whole list of services that Internet users are clamoring for. However, Java aims at becoming *the* Internet protocol. It will be important to understand how to get a site up and running which can deliver Java in preparation for the future.

Quick Review

You have explored Java so far as an end user would, pointing out the benefits and learning how to use the technology passively. This is the first point of contact for someone on the Internet with Java. Most people, when first acquainted with the World Wide

Web aren't shown anything about HTML documents. They merely realize that what was once a cryptic series of commands and different protocols, is now interfaced through an easy-to-use graphical front end, which brings together text, images, and movies, and allows the user to download files and view newsgroups seamlessly. *How* this happens doesn't really matter. The fact that it can happen does.

Java is the same way. It will become the ubiquitous method for providing dynamic content over the web. It is precisely at the point when people no longer realize it is there that Java will have attained its goal. However, the luxury of allowing underlying technologies to take care of everything is not to be for everyone. Someone has to both develop the content and applications, and deliver them over the Internet. These jobs fall to the programmers and site administrators who will provide the future that Java promises.

The future that Java implies is one of seamless interconnectivity of information and interface. Users will no longer be hassled by making sure they have the right viewer for a document, or converting from one format to another so that they can print a document. The information provides its own means of manipulation—with the help of Java. In addition to using information, the promise of *finding* information is just as important. Information overload is perhaps the biggest challenge for the advancement of the Internet, and while many services such as robots, spiders, and worms have been developed to search through the tangled web and create vast databases, the promise of intelligent agents to carry out tasks might be a possible solution.

Java's architecture has been designed to provide the extensibility, portability, and high-performance that programs need for the emerging demands of the Internet. First and foremost, Java provides the portability necessary for the Internet. In addition, the security features it employs are fundamental to its acceptance as a distribution platform for executable content. Finally, it fits into the modern architecture of robust, multithreading operating systems. Java's ease of use and functionality also make it an ideal platform for program development. These features make Java a promising technology, and its early acceptance by the Web in such areas as VRML is sure to solidify its hold on the future of the Internet.

For the end user, Java's functionality can be seen in the Java interpreter and HotJava browser. These two tools provide the run-time environment needed for the execution of Java applications. The previous chapter covered the use of these two tools. It also provided an introduction to including Java applets in HTML pages. For the majority of Internet users, running Java applets and stand-alone applications is how they will come to know Java. It will provide the seamless distribution of interactive content and new media on a host of different platforms, freeing the exploration of the Internet from worrying about what format a file is in, or what platform a program was compiled for. The goal of the Internet to provide universal connectivity is finally possible.

What This Chapter Covers

Providing easy to use, seamless integration of distributed applications for the end user does not mean that a system administrator's job will get any easier. The demands of high-performance distributed computing will push the limits of present day networked hardware. Providing the ability to use and distribute Java executables will fall to the site administrator. This means that not only setting up clients with the proper software to view Java content, but also preparing the traditional Web servers for dynamic content will be necessary. In addition, site administrators will have to concern themselves with making sure that they have a secure facility against possible errant executables or attacks through Java.

This chapter covers the following topics:

➤ Setting up the Java environment on a client system for running applications

➤   Client-side security and optimization

➤   Server-side administration

➤   Java delivery

➤   Network-wide security management

➤   Overall network enforcement

Java provides diverse functionality by providing stand-alone applications, applets, and content and protocol handlers. Learning how to provide all of these effectively will be important to making your site an effective Java medium. By creating safe clients, administrators can solve many of the security problems of distributed executables without relying on firewalls and restrictions on Internet access. It is this balance between security and access that is the most important job for the administrator. If you make your site too open, you make it a playground for breaking and entering; if you make it too restrictive, you defeat the purpose of the Internet itself.

As you look toward setting up your site for using Java, it is important to remember that what might appear to be just one more protocol on a long list of protocols will in fact free the site administrator from many of the hassles of providing content for the Internet. Up to now, if you wanted any type of interaction such as forms or image maps, you had to deal with CGI scripts and other ad hoc attempts to make the Web interact with a user. This reliance on CGI scripts did two things, it placed all the processing burden on the server side, and made delivering content a mess of directories and additional executables. Instead, Java takes care of all interactions on the client computer, and encapsulates delivery and interaction in a single file. Java can only make it easier for the future site administrator.

After You Finish This Chapter

After you finish this chapter you should be able to set up Java on a client system, administrate a site, and provide Java content in the form of applets, stand-alone applications, and handlers. This chapter covers these steps in detail, and will take you through the steps necessary build a secure, dynamic site based on Java.

Setting Up the System

Setting up the system for both client- and server-side computing involves installing the software for the Java run-time environment. In addition, if you want to program in Java, all of the necessary tools for compilation and automatic document production are included with the Sun Java release. If you are planning on using any other browser such as Netscape Navigator, you will have to follow the instructions provided with it for installation. However, the methods should be straightforward, and if you have used a browser with the World Wide Web, you should be familiar with the process.

Hardware Requirements

The hardware requirements for using the Java programs are different depending on what machine you are using. There are at the time of writing two systems that will support the Java environment: Solaris 2.3 and above for the SPARC processors, and Windows NT 3.5 for the Intel $x86$ family.

Hardware Requirements for Programming in Java	
Sun Workstation	Windows NT Workstation
SPARC processor	Intel $x86$ processor (486+ recommended)
Sun Solaris 2.3 or above	Windows NT 3.5 or above
32 MB Memory	16 MB Memory
16 MB+ Hard Drive Space	11 MB+ Hard Drive Space
	8-bit color
Sound capabilities	16-bit SoundBlaster (for sound)

The requirements listed in the previous table do not include room for your own files, so be sure to have plenty of space on your hard drive. Although these are presently the only platforms for which the interpreter and browser are available, at the time of writing ports were underway for Windows 95 and MacOS 7.5 at Sun, and others were working on Linux, Amiga, and NEXTStep ports. The many features of Java make it difficult to port to other systems, so it would be good to keep up on the present state of the environment since ports to new systems will be in a constant state of flux, with new hardware and operating systems coming into the Java fold. For the purposes of this book, we will be dealing only with the Solaris and Windows NT versions of Java.

The Java version for Solaris will work if you have Solaris correctly installed. Java for Solaris supports a wide range of hardware options. Unfortunately, the Windows NT version supports a much more limited hardware set. 1-, 4-, 16-, and 24-bit color support are being worked on for Windows NT. Sound support is especially limited at the time of writing.

It should be noted that running Java under Windows NT with an incompatible sound card will hang the system. If you have an incompatible sound configuration, or are having problems with your system hanging, be sure to check out the troubleshooting section in the Windows NT software setup.

Once you have assured yourself that you have the proper hardware for running Java, you can to proceed with getting the software and setting it up on your system.

Setting Up the Software

The procedure for setting up the software is similar for both Solaris and Windows NT; however, due to the limited support at present for the Windows NT platform, care should be taken to ensure a proper system configuration.

SunSparc/Solaris 2.x

The Java file for Solaris comes as a compressed tar file about 5.4 MB in size. When you have completed the download, uncompressed and unpacked the file, the resulting files and directories take up approximately 16 MB of disk space. The files can be transferred through FTP from either of the following sites:

➤ sunsite.unc.edu (198.86.40.81) in the /pub/sun-info/hotjava directory

➤ java.sun.com (198.70.96.253) in the /pub directory.

The files can be mirrored at other locations, so an Archie search might uncover a closer (and faster) site.

Downloading Java

The current version of Java for Solaris is the Alpha3 release. The complete file name is hotjava-alpha3-solaris2-sparc.tar.Z. To download the file from java.sun.com:

```
$ ftp java.sun.com
Name (java.sun.com): anonymous
331 Guest login ok, send your complete e-mail address as
password.
Password: username@domain-name
...
ftp> binary
200 Type set to I.
ftp> cd pub
...
CWD command successful.
ftp> get hotjava-alpha3-solaris2-sparc.tar.Z
200 Port command successful.
150 Opening BINARY mode data connection for hotjava-alpha3-
solaris2-sparc.tar.Z
    (5476079 bytes)
226 Transfer complete.
local: hotjava-alpha3-solaris2-sparc.tar.Z remote: hotjava-
alpha3-solaris2-sparc.tar.Z
5476079 bytes received in xe+xx seconds (xx Kbytes/s)
```

The previous commands will be similar on whatever system you are downloading from. Merely replace the site name and directory where the file resides.

Note

It should be noted that Sun is constantly releasing newer versions of the Java language, and the file names might have changed.

Uncompressing Java

Once you have downloaded the files, you must uncompress and unpack the files. The following command uncompresses the file and sends it to the tar utility, which will then unpack the file into the necessary directories. The command creates a directory hotjava/ with subdirectories including all of the executables and documentation.

```
$ zcat hotjava-alpha3-solaris2-sparc.tar.Z ¦ tar xf -
```

You also need to set up your shell so that the hotjava/bin directory is in your path. This varies depending on what shell you are using, so check your specific software documentation. Once you have completed these steps, the browser, compiler, and tools are ready to be used for running Java applications on the Sun platform.

Intel x86/Windows NT

The Java release for Windows NT is much more recent than the Solaris version. At the time of writing the Solaris version is in release 3, while the Windows NT version is in release 2. It should be noted that release 2 of the Windows NT version has several missing features. These include the lack of printing ability, support for only 8-bit color, and limited sound support for only the Sound Blaster 16. Release 3 for Windows NT is due out soon, and should solve many of these problems. It is important to keep these missing features in mind, however, when using early versions of software.

The Java file for Windows NT comes as a self-extracting archive file about 3.6 MB in size. When you have completed the download, uncompressed and unpacked the file, the resulting files and directories will take up approximately 11 MB of disk space. The

files can be downloaded from java.sun.com (198.70.96.253) in the
/pub directory. The files can be mirrored at other locations, so an
Archie search might uncover a closer (and faster) site.

Downloading Java

As mentioned before, the current version of Java for Windows NT
is the Alpha2 release. The complete file name is hotjava-alpha2-
nt-x86.exe. To download the file from java.sun.com:

```
$ ftp java.sun.com
Name (java.sun.com): anonymous
331 Guest login ok, send your complete e-mail address as
password.
Password: username@domain-name
...
ftp> binary
200 Type set to I.
ftp> cd pub
...
CWD command successful.
ftp> get hotjava-alpha2-nt-x86.exe
200 Port command successful.
150 Opening BINARY mode data connection for hotjava-alpha3-
nt-x86.exe
     (3618772 bytes)
226 Transfer complete.
local: hotjava-alpha2-nt-x86.exe remote: hotjava-alpha2-nt-
x86.exe
3618772 bytes received in xe+xx seconds (xx Kbytes/s)
```

As mentioned in the section for retrieving the Solaris version, the
previous commands will be similar on whatever system you are
downloading from. Merely replace the site name and directory
where the file resides. It should be noted that Sun is constantly
releasing newer versions of the Java language, and the file names
might have changed.

Uncompressing Java

The file must be uncompressed once it has been downloaded. Because it is a self-extracting archive, you simply need to enter the name of the file at the command prompt.

```
C:\> hotjava-alpha2-nt-x86
```

You will also need to set up Windows NT so that the hotjava/bin directory is in your path. You can do this by entering the following:

```
C:\> set PATH=drive:path\hotjava\bin
```

Once you complete these steps, the browser, compiler, and tools are ready to be used for running the Java applications on the Windows NT platform.

Setting Environment Variables

When you set environment variables from the DOS prompt in Windows NT, they only affect the current session. If you want to make permanent changes to the environment variables, you must do so from the Control Panel. From Program Manager, select the Control Panel icon (usually in the group Main). Once the Control Panel is up, select the System icon. You will be presented with the System dialog box as illustrated in figure 4.1.

Make sure that you have selected the User Environment Variables area by clicking on one of the existing variables there. At the bottom of the dialog box, enter the name of the new variable in Variable, and its value in Value. Because you need to select an existing variable in the User Environment Variables area, simply replace the name and value with the new settings, it will not remove the old environment variable.

For the Solaris system, setting environment variables are different depending on what shell you are using. Please refer to the documentation for your specific setup for setting environment variables.

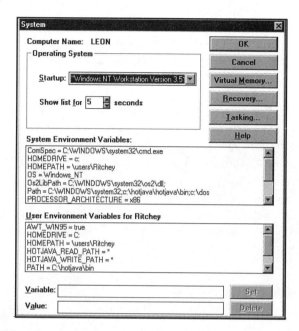

Figure 4.1

The System dialog box.

Setting Up a HotJava Icon in Windows NT

If you want to set up the HotJava program as an icon in Windows NT, from the File menu in Program Manager, select New.... The New Program Object dialog box will appear (see fig. 4.2).

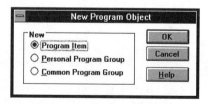

Figure 4.2

The New Program Object dialog box.

Select the Program Group radio button, either personal or common, depending upon whether you want it to be available to everyone (common) or to only come up when you log in (personal), and then the OK button. When the Program Group Properties dialog Box appears, enter the description of the program group and click OK.

After you have created an empty program group and opened it up in Program Manager, select File, New..., and this time select Program Item. The Program Item Properties box will appear, and you can enter the specifics for the program. Use the Browse... button to find the path to the HotJava executable, which is in the /bin subdirectory of the /hotjava directory. Select OK when you have completed the information. A DOS icon should appear in the Program Group you created with the name you entered for HotJava.

Problems with the Windows NT Version of Java

The Alpha2 release of Java for Windows NT has several problems that might arise in the installation or running process. Table 4.1 lists the most common, and gives you the work-around for them.

Table 4.1   Troubleshooting the Alpha2 Release of Java for Windows NT

Error	Solution
The System Hangs Windows NT	This situation is typically caused by an incompatible sound configuration. HotJava will only support Windows NT 3.5 with a SoundBlaster 16. If you are running HotJava under any other configuration with sound enabled (which is the default) the operating system will hang. If you do not have the correct configuration, set the HOTJAVA_DISABLE_SOUND environment variable equal to TRUE. C:\> **set HOTJAVA_DISABLE_SOUND=true** It should also be noted that having sounds enabled on any build of Windows NT 3.51 will hang the system. You can download new SoundBlaster drivers from java.sun.com. The file is pub/sb_nt.exe. If this does not solve the problem, you must disable the sound. This problem might be fixed in the Alpha3 release.

Error	Solution
HotJava/NT deadlocks	There are certain situations involving applets and the thread that deliver events from Windows that will lock up HotJava, but not the system itself. You can try to avoid resizing the window, especially while applets are loading. In addition, turning off full-drag improves the problem. You can turn off full-drag by opening the Control Panel and then opening the Desktop Icon. In the Applications group box, uncheck Full Drag.
HotJava displays an error when trying to create the file .hotjava	This is the most common error to occur, and has to do with invalid HOMEDRIVE and HOMEPATH environment variables. You can solve this problem by making sure the variables point to an existing, valid directory. You can reset these variables with C:\> set HOMEDRIVE=a *valid drive* (c:) C:\> set HOMEPATH=*a valid path* (/user/name)
HotJava says it won't run on Win95	This error occurs if you are running the Win95 Shell under Windows 3.51. Enter C:\> **set AWT_WIN95=true** and restart HotJava/NT. You can enter all of these commands into the System dialog box to make them permanent as discussed in the section on Setting Environment Variables.

You might be thinking, having looked over the list of possible errors and bugs, that Java is a little unstable. Keep in mind, however, that this software is in the *Alpha* stage. In product development, this is the stage typically reserved for in house usage, not for general consumption. It is only when software enters the *Beta* stage that it is even released in limited numbers to beta testers. Why then is Java out? Sun wanted people to begin using the Java language as early as possible. It is precisely for users such as yourself that Sun released this product—to help content developers get a head start on programming in Java. Second, the problems mentioned are for the specific releases mentioned. It is highly possible that later releases will have fixed most, if not all, of the problems mentioned by the time you read this book. It is important to keep abreast of where the Java environment is presently at, and where it is going.

Setting Up the Client

Once you have the software installed, you should be able run the Java interpreter and HotJava browser right away. There are two main issues for the site administrator to deal with in setting up the software on clients—environment variables and security. Making sure that the environment variables are set correctly makes using the software much easier. By determining early on how to set up the security for the software, you can have a better understanding of what is going on in your site, and where possible weak points are located.

Environment Variables

The environment variables for HotJava and the Java interpreter determine how the run-time environment, and the applications Java is running, sees your system. By setting these variables, you can create your first line of defense against Java programs that either intentionally or unintentionally attempt to invade the client system. Table 4.2 displays the environment variables that affect HotJava and Java.

Table 4.2   The Java Environment Variables

Variable	Function
HOTJAVA_HOME	This is the directory where HotJava will look for the resources necessary to run. The default is the directory in which it was installed.
WWW_HOME	This variable tells HotJava what URL to use as the homepage.
HOTJAVA_READ_PATH	This variable tells HotJava where applets can read files from. The default is<install-dir>:$HOME/public_html/
HOTJAVA_WRITE_PATH	This variable tells HotJava where applets can write files to. The default is/tmp/:/devices/:/dev/:~/.hotjava/
CLASSPATH	This variable tells Java where classes can be imported from. The directories are separated by semicolons.
NNTPSERVER	Set this variable to your News server for HotJava to be able to read newsgroups.

While the HOTJAVA_HOME and WWW_HOME variables are pretty self explanatory, the HOTJAVA_READ_PATH, HOTJAVA_WRITE_PATH, and CLASSPATH variables should be discussed in more detail.

HOTJAVA_READ_PATH Variable

The HOTJAVA_READ_PATH variable tells HotJava where applets can read files from. It uses the paths given to match the files that an applet wants to open for reading. HotJava okays a read if the file either is a directory or subdirectory of a path in the variable statement or matches a specific file in the variable statement.

One way for an applet to get into a file it shouldn't is for the file to reside in a subdirectory of a directory that does have permission. For example, if you have a file known as My_Secret_Diary.doc in the directory users/Ritchey/Documents/PersonalStuff/ and gave permission for HotJava applets to read documents in users/Ritchey/Documents/, It would be possible for an applet to gain access to that file.

Instead, make sure you keep public and private documents separated, and that paths in your HOTJAVA_READ_PATH variable explicitly state which subdirectories you want read. You could create two subdirectories in every directory, one public, one private, and only refer to the public directory; however, this means making sure you are placing files in the right spot over dozens of places. A more useful method would be to create a single public directory, and place subdirectories in it that hold the information you explicitly want the world to see. This way, you must actively place a file in the public directory for it to be accessed, and you have a much easier time keeping track of what permissions are on your system.

HOTJAVA_WRITE_PATH Variable

The HOTJAVA_WRITE_PATH variable works the same way as the HOTJAVA_READ_PATH variable except it gives applets permission to write files in these directories. The default includes areas where HotJava sends log information an applet might issue;

/.hotjava/, and the /temp/ directory, in addition to necessary directories for Unix workstations such as /devices/ and /dev/. Again, you can attempt to create different areas where you want applets to be able to write to, but the easiest thing to do is to create a single area where applets can read and write files for their use. That way you can easily keep a handle on applets on your system.

Note The HOTJAVA_READ_PATH and HOTJAVA_WRITE_PATH can also be set in the Properties... dialog box under Options on the menu bar.

CLASSPATH Variable

The CLASSPATH variable controls where the interpreter and browser will import classes from. The default is for only the install directory and subdirectories to be available for import; however, if you have created your own classes, or keep classes you use somewhere else, make sure you have those directories in the CLASSPATH variable so that the class-loader is able to import them. This only affects classes that are being imported by other classes. You get an access violation if a class attempts to import another class that isn't in the CLASSPATH variable.

Note The CLASSPATH variable uses semicolons ; not colons : to separate directories as in the HOTJAVA_READ_PATH and HOTJAVA_WRITE_PATH variables.

Once you have created the proper read and write access restrictions, you can be sure that information on your computer will not be susceptible to Java applets. The Java environment, because it is interpreted, can check all actions before they are carried out. As mentioned in Chapter 2, "An Introduction to Java," the Java run-time security features ensure that only validly accessible paths are available to programs.

Security

In addition to setting the environment variables, there is a Security dialog box under the Options menu (see fig. 4.3). This dialog box allows the users to determine how they want Java to enforce its security measures.

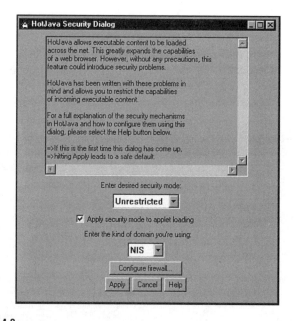

Figure 4.3

The HotJava Security dialog box.

The security mode drop-down list provides four choices for how applets can access URL's from your computer. Table 4.3 explains these choices in detail.

Table 4.3	Security Modes for Java Applets
Mode	**Restrictions**
No Access	This stops applets from loading URLs from any location, even your own computer.
Applet Host	This mode allows an applet to use URLs that refer to the system they came from.
Firewall	This mode restricts URLs to those behind the firewall. Applets that are inside the firewall can access any URL, but applets outside the firewall can access only those URLs that are also outside the firewall.
Unrestricted	This mode allows an applet access to any URL it requests.

In addition to restricting applications from accessing specific classes of URLs, you can use the Apply security mode to applet loading check box to further restrict even the loading of the applets themselves. Table 4.4 lists the restrictions that are enforced when this box is selected.

Table 4.4   Restrictions to Applet Loading

Mode	Restrictions
No Access	In this mode, HotJava cannot load any applets.
Applet Host	This mode restricts HotJava to running applets that are on the machine itself.
Firewall	This mode restricts HotJava from loading any applets outside the firewall.
Unrestricted	This mode allows HotJava to load any applet.

The next drop-down list in the Firewall dialog box after the security mode drop-down list allows you to specify the type of naming service you use: DNS or NIS. This is specific to your site, but most Internet services use the Domain Naming Service (DNS).

At the bottom of the dialog box are four buttons. Configure Firewall... presents another dialog box for setting up the safe systems you want your computers to access. (See the next section on Configuring a Firewall.) The Apply button sets HotJava's security configuration as you have specified. The Cancel button closes the dialog box, and returns the settings to what they were before. The Help button loads the help files for using the dialog box into HotJava where you can find more information on the HotJava security features.

Configuring a Firewall

If you are using the Firewall configuration in the Security dialog box, you must specify which systems are within the firewall. Typically, a firewall is a set of computers that share a domain name, such as cam.ac.uk or mcp.com. These computers are all considered safe while all addresses outside of this domain are unsafe. If your firewall were mcp.com, applets that called URLs from addresses with this extension would be allowed.

HotJava allows for the firewall specification to be much more detailed, giving the site administrator control over specific sites in the firewall. The HotJava Configure Firewall dialog box (see fig. 4.4) allows the administrator to enter hosts or domains for inclusion behind the firewall. The domain name can be either a specific domain, such as mcp.com, or a . that specifies all local hosts as being members of the firewall. If you can address a host with just its name (newriders instead of newriders.mcp.com) it is considered a local host. Essentially all computers with the domain of your system will be included. Additionally, you can specify specific hosts to include behind the firewall. Use either their full symbolic name (newriders.mcp.com) or their numeric IP address.

Figure 4.4

The HotJava Configure Firewall dialog box.

Once you have selected the type of entry in the drop-down list (domain or host) and entered the new selection, use the Add button to add the new entry to the firewall list. If you want to change an entry, select it in the list, type in the new entry, and hit the Change button. To remove an entry, select it, and hit the Delete button. The bottom three buttons, Apply, Cancel, and Help are the same as for the Security dialog box. Selecting Apply causes your selection to be used as the firewall configuration. Cancel exits the dialog box, and returns it to the previous configuration. Help brings up information on using the firewall configuration settings.

Setting Up a System Security Configuration

If you are on a multiuser system, you might want to restrict the type of access users have with the HotJava browser. You can do so by creating a system security configuration. By using a system security configuration, you can be sure that those running HotJava are doing so at a minimum security level that you specify. They can create a more restrictive setting, but never a more open one.

To create the System Security Configuration you must be logged on as root or administrator, and be able to set permissions on files. First, go into HotJava, and set the system security for the minimum level you would like everyone to use, using the normal dialog boxes mentioned previously. In the HotJava install directory (typically /hotjava/) create a directory called security_config. Your directory structure should look similar to figure 4.5.

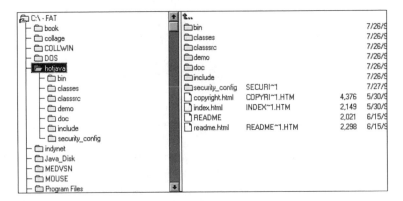

Figure 4.5

Directory structure for security configuration.

Once this directory has been created, copy the files access_mode and firewall_hosts from your $HOME/.hotjava directory, into the new security_config directory. The HOME directory is a combination of the HOMEDRIVE and HOMEPATH environment variables that were set while installing the program. Make sure that the new files are only alterable by the root or system administrator. HotJava now loads with these security defaults, and users are not able to downgrade the security precautions set for the system. They can, of course, create more restrictive environments, but never less.

As long as you set up HotJava correctly, you should have no problems with security at your site because of any failure in the Java protection. Remember, there is more to Java security than file system protections. First, the language and compiler limit what a programmer can actually do with memory. Second, all bytecodes are verified as being safe before execution. Third, the class loader separates loaded classes from each other and the rest of the system. With the file system security on top, Java provides four levels of overlapping security to ensure that loaded applets cannot violate system integrity.

Setting Up the Server

Setting up your server for providing Java content is no different than for any other Web service. Java is delivered over the http server within HTML files as if it were an inline image or sound file. You should make sure that all of your normal HTTP services are working well, and Java should present no problems. There are many good books out on the market for setting up and administrating Web servers. For now, the assumption will be made that there is a working http server, and Java will be distributed over this.

Serving Applets and Code Pages

In order to distribute applets and their code pages, the HTML and class files must be where browsers have permission to download the files. Typically there is a root data directory where all files and subdirectories that are available over the Web are kept. When you are giving out URLs that point to your pages, remember that they are relative to this directory. Otherwise, users who want to provide Java content in their pages need only to be told where they can place their files and code pages if they want to make their source code available.

That is all there is to providing applets. There is no need to get CGI scripts up and running, or to teach users what programs to run, or what directory everything is in. Be sure to keep track of what files people are serving over your system— this isn't Java specific, just good practice.

Serving Handler Applications

In order to make Java protocol handlers available, you must provide the directory structure and CLASSPATH settings to ensure that HotJava can find the classes necessary for importing the handlers. Create the directory structure shown in figure 4.6.

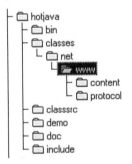

Figure 4.6
The handler directory structure.

Once you have created the directories, make sure the CLASSPATH environment variable is set to the classes directory at the root of the structure.

For creating protocol handlers, you will add a new directory for each new protocol, under the /protocol/ directory. The programmer providing the code for the new protocol handler (named

Handler.class) will place the Java bytecode file in this directory. To implement the new protocol in HotJava, you run it like any other URL. For example, if someone had developed a protocol named henry, you would use it by referring to:

    henry:location/filename

It is identical to the way you would issue an ftp: or news: URL.

In order to deal with a new content handler type, you must create a subdirectory under the /content/ directory names exactly after the MIME type of the document. The programmer provides the Java compiled .class file that has the name of the MIME sub-type. When a file comes across with the new type, Java knows how to handle it. If you are serving new content types, make sure your http server sends the correct MIME type details for the file. Check your http documentation for how to add new MIME types.

Providing new handlers is discussed in more detail in Chapter 12, "Java for the Internet." For now, your system should be ready to deliver dynamic content as both HTML and handler applications.

As a site serving web content, there are common security procedures you should always follow. Make sure you have a Physical protection scheme such a UPS boxes, tape backups, and a locked door between your server and the rest of the world. All of the precautions in the world won't help if someone walks up to the server terminal after a root user has left his account running. In addition, if you are running on Windows NT, make sure you use the NT File System (NTFS). While Unix file systems set restrictions on access, DOS's FAT does not. However, NTFS is a secure file system that safeguards your disks well beyond what FAT can provide. Additionally, it can recover from hard disk crashes and other catastrophic failures. In addition, you can even create a separate partition for all files you are going to make available over the Internet. You might also want to set up a Firewall or Proxy between your site and the Internet for added security. By following safe practices, you should have no problems with Java and your networked system.

Summary

This chapter focused on site administration as both client setup and server administration. From the client setup side there are many new security and software issues to deal with—most importantly how restrictive or open you want your network to be. By dealing with these issues early, and planning for the integration of Java, you can assure yourself that the system won't fall to a Trojan horse or virus. In addition to setting up the clients on your system, you must also prepare your http server for distributing the Java enabled documents your users will be clamoring for. Hopefully you can see that this is essentially no job at all. Java works just like any other inline image or sound file. However, by making sure that your system is set up properly, you can help lead developers of new content in the right direction for getting their pages out onto the web quickly and easily.

As a site administrator, you rarely have the luxury of playing around with new technology. It is the administrator who has to make all of it possible. By getting a feeling for Java early on, you should be able to prepare your site, and yourself, for a smooth transition to what Java has in store. Hopefully the discussions on security in earlier chapters, and the safeguards mentioned here reaffirm the position that Java is a powerful, robust, *secure* system for providing dynamic content over the Internet.

Chapter 5

Getting Started on Your Own Java Code

The Java environment is a portable, robust, high-performance, advanced language, while still maintaining the ease of use and functionality that object-oriented languages have always promised but never quite attained. By providing a portable, dynamic, multithreading language, programmers can develop advanced applications across heterogeneous networks such as the Internet. At the same time, the class libraries impart the ease of use and functionality of more open platforms while providing a secure environment for distributed systems. These features in combination are sure to make Java the dominant technology of the Internet in the next decade.

Quick Review

Up to now, Java has been discussed from the viewpoint of the end user or administrator. You have learned about the evolution of the Internet, and where Java fits into its future. HTML, VRML, Intelligent agents—all of these technologies will undoubtedly be controlled by the Java programming language and environment. Any understanding of the future of the Internet will be predicated by an understanding of this technology.

With this information in mind, understanding the ways in which to both use and serve Java content becomes imperative. For most users, the primary use of Java will be either as stand-alone applications or as extensions and applets in a browser environment. In fact, end users will most likely not even know that they are using Java—it will become as widespread as e-mail or HTML, appearing in all aspects of computing on the Web. The site administrator, however, has a new job with Java. Setting up clients and servers, providing Java content in addition to the many other networking protocols, and helping users develop or include Java content in their own documents will all be required. In addition, although Java provides a secure environment and many safety features, distributed applications invariably bring to mind viruses, Trojan horses, worms, and worse—making site administration and security a top priority. This work pays off in the end, however, by providing a more seamless incorporation of content and protocols for both client-side and server-side computing.

At this point, the book has covered what you need to know to use Java applets, applications, and handlers. But what if you can't find an applet or handler to do what you want? Before Java, you had to sit down with a development environment such as Visual C++, a commercial TCP/IP class library, and so on, and write your own stand-alone helper application or, heaven forbid, your own browser to implement your ideas. Even then, for everyone on the Internet to use it, you would have had to get it to them, and make sure that it supported all the other protocols. Back then, the individual was precluded from developing innovative products in any reasonable time.

What This Chapter Covers

You've seen the applets, you've run the applications, and now you want to go out on your own. This chapter provides a basic introduction to programming in Java. First, you will set up your hardware and software for programming. At this point, you should be on either a Sun SPARCStation running Solaris 2.3 or later, or an Intel x86 running Windows NT 3.5. If you are using Sun's HotJava Browser, you likely have the compiler and interpreter up and running already. If you are using Netscape's Browser, however, you need to get the correct software for compiling and running in Java from Sun.

After the system is set up, you will proceed to cover the fundamentals of creating applets and stand-alone applications in Java. You will implement the now-famous "Hello, World!" program used as perhaps the first example in every programmers repertoire. This example will give us a good place to start in showing off the programming environment and the fundamentals of the programming language, while enabling us to create a framework for the more detailed explanations. Specifically, this chapter will cover the following:

➤ Introduction to Classes

➤ Creating the HelloWorld Applet

➤ Creating the HelloWorldApp Stand-Alone Program

➤ Troubleshooting Your Code

If, by some misfortune, you do have any problems, you can refer to the last section, which covers troubleshooting the compiler and interpreter. Of course, you hope that this section isn't needed, but it is inevitable that something will go wrong at some point. A quick guide to the most common problems should get you through most of the errors that arise, and get you up to speed on dealing with more difficult problems if they appear.

After You Finish This Chapter

After you finish this chapter, you should be familiar with the compiler, interpreter, and general environment for programming in Java. You should be able to get small applets and stand-alone applications up and running, and be able to deal with most errors that will pop up from syntax errors and the like. In the next chapter, the fundamentals of the Java language are presented, including types, expressions, and control flow. This information provides the basics needed for implementing your ideas in the Java language. Later chapters introduce the class structure, libraries, and more advanced topics used to implement all the features of Java. Although the examples in this chapter could be considered synthetic, they provide you with a good basis for learning the Java language.

Setting Up Your System for Programming in Java

The first step in developing for the Java language is getting the programming environment up and running. You need the javac compiler, the Java interpreter, and a Java-enabled browser for this stage and for the next few chapters. The steps for getting and setting up the software are covered in Chapter 4, "Server Admin-istration for HotJava and Java." The compiler and interpreter as well as the browser are all included in the Sun release. If you properly installed the software earlier, you are all set to go; otherwise, return to Chapter 4, and install the Java release for your hardware platform.

Your First Java Program—Hello, World!

By now you should have the Java environment up and running correctly without too much suffering. You are finally ready, therefore, to start coding your first programs. The next two sections cover general ideas about programming in Java, detail what you need in order to get a program to run, and demonstrate the "Hello, World!" program as both an applet and a stand-alone program.

Your first Java program will be quite a simple one. It will print the words Hello, World! on-screen. Although the result of the program is not that fantastic, what actually goes on in the background to get it to do what it does *is*. The source code for the HelloWorld class is relatively short, and displays the built-in power of the Java language classes. It also provides a good example to demonstrate some of the features of Java.

If you flip ahead to the source code for HelloWorld, you will notice that there are several words such as import and extends. These declarations are fundamental to implementing the object-oriented nature of Java, and bring us to a basic problem in teaching the language. The problem revolves around classes—Java's representation of an object. An object-oriented language can be approached in essentially two ways: by teaching about classes first and the rest later; or by teaching declaration, types, and control flow first, and classes later. For those coming to a new language without any experience, it is generally believed that teaching the way in which classes work first is fundamental to creating good habits, and programmers, from the start. The problem with this approach is that classes are a more difficult concept than the basic structure, and an understanding of the fundamental types and control flows is necessary to properly demonstrate programs. If you learn the basics of classes and objects early, however, creating good object-oriented code later becomes easier.

The second method, however—teaching the fundamentals of the language first, and then introducing classes later—is the method I have chosen in this book for two reasons. First, I believe that most people attempting to tackle Java will not be new to programming, but will have at least some programming experience, especially in C and C++. Programmers who already have a good idea of what is in the language will be able to use the next two chapters as a quick guide comparing the environments and languages of C/C++ and Java. Toward this end, I have included notes on similarities and differences between the languages. These notes appear next to the text of the relevant sections. Second, although tutorials on classes and objects would require understanding some of the fundamentals such as types, expressions, and control-flow, a single class will be able to encapsulate the ideas presented in these two chapters and enable us to get the basic house-cleaning chores out of the way before you begin to get into the meat of the Java language.

However, it is not worthwhile to ignore the whole class issue until you are ready for more detailed coverage. Java as a language requires the use of classes from the beginning; however, the necessary class structure can be kept to a minimum, and an explanation of the object-oriented techniques will provide a good impression on which to begin learning the language. It would also be useful if you have read Chapter 2, "An Introduction to Java," because general properties of the Java classes are discussed there. If you understand classes, or are an experienced programmer and will be using these two chapters only as a general overview before diving into Java, feel free to skip the next section.

Introducing the Concept of Classes

First and foremost, you should notice that the HelloWorld application is called a class. That is exactly what it is. In fact, the output of the compiler is HelloWorld.class. Java is an object-oriented language to the extreme. All aspects of the language revolve around classes of objects. When you run either the interpreter or the browser, it implements a class—not a file.

A class is, generally speaking, composed of two kinds of items: *instance variables* and *methods*. Instance variables are what describe an object. For example, if you have an object such as a light bulb, you need to store its state, such as on or off, or perhaps its wattage. These values—on or off, and wattage—are stored in the instance variables. An important idea to remember is that these instance variables are typically *encapsulated*. This means that only the objects themselves can change the variables. Of course, such things as the light bulb knowing whether it is on or off, and being able to turn itself on and off, are well and good, but how does anything else tell it what to do? This is where methods come in. The light bulb would provide methods for turning itself on and off, such as TurnLightOn() and TurnLightOff(). Just as you cannot directly force the electrons to stop flowing through the tungsten filament in a bulb and must use the light switch, other objects must turn the light on and off using the light's methods. The imaginary light bulb might look something like this:

```
class LightBulb {
    boolean LightOn;
    int Wattage;
    public void TurnLightOn(){
        LightOn = true;
    }
    public void TurnLightOff() {
        LightOn = false;
    }
    public void ExpelPhotons() {
        if(LightOn) //do something to draw a lit bulb on the
                        //screen
        else //do something to draw an unlit bulb on the screen
    }
}
```

Of course, this is an incomplete example—it doesn't explain the way in which the bulb actually lights up, for instance. But this example does give a good picture of the kinds of class definitions you will be looking at. If you don't understand the format, or specific lexical issues, don't worry; they will be explained in later sections. The idea here is to get an idea of what a class looks like, and in general the way in which it works.

You need to know about one other thing to write our HelloWorld applet and application: inheritance. Say you really like your light bulb, but think it is a little boring. You decide to include a little bell that goes off every time it is turned on to really get the attention of the user. Do you have to throw away all the code you have just worked so hard to produce? Not at all. You can use the extends modifier to show that our new class LightBulbWithBell is an extension of the old class. Our new class might look something like this:

```
class LightBulbWithBell extends LightBulb {
    public void ExpelPhotons() {
        if(LightOn) {
            ...//do something to draw a lit bulb on the
            screen
            SoundBell();
        }
        else //do something to draw an unlit bulb on the
        screen
    }
}
```

You have added functionality to the ExpelPhotons() function to make it sound a bell. Again, the exact details of the way in which it lights up, or sounds the bell, don't matter. The important idea is that you can *inherit* objects and their features and update them. The specific type of updating performed is called *overriding* because you overrode the previous declaration of ExpelPhotons(). You also can add new methods and instance variables if needed. This capability to inherit properties from previously coded classes is just one of the many powerful features of object-oriented computing. This leaves you with two important points needed for beginning to study the Java language:

➤ All Java variables and methods must be members of a class.

➤ Classes encapsulate these members, and provide methods for inheritance.

A general understanding of classes at this point will make reading the code easier in the future, because so much of it revolves around the creation of classes. For the next few chapters, however, you will be dealing with only a single class instance.

A deeper investigation of objects and classes can be found in Chapter 7, "Getting It Together—Classes, Interfaces, and Packages."

Note

With this brief introduction to classes behind you, you are now ready for your first Java program.

HelloWorld as an Applet

For most users of Java, the goal of programming in the language is to provide applets over the Internet to be used by Java-enabled browsers. Therefore, our first incarnation of the HelloWorld class will be just that—an applet. Using the browser environment requires using some of the class libraries that deal with the windowing environment. In particular, you will be using the awt (Another Windowing Toolkit) class to control the appearance of our applet on-screen. You will override the paint() method of the awt.Graphics class in order to place the text "Hello, World!" in the window.

All applets are inheritances of the base class browser.Applet. You will override the init() method of this class in order to resize the window before you display the text. You will depend on the base classes to receive window calls, repaint themselves when the window is uncovered or resized, and in general provide for all housekeeping chores. All in all, our code will be only 10 lines, and half of those are there merely because of aesthetics and readability. Not a bad return for such little work on our part.

Setting Up the Environment

The first step in creating your HelloWorld class is to create the directories where the files will reside. Because you are going to serve our applet from an HTML page, you need a directory to store it. In addition, you will need a subdirectory to hold the class files generated by the javac compiler. When you finish the steps in table 5.1, the directory structure should look as shown in figure 5.1.

Figure 5.1

Directory structure for the HelloWorld class.

Table 5.1 Creating Directory Structure in Windows NT and Solaris	
Windows NT	**Solaris**
C:\> mkdir c:\Html	$ mkdir ~/Html
C:\> cd c:\Html	$ cd ~/Html
C:\> mkdir classes	$ mkdir classes
C:\> cd classes	$ cd classes

The directory structure used in these examples is for local machine use only. If you want to make your applet pages available to the wider Internet, you should talk with your system administrator about where you can place your files for world access. Be sure to find the correct directory structure to use, and the resulting URL necessary to find the document externally.

The Source Code for the HelloWorld Class

When you have the directory structure finished, you can begin to code the HelloWorld class. First, you must create a file called HelloWorld.java in the classes directory. The java extension is the standard method for indicating a Java source code file. In Windows NT you can either use the edit command or use the Notepad in the Windows environment. In Solaris, you can either use a command-line editor, such as vi or emacs, or use an OpenWindows editor, such as the TextEditor. Refer to the software documentation for details about creating a plain ASCII text file for your environment. Whichever editor you use, make sure that you are familiar with all the editing features. Correcting a typo in a command-line editor can be the most frustrating problem in the world when you don't know the commands.

Here is the source code you need to enter:

```
import browser.Applet;
import awt.Graphics;
class HelloWorld extends Applet {
    public void init() {
          resize(150,25);
    }
    public void paint(Graphics g) {
        g.drawString("Hello, World!", 50, 25);
    }
}
```

When you have finished typing the code, save it in the classes subdirectory under Html.

Look at what you have line by line. First, you have the following:

```
import browser.Applet
import awt.Graphics
```

These lines tell the compiler that you will be using these classes and to be ready to use them. In fact, the compiler will bring in the class definitions and include them with the source code you have written.

```
class HelloWorld extends Applet {
```

This line declares a new class, HelloWorld, and tells the compiler that it is a subclass of (extends) the Applet class.

```
public void init()
```

This line overrides the init() function of the Applet class. public means that objects outside of this class can invoke it, and void means that the method returns no value. The empty parentheses show that this method also takes no arguments. When the Applet is created, methods in the superclass Applet will call this function, invoking the next line:

```
resize(150,25);
```

This line tells the browser to resize the window to 150 by 25.

```
public void paint(Graphics g) {
```

This line is another overriding method. It is overriding the method paint from the Applet class. When the Applet is told to paint itself, this is the method it calls. Again, the method is public and has no return value. You do, however, have an argument. When paint() is called, it needs to be sent an object of class Graphics; in this case, the method refers to it as g. g is sent by the methods you don't see in the superclass Applet that handle Graphics objects.

```
g.drawString("Hello, World!", 50, 25);
```

In this line, the Graphics object g is told to invoke its method drawString() with the arguments Hello, World!, 50, and 25. This tells the method to print the text Hello, World! at location 50, 25.

When the applet has completed running, the automatic garbage methods of the Java environment ensure that memory allocated is freed and generally make sure that the program exits cleanly.

Compiling

After you have written the source file, and saved it into the classes directory, you are ready to compile the code. The command for compiling in both Solaris and Windows NT is this:

```
C:\> javac HelloWorld.java
```

If compilation succeeds, you should have a file named HelloWorld.class in the classes directory. If you have any problems, make sure that you have typed all commands correctly. If you still can't get the file to compile, check out the section at the end of the chapter on troubleshooting the compiler.

Creating the HTML File

After you have completed the compilation steps and created the HelloWorld.class file, you are ready to place it into an HTML document. Again, in your editor, create a plain ASCII text file in the Html directory called HelloWorld.html. The file will be a standard HTML file that includes the <APP> directive. For more information on writing HTML documents that include applets, look in Chapter 3, "Using the Java Environment," in the section titled "Providing Applets." For our purposes, you need only the basic structure:

```
<HTML>
<HEAD>
<TITLE>Hello, World!</TITLE>
</HEAD>
<BODY>
Say Hi to Everyone:

<APP CLASS="HelloWorld">
</BODY>
</HTML>
```

As mentioned in Chapter 4, "Server Administration for HotJava and Java," The <APP CLASS=class_name> directive tells the browser to load and run the class *class_name* from the classes subdirectory in the HTML file logical directory. Note that you refer to classes and *not* to file names. The file name is HelloWorld.class, and you refer to it simply as HelloWorld.

Loading the Applet

After you have completed the HTML file, you are ready to run the applet in the browser. Begin the HotJava browser by either clicking on the HotJava icon or invoking the browser from the command line with **hotjava**. There is currently a bug in HotJava that does not enable it to reload an applet if you have recompiled the code when it is invoked from the command line. If you are running it from the command line, move to a different directory before entering **hotjava**.

Do not invoke the Java browser HotJava from the classes directory. Due to a bug in the program, HotJava cannot reload an applet when invoked from the directory that contains the applet's compiled code.

After you have HotJava running, you can load the HTML file and see the fruits of your labor. Load the HTML file by entering the URL in the Document URL field toward the top of the HotJava window:

```
Document URL: file:/path/Html/HelloWorld.html
```

If everything goes as planned, you should see what's shown in figure 5.2.

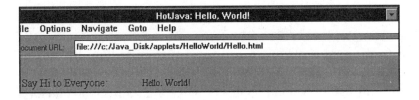

Figure 5.2
The Hello, World! applet displayed in HotJava.

Congratulations! You have finished your first applet and have completed all the steps necessary for creating your own Java applets for the Internet. Obviously, there is much more to programming more complicated applets, but in essence, you have learned all there is about the process, illustrated in the following steps:

1. You develop the code, compile it, and check for compile-time errors.

2. You develop your HTML pages, including the new applets.

3. You test the pages with a browser such as HotJava.

Of course, that is not all that the Java language is good for. By using the interpreter java, you can write stand-alone applications in addition to browser applets. To help you understand the differences between creating an applet and creating an application, you will recode the HelloWorld class as a stand-alone application to be run on the interpreter.

The HelloWorld Class as a Stand-Alone Application

The HelloWorld class can also be run as a stand-alone application using the java interpreter. Although most Java work will be seen as applets and, as you will see later, as handlers for types and protocols, the language can also be used to create stand-alone programs. Of course, these programs are not stand-alone in the true sense of the word because you still need the java interpreter on your system to run them. To differentiate our applet from our application, you will refer to the new class as HelloWorldApp.

For the HelloWorldApp class, you will not require the classes used in the applet form of the program. Instead, you will create a new class from scratch. If you look ahead at the code, you will notice that our program does not *extend* any other class. In fact, this is misleading; you are in fact extending the class *Object*.

When a class is defined without specifying the inheritance class, the class Object is taken as the default.

Note

Thus, even though you seem to be creating a new class, you can still use many powerful features built into Java. In fact, all classes are derived from the Object class, as discussed in Chapter 7, "Getting It Together—Classes, Interfaces, and Packages." Suffice it to say here that the Object class provides the garbage collection and system utilities basic to all Java implementations.

Our HelloWorldApp class this time is only five lines long, half the length of the applet version, and still much of that is spacing for aesthetics and readability. For that, you get a program that will run on any platform the Java language has been ported to, along with all the features of the language.

Setting Up the Environment

Your HelloWorldApp does not require us to create any special directory structure for holding the class files. Instead, you can work in any directory you choose. For now, create a directory HelloWorldApp to hold your work. In this directory, create a file named HelloWorldApp.java. Using any editor you choose, create the file in plain ASCII text.

The Source Code for the HelloWorld Class

The source code for the HelloWorldApp is relatively simple:

```
class HelloWorldApp {
    public static void main (String args[]) {
        System.out.println("Hello, World!");
    }
}
```

After you have finished typing the code, and ensuring that it is correct, save the file to the HelloWorldApp directory.

Again you will go over the source line by line.

```
class HelloWorldApp {
```

As mentioned before, this line declares the class as HelloWorldApp. The declaration does not specify what class HelloWorldApp extends, so the default is taken as Object. Again, every class, except for Object, has a superclass. In other words, every class is an inheritance of another class, except for Object. This line could also have been written like this:

```
class HelloWorldApp extends Object {
```

Writing it the first way is easier, however, and the Object extension can always be assumed.

```
public static void main (String args[]) {
```

This line has several new features not in the applet.

➤ The modifier static appears. This keyword tells the compiler that this method refers to the class itself, not to a specific instance of the class. This enables the method to be invoked without a HelloWorldApp object having been created first. This topic is covered in Chapter 7.

➤ Notice that the method takes an argument, args[], that is an object of String. In fact, this object holds the arguments typed after a command when it is entered.

➤ Notice the name of the method itself—main(). This method, as in C and C++, is required of all applications to tell the interpreter where to start. The interpreter is what calls the main() method and passes the command-line arguments to it.

```
System.out.println("Hello, World!");
```

This line outputs the text Hello, World! to the standard output, usually the screen. In this case, the class System has the method out, which in turn has the method println, which outputs the argument to the screen. Notice that the call uses the dot (.) operator as in C and C++.

Compiling

By now you should have completed the HelloWorldApp.java file and saved it to the HelloWorldApp directory. As before, you need to compile the class using the javac compiler.

```
C:\> javac HelloWorldApp.java
```

The compiler should create the class file HelloWorldApp.class in the directory HelloWorldApp. If you have any problems, check for typing errors, and if they still persist, check the troubleshooting guide at the end of the chapter.

Running the Interpreter

After you have completed the compilation and javac has created the class file, it is time to run the application. You invoke the interpreter with the java command. As with putting classes into HTML files, remember that java refers to the class, not the compiled file. To run HelloWorldApp, enter this:

```
C:\> java HelloWorldApp
```

If all goes well, you should see the output shown in figure 5.3.

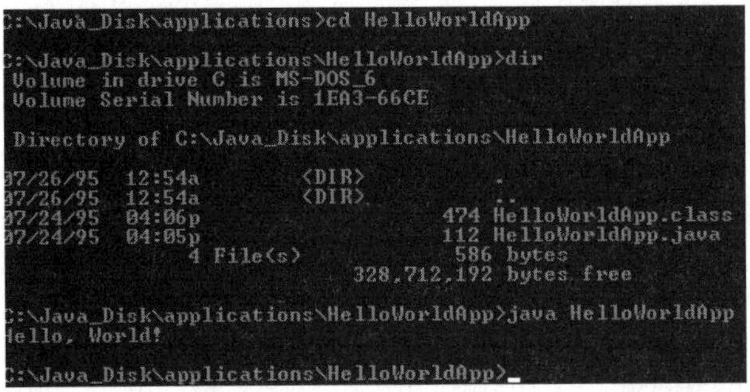

Figure 5.3

Output from the HelloWorldApp and Java Interpreter.

Again, congratulations! you have completed your first stand-alone Java application. In many ways, the process is an easier one than that of creating applets. You didn't have to mess around creating an HTML page with <HEAD>, </TITLE>, or <APP> declarations, or run HelloWorldApp through HotJava. Very quickly, you have created a sophisticated program capable of running on many different systems. Although HelloWorldApp doesn't seem all that sophisticated, in fact, the Java language is hard at work in the background delivering a robust, high-performance application. In the next few chapters, you will begin to piece together the fundamental aspects of the Java language needed for developing your own ideas into Java classes.

Troubleshooting

Presented here is a list of errors you might confront and solutions you might find helpful when running the Java compiler javac and interpreter java. This is not an exhaustive list, but it should enable you to work through most of the error messages that appear as you try to compile and run the examples and your own code. For a more complete list, see the section on using Java tools in Chapter 13, "Interfacing with C and Using the Java Tools."

Compiling Errors

This list of compile-time errors covers the most common mistakes made during program compilation. Any time the compiler outputs an error message, it will not output the .class file. If you are trying to compile a program and don't seem to be getting the .class file, the compiler is most likely encountering an error somewhere in your code. Most of these mistakes are typographical errors, but they are not always easy to find. Be sure to check your code carefully, especially for semicolons at the ends of statements. Semicolons are used to tell the compiler where a statement ends; however, sometimes it is not clear if you should use a semicolon at the end of some lines. In the next chapter, as the language is discussed, the usage of semicolons is covered. For now, think of them as the equivalent of periods at the end of sentences.

➤   `javac: Command not found`

This error occurs on Unix systems where the path isn't set properly. Make sure that your path statement includes the directory where the Java binaries are kept. This is typically the hotjava/bin directory. Use setenv or a similar command to set your path variable to the javac directory. An example path statement might be:

PATH=C:\hotjava\bin;C:\users\Ritchey\hotjava\classes;

Check with your shell documentation for the specifics of your configuration.

```
filename:linenumber: ';' expected
    some line of code
                    ^

n error(s)
```

You receive this error when you have forgotten to include the semicolon (;) at the end of a statement or declaration. This error message occurs only if the compiler figures out what you were trying to do. Many times, however, the compiler cannot guess what is missing, and might output strange error messages—such as `Invalid type expression` or `Invalid declaration`—on the following lines of code. If the lines in which the compiler finds an error look correct, check the lines immediately preceding those with the errors for missing semicolons.

```
filename:linenumber: Variable variable_name
may not have been initialized.
        variable
              ^

n error(s)
```

Any time a variable is used without first being initialized, the compiler throws an error message and the .class file is not created. Make sure that all variables are initialized. You will learn about initialization in Chapter 6. Initialization is the way you tell the compiler what kinds of variables you will be using.

Interpreter Errors

Many times, programs will compile, yet still not run under the java interpreter. The interpreter commonly issues two types of errors:

➤ `Can't find class classname.class`

This error is produced when the user tries to run a class by giving the interpreter the class file name rather than the class name. Be sure to drop the .class extension when running classes through the interpreter. For HelloWorldApp, you should enter `java HelloWorldApp` not `java HelloWorldApp.class`.

➤ `In class classname: void main(String argv[]) is not defined`

This error occurs when a class does not have a main() method defined. All applications must have a main() method defined in order to give the interpreter a place to start execution. You will learn the main declaration in more detail in Chapter 6.

Summary

You have learned the basics of developing Java code into either an applet or an application. By now, you should be comfortable using the Java compiler and interpreter, as well as using applets in HTML pages. Spend time with the Hello, World! applet and application. Change lines to get error messages, and see what the compiler and interpreter do. Try to see whether you can reproduce the errors shown in the troubleshooting section. Also, try to change the arguments used in resizing and placing text, or try outputting multiple lines of text. The best way to learn is by trial and error. Of course, the goal here is to help you get all the trial, with as little of the error as possible.

Now that you have mastered the Hello, World! app, what now? In the next chapter, you learn the basics of the language. That text discusses declaring and using the basic types, such as numbers, strings, and arrays with operators. In addition, the guts of a program—control flow—are presented. This section covers all the ways to control the movement of the program.

In later chapters, you start learning more advanced topics. Classes and the ways in which to use them to their full extent are presented. You learn threads, exceptions, and the use of the standard class libraries. Eventually, you look at developing content in more detail, including not only applets and stand-alone applications but also content and protocol handlers.

The HelloWorld examples are intended to show the ways in which Java provides a powerful environment for developing applications. The portability allows for a single compile environment while allowing distribution across a heterogeneous network. The robust, high-performance execution means that the performance hit for such portability is kept to a minimum. In addition, the built-in security features allow for easy development of innovative content. Most of all, these examples should give you a feel for what developing in the Java environment is like.

Chapter 6

The Fundamentals—Types, Expressions, and Control Flow

Now that you have written and compiled your own code and seen it run, you should feel familiar enough with the javac compiler and java interpreter to begin working on more substantial projects. Of course, to begin working on more complicated programs, you will need to learn more about the Java language itself. This chapter aims to familiarize the reader with the foundations of the language—types, expressions, and control flow. These items are essentially the guts of any program, and are basic to any programming language.

For those who are familiar with programming, especially C and C++, the following chapter will be quite familiar. Except in a couple of places where Java sticks more closely to the object-oriented paradigm, almost all the C fundamentals are the same. For those experienced programmers, special indicators flag areas where Java is diverging from C or C++. Those who are coming at Java as their first programming language should read this chapter carefully. This chapter's topic is deceptively simple; and, although a cursory read might impart the feeling that you know the material, as rare as natural programmers are, photographic memory is even rarer. Be sure to go over the examples. Spend time with the code to make sure you understand what is going on. A detailed understanding of the basic structures makes later programming easier and much less frustrating.

Quick Review

Up to now, you have covered the Java language and environment from a conceptual standpoint. You looked at the features and capabilities of the Java specification with respect to portability, performance, and ease of use in Chapter 2, "An Introduction to Java." The interpreter and browser environments were discussed from both the end user and the server sides in Chapters 3 and 4, "Using the Java Environment" and "Server Administration for HotJava and Java." Finally, in the preceding chapter, you learned the compiler environment and the general procedure for writing, compiling, and using your own Java programs. With this background, you should be able to place this chapter within the context of the entire Java framework.

In the preceding chapter, you learned the rudimentary skills needed for producing applets and applications. In addition, you learned the basics of the class structure of Java. An understanding of these topics is necessary for working through this chapter. In particular, using the javac compiler and the run-time interpreter Java will be important to completing the exercises presented in the following sections. For this chapter, you primarily use the interpreter and stand-alone applications, rather than the browser and applets, for development. The reason for this choice is that the overhead of writing code for the interpreter environment is much less than that for writing applets for HotJava or Netscape. If you felt comfortable with getting the HelloWorldApp class running, you should have no problems running the examples in this chapter.

What This Chapter Covers

This chapter presents the fundamental data type, expressions, operators, and control-flow declarations of the Java language. In addition, the standard input and output are covered for reasons of program usage. For our programs in this chapter to be at least correct, if not precise, you must do three things. First, you must encapsulate them in a class structure. What you learned in the preceding chapter is more than enough to provide a rudimentary class for the examples here. Second, our programs must be able to output the results of their work to the user so that you know whether they have worked. In this case, you will use the method System.out shown in the preceding chapter. Third, you need to provide our program with information at run-time. This will be accomplished by using the System.in method. You could, of course, provide any data you needed in the program itself; however, if you wanted to test under different situations, you would need to recompile the code every time. Instead, by using the standard input methods, you can check that our application works for a range of input variables without recompilation.

After you develop the basic structure of the programs, you will use them to discuss the fundamental aspects of the language. Types such as numbers, characters, and arrays will be defined, along with operators, declarations, and expressions. These elements are what could be called the calculating engine of Java. They provide the means for solving equations and testing or changing the state of a variable. In addition, control-flow will be discussed. This aspect of the language provides the methods for making decisions based on the calculation portion of the code. In essence, this is where the real "computing" goes on. These elements exist in every programming language, and are the basis of modern computing. Because all languages share these common elements, having a good understanding of the way in which they work not only makes an understanding of the rest of the Java language simpler but also makes learning a new programming language easier.

After You Finish This Chapter

The information in this chapter does not tell you everything there is to know about programming in Java. Even though our programs will run and do what you ask them to do, it is important to realize that you are producing a synthetic environment in order to discuss certain features of the language. After you have completed these fundamentals, you can use the framework developed to build the complete picture of the Java language. When you have finished this chapter, you should be ready to learn more about the class elements of the Java language, including instance variables, methods, constructors, and inheritance, along with more advanced features such as threads and class libraries. But to get there, you must start at the beginning.

The Architecture of Java Code

When you write a program in Java, you create at least one file with the extension .java that holds your source code. This file is called a *compilation unit*. All Java programs are composed of at least one, and typically more, of these units. Each unit comprises combinations of four different elements: package statements, import statements, class declarations, and interface declarations. For our programs in this chapter, you mainly use the class declaration. The other declarations are covered in more detail in Chapter 7, "Getting It Together—Classes, Interfaces, and Packages." The class declaration is composed of instance variables and methods, along with static variables and methods. All applications must have a main() method defined, which is where the interpreter starts to run the program. Altogether, these elements will look as shown here:

```
class ClassName {
    public static void main (String args[]) {
        //add code here
    }
}
```

This is the basic structure of the Java code you will be working on. All the examples in this chapter add code to the main() method. Recall the earlier discussion of the main() method in Chapter 5, "Getting Started on Your Own Java Code." The method must accept the command-line arguments from the interpreter (String args[]), and does not return any variables (void). The method is the same for all instances of the class (static) and can be invoked by any other class (public).

In addition to the class declaration, you will also use the import statement to allow the program the use of certain classes provided with the Java environment. If the code requires the use of a class's method, it will appear as shown here:

```
import ClassName

 class ClassName {
     public static void main (String args[]) {
         //add code here
     }
 }
```

Any imported functions will be explained in the text along with the code examples.

The Java Token Set

The javac compiler takes the code written in the *Unicode* format that you give it, and extracts individual elements known as *tokens*. These tokens can be divided into five types: *identifiers*, *keywords*, *literals*, *operands*, and *separators*. In addition, the compiler removes *comments* and *white spaces* (spaces, tabs, and line feeds) which are not a part of the token set. Each of these tokens is discussed in more detail in the next section.

The Unicode character set replaces the standard ASCII set, expanding the number of bytes from 8 for ASCII to 16 for Unicode. Unicode extends the character set to provide for many non-Latin language characters.

 Note

After the compiler has extracted the tokens from your code, it proceeds to create the machine-independent Java bytecode, which is capable of execution in either the interpreter or the browser environments. All of your programs will be written using the following types: identifiers, keywords, literals, operators and separators; in addition to the non-token comments.

Comments

Comments in Java come in three styles. The older /* */ style was originally used in the ANSI-C standard. This comment is useful for multiple-line comments, for example, at the beginning of a code fragment:

```
/* The following class will output the
   words Hello, World! to the screen
   when run on the interpreter         */
class HelloWorldApp {
...
```

The // comment method was added to C++ as an easier way to comment out individual lines. If a line of code does something important, it is always useful to make a short comment. Here's an example:

```
System.out.println("Hello, World!");  //note the use of
quotation marks
```

The /** */ comment, which is the third style, is a new addition to Java, and is used by the javadoc automatic document creator. Its use is covered in the "Using the Java Tools" section in Chapter 13, "Interfacing with C and Using the Java Tools." The full set of comment types is shown in table 6.1

Table 6.1	The Different Comments in Java
Comment Type	**Description**
// comment	All characters after the // to the end of the line are ignored.
/* comment */	All characters between /* and */ are ignored. These comments can extend onto multiple lines.
/** comment */	All characters between the /** and */ are ignored as in the /* */ comments; however, these comments should be used only before declarations, because they will be used by the javadoc tool in creating automatic documentation. See the section on "Using the Java Tools" in Chapter 13.

Including comments in code is an important habit to get into. Even though it seems as though everything is perfectly clear when you are writing your code, someone else who wants to use it might have great difficulties in determining exactly what you were trying to do. It will also save you many headaches later when you decide to update that class that you spent weeks creating, only to find that you can't figure out the way to work in new code without disrupting what you've done. Comments are perhaps the easiest and most powerful method for ensuring that code is reusable.

Identifiers

Identifiers are the names given to variables, classes, and methods to identify them to the compiler. HelloWorldApp, main and LightOn are all examples of identifiers used in previous Java code. What, then, makes a valid identifier? In Java, all identifiers must begin with a letter, the underscore character (_), or the dollar sign ($). All subsequent characters can also include digits (0–9). Letters are considered all the upper- and lowercase alphabet from A to Z, and all Unicode characters with numbers above hex 00C0. This enables non-Latin characters such as "Ç" and "ø" to be used in names; however, characters such as "¶" are not included. Check out the Appendix, "Further Information," for information on where you can find details for the Unicode character set.

In addition, those words designated as *keywords* in the next section are unusable. Table 6.2 gives examples of valid and invalid identifiers in Java.

Table 6.2	Valid Identifiers	
Valid	Invalid	Valid, but Not Recommended
watts	wattage #	WATTS
lightOn	light-on	lighton
monthsWith_31_days	5dogs	_number
x	abstract	$_243_fubar

Of course, unless you have a non-American standard keyboard, using anything other than the "_", "$" and "a"–"Z" letters would merely create difficulties in editing. Unless you have good reason, it is not advisable to use the "$" at all, and only to use the "_" in the middle of identifiers (between words) to improve readability. One reason for this guideline is that later, when you are linking in C code, the "_" and "$" are typically used by library routines. Not using them in your code helps to quickly narrow down problems to specific libraries. Using descriptive names should provide you with all the flexibility you need. The standard is to make all letters lowercase except for the beginning of words that appear in the middle of an identifier (such as in lightOn).

Note

In C and C++, the standard is to name #define identifiers with all upper-case letters. Java does not implement a #define, so for ease of transition, all-uppercase identifiers should not be used. This rule will come in handy when you are linking in C code later.

Keywords

Keywords are identifiers used by the Java language, and cannot be used in any other way than that defined by the Java language. You won't be able to remember every single keyword, so if you are having a problem with an identifier that is a single lowercase word, be sure to check out the keyword list in table 6.3.

Table 6.3	List of Reserved Java Keywords		
abstract	double	int	super
boolean	else	interface	switch
break	extends	long	synchronized
byte	false	native	this
byvalue*	final	new	threadsafe
case	finally	null	throw
catch	float	package	transient
char	for	private	true
class	goto*	protected	try
const*	if	public	void
continue	implements	return	while
default	import	short	
do	instanceof	static	

* reserved keywords, but currently unused by Java

Literals

Literals, which are used when entering explicit values into your code such as 5 or x, refer to the basic representation of two types of data in the Java language:

1. numbers
2. characters

The number literals can be categorized into two subtypes: integers (numbers without a decimal point) and floating point (numbers with decimal values). The character literal refers to a single value of the Unicode character set, whereas strings refer to collections of characters. In addition, there is a special literal known as boolean. The boolean literal is included under numbers because in C there was not boolean, instead, the integers 1 and 0 were used for true and false respectively.

Literals are closely linked with types, which are discussed in the next section. The difference between types and literals is that literals are explicit values entered into the code of your program, whereas types represent an amount of memory large enough to hold that information. Think of the small child's toy that has different pegs to put into the right shaped hole. It has round, square, triangle, and star-shaped pegs, and a set of holes to match. The holes that can accept the different pegs are the equivalent of types. They are an indication of the kind of data that can be stored. Literals are the equivalent of the pegs, or data, actually placed in those holes.

Integers

The first literal is the integer. This literal, the most common, comes in three guises: *decimal*, *hexadecimal*, and *octal* format. The decimal, or base 10, integer is the most familiar, appearing as you would expect it. The important thing to note about the integer is that it does not have a leading zero. The hexadecimal, or base 16, integer is typically used as a binary shorthand, each digit grouping four binary ones and zeros. Hexadecimal integers are represented by the digits 0–9 and the upper- or lowercase letters A–F, which represent the numbers 10–15. These integers are preceded by 0x or 0X. Octal, or base 8, integers are represented by the presence of a zero (0) in front of the digits. Table 6.4 gives examples of several numbers in the different formats.

Table 6.4   The Decimal, Octal, and Hexadecimal Representations of Integers

Decimal	Octal	Hexadecimal
0	0	0x0
2	02	0X2
63	077	0X3f
83	0123	0x53
63l	077l	0x3Fl

Integer literals are stored in the int data type, which provides for 32 bits of information. This limits the range of values from (decimal) -2,147,483,648 to 2,147,483,648. If for some reason you need to represent a larger number, the long integer type is 64 bits in size, which should be adequate. If you want to force an integer to be stored as a long, you can append an l or L to the end. The section on types discusses the storage of values in more detail.

Floating-Point

The floating-point literals are used to represent decimal numbers with fractional parts such as 1.5 or 43.7. They can be in either standard or scientific notation. Following are some examples:

3.1415, 0.1, .3, 6.022e23, 2.997E8, 1.602e-19

The standard storage of a floating-point literal is called the float for single precision, and takes up 32 bits of space. There is also a 64-bit double for double precision. You can specify which type you want with the f/F or d/D suffix:

3.1415f, 6.022e23d, 2.997E8F, 1.602e-19D

Boolean

The boolean literal has two states: true and false. These states are represented by the keywords true and false. This value is used to represent the state of something that can have only one of two values. The values are typically used as flags for determining whether to take a certain action. The boolean value is a true literal, and not a representation of the integers zero or one as in C or C++.

Character

The character literal is a character enclosed in single quotation marks (such as x). It can be any character from the Unicode character set. In addition, the backslash (\) is used to represent nonprinting or conflicting characters. Table 6.5 lists the various nonprinting control character combinations Java will accept:

Table 6.5 Special Character Representations

Description	Standard Designation	Sequence
Continuation	<newline>	\
New-line	NL(LF)	\n
Horizontal tab	HT	\t
Backspace	BS	\b
Carriage return	CR	\r
Form feed	FF	\f
Backslash	\	\\
Single quotation mark	'	\'
Double quotation mark	"	\"
Octal bit pattern	0ddd	\ddd
Hex bit pattern	0xdd	\xdd
Unicode character	0xdddd	\udddd

String

String literals are any number of characters enclosed in double quotation marks. Strings are in fact implemented by the class String, not as an array of characters as in C++. Each String literal creates a new instance of the class String. Don't worry about the fact that Strings are classes. Because of the very nature of classes, you don't need to worry about how to implement them—they take care of themselves. Mentioning the fact that Strings are classes here is merely for the sake of correctness. Table 6.6 gives examples of some Strings and their printed output.

Table 6.6 Examples of Valid Strings

The Declaration	The Result
""	
"\'"	'

The Declaration	The Result
"Your Ad Here"	Your Ad Here
"Multiple\nLines"	Multiple
	Lines

If you would like to see what some Strings would look like on-screen, you can take our HelloWorldApp and change the String in the line:

```
System.out.println( place your String here );
```

Compile the file as before, and run it through the interpreter. You should be able to check out all the nonprinting characters and the Unicode set.

Operators and Separators

Many characters and character combinations are used in Java as operators and separators. Operators are used to perform some type of computation on objects, whereas separators are used to tell the compiler where groups of code are divided and arranged. Table 6.7 presents all the valid operators and separators.

Table 6.7	A List of Operators and Separators						
+	-	!	%	^	&	*	|
~	/	>	<	(	)	{	}
[	]	;	?	:	,	.	=
++	--	==	<=	>=	!=	<<	>>
>>>	+=	-=	*=	/=	&=	|=	^=
%=	<<=	>>=	>>>=	||	&&		

You have now seen all there is to the Java Language. The previous sections presented all the possible character sequences you can use to create a Java application. Of course, this doesn't help you when it comes to learning the way to program in Java. The correct combination of the previous elements is what creates the application you want to run. You should, however, be able to recognize which functions specific elements have before trying to figure out what they are doing in combination. As you proceed through the language, you will refer to these basic types. You need not have them memorized, but you should at least be familiar with the different classes of tokens so that when you refer to operators or identifiers, you will know what to expect.

Declaring Variables

To store a value in Java, it must be contained in a variable. For a variable to be used, it must have two items associated with it: a type and an identifier. You assign these in the declaration statement:

```
type identifier [, identifier];
```

This statement tells the compiler to create a variable with the name *identifier* of type *type*. Note the semicolon telling the compiler that this is the end of the declaration; also, the optional identifier in square brackets indicates optional declarations. In this case, you can string together the declaration of several variables with the same type by separating their names with commas. After you have created a variable, you can assign it values, or perform calculations on the value it holds with operators.

The type, as mentioned in the section on literals, determines what kinds of values variables can hold, what can be done to those variables, and what these actions do to the variables. In Java, there are two kinds of types. At the first level are the types that are called *simple*. They are not built on any other type. The integer, floating-point, boolean, and character types are all of this kind. They are as basic as you can get. In addition, Java defines what are known as *composite* types. These types are built on the simple types, and consist of arrays, classes, and interfaces. You learn the array type in this chapter and save the class and interface types for Chapter 7, "Getting It Together—Classes, Interfaces, and Packages."

The Java type, unlike C, C++, and many other languages, does not actually affect its memory allocation. Instead, the type controls the variable's arithmetic properties and the legal range of values. If the variable is outside of the legal range it is divided by the range, and the remainder is used.

Note

Declaring Integer Types

There are four integer types, each referring to variables with different bit lengths. The shortest is the byte integer, which is 8 bits long. Next is the short integer, which is 16 bits long. The int type integer is 32 bits long, and the long integer is 64 bits. All types are signed. Following are some sample integer declarations:

```
byte x;
short numberOfChildren;
int wattage;
long WorldPopulation;
int x, y, z;
```

Note the use of the commas in the last example to declare three variables, x, y, and z, at the same time and all of type int.

Declaring Floating-Point Types

The floating-point type is declared using either the float or the double keyword. The float keyword stores the variable as a 32-bit single-precision floating-point number, as defined by IEEE 754. the double keyword stores the variable as a 64-bit double-precision, as defined by IEEE 754. Here's an example:

```
float pi;
double avagadroNumber;
```

Declaring Character Types

Java uses Unicode, which is a 16-bit character set; therefore, the Java char type is a 16-bit unsigned integer. Char variables would be used to store single characters, not entire strings, which is done by the String class. Following is an example:

```
char c;
```

Declaring Boolean Types

The boolean type holds the logical values true and false. This type is typically returned by methods that want to indicate the success of their operation. In addition, the logical operators return values of type boolean. Here's an example:

```
boolean lightOn;
```

Note

The boolean type is a type all its own. It is not like Boolean in C or C++, where it is an enumeration representing the integers zero and one. For this reason, boolean values cannot be converted into numbers by casting.

Declaring Arrays

Arrays are special types in Java. They hold a list of objects that can be referenced by indexing. In addition you can have arrays of arrays. Following are some examples:

```
int i[];       //one-dimensional array
char c[][];    //two-dimensional array
float[] f;
```

Notice that you do not include the number of variables to be held in the array, and notice also the optional placement of the square brackets. Allocation of an array must be explicit using the new operator, which is discussed in the next section.

Note

Unlike C and C++, Java does not use pointers; therefore, boundary-checking problems that are so common on these platforms do not occur in Java. Because of this, the array must be allocated explicitly with the new command.

Scope

When you declare a variable, it is introduced into a scope. The name can be used only in that specific part of the program. The scope of a variable is from the point it was declared to the end of the block it is in. A block is defined by the two curly braces { }. For example:

```
class App { // beginning of class App block
    public static void main(String args[]) { // beginning of
    main
        int i;                              // method block
        ...
    }                         // end of main method block
    public void method1() { // beginning of method1 block
        char c;
        ...
    }                        // end of method1 block
}                            // end of class App block
```

int i has been declared in the method main. Because main's block does not include the method1 block, any reference to i in method1 would be an error. The same would go for char c.

In one special situation, a variable can be *hidden* by other variables. This is the case in which a variable is declared in a block; then, another scope is created within the original block, and a variable with an identical name is declared. While the program is in the second block, the first variable is hidden from use. This situation occurs in the following code:

```
class App {
    public static void main( String args[] ) {
        int i;
        boolean test = true;
        // int i is in scope
        while( test ) {
            int i;
            // the first i is now hidden, and the second i
            // always referred to
```

```
        }
        // the second i has fallen out of scope, and you
        // are now back to our original i
    }
}
```

Be careful when you are declaring variables, and keep track of what you have done. This is one reason it is important to use comments and descriptive names. You will be able to tell the difference between variables, and the problem of hidden variables will be less frequent.

Operators

After you have created your variables, you must be able to assign them values, make changes to them, and perform calculations. These are the roles of the operators. Table 6.8 lists the operators, from highest to lowest precedence.

Table 6.8	Operators from Highest to Lowest Precedence			
.	[]	()		
++	- -	!	~	instanceof
*	/	%		
+	-			
<<	>>	>>>		
<	>	<=	>=	
==	!=			
&				
^				
&&				
||				
?:				
=	op=			
,				

Precedence refers to the order in which multiple operations will be computed. Operators on the same level have equal precedence. For example, the calculation

```
a=b+c*d/(c^d);
```

would proceed by working from left to right on all binary operations (those involving two variables), computing those operations at the top of the list and working down. In this case, because the ( ) has higher precedence than anything else, the c^d would be computed first. Next, the c*d and the result of that divided by the result of the first operation would be computed. Finally, all this would be added to b and the result placed in a. Whenever you are in doubt about the order in which something is calculated, be sure to use the parenthesis () to specify to the compiler the way to do things.

Of course, the first operator you need to know is the assignment operator (=). This does exactly what you think it does. It takes the values on the right side of the equal sign and places them into the variable on the left side of the equal sign. Even though this is the easiest operator, it can get you into lots of trouble. Make sure that the lefthand variable is big enough to hold the results of anything that occurs on the righthand side.

Operators on Integers

Operations on integers fall into two categories: unary and binary. Unary operators act on one variable at a time. Binary operators act on two variables at a time. For operations in which the result is an integer if any of the variables, or *operands*, is long, then the result is a long; otherwise, the result is an int. Even if the operands in question are byte, short, or char, the result is an int.

Table 6.9 lists the unary operators.

Table 6.9	Unary Integer Operators
Operator	Operation
-	Unary negation
~	Bitwise complement
++	Increment
- -	Decrement

The unary negation changes the sign of an integer. Bitwise complement changes each bit of the variable to 1 if it was a 0, and to 0 if it was a 1. Increment increases the value of the variable by one, and decrement decreases the value of the variable by one. Following is an example:

```
class Unary {
    public static void main (String args[]) {
        int i = 0;
        int j = 10;
        for(i = 0; i<10; i++) {
            j--;
            System.out.println(i+"\t"+j+"\n");
        }
    }
}
```

This application runs increasing numbers in one column and decreasing numbers in the other. Note the use of ++ and - -. Each time these occur, the system either raises or lowers the value of the operand by one. This is the way in which unary operators work—they change the value of the variable they are used on. For the negation and bitwise complement, the variable is not changed; for the increment and decrement, the variable is changed. The following code gives an example of the way this works:

```
class Unary {
    public static void main (String args[]) {
        int i = 10, j = 10, k = 10, l = 10;
        System.out.println(i+"\t"+j+"\n");
```

```
        j++;
        i--;
        ~k;
        -l;
        System.out.println(i+"\t"+j+"\t"+k+"\t"+l+"\n");
    }
}
```

Notice that j and i have been changed, and print out their new values, but k and l have reverted to their original values. When using the unary negation and bitwise complement in a compound operation, you are actually using a temporary variable, holding the new value of the operand. The increment and decrement operators are both prefix and postfix—that is, they can be placed before (++x;) or after (x++;) the operand. If they are used in compound statements such as

```
i=x++;
```

or

```
i=++x;
```

then the first line increments x *after* assigning its value to i, and the second line increments x and then passes the new value on to i.

The second type of integer operator is the binary operator. These operations do not change the values of the operands. They return a value that must be assigned to a variable. Table 6.10 lists the binary integer operators

Table 6.10	Binary Integer Operators
Operator	**Operation**
+	Addition
-	Subtraction
*	Multiplication
/	Division

continues

Table 6.10 Continued	
Operator	**Operation**
%	Modulus
&	Bitwise AND
|	Bitwise OR
^	Bitwise XOR
<<	Left shift
>>	Right shift
>>>	Zero-fill right shift

The following program prints the values of some operations:

```
class Binary {
    public static void main (String args[]) {
        int i = 5;
        int j = 10;
        System.out.println(i+"\t"+j+"\n");
        j = j + i;
        System.out.println(i+"\t"+j+"\n");
        j = j * i;
        System.out.println(i+"\t"+j+"\n");
        j -= i;
        System.out.println(i+"\t"+j+"\n");
    }
}
```

Notice the last operation. It is a combination of the binary operator and the assignment operator. This is equivalent to writing `j=j-i;`. This can be done with all the binary operators. Take the time to place your own equations into the code. Add variables and try different combinations.

Some further notes on the integer operations. First, division of integers rounds toward zero. Second, if you divide or modulo by zero, you will have an exception thrown at run-time. If your operation exceeds the lower limit, or underflows, the result will be a zero. If it exceeds the upper limit, or overflows, it will lead to wrap-around. Moving past the upper limit will place you at the very bottom value—approximately –2.1 billion.

There are also additional relational operators that produce boolean results. These operators are shown in Table 6.11.

Table 6.11	Relational Integer Operators Producing Boolean Results
Operator	**Operation**
<	Less than
>	Greater than
<=	Less than or equal to
>=	Greater than or equal to
==	Equal to
!=	Not equal to

I will point out immediately here that the equal-to operator (==) will cause you endless suffering. I still replace the double equal sign with just a single equal sign when I mean to compare two values instead of assigning the value of the right operand to the left. Make sure that you use the double equal sign for comparison. Try this application:

```
class Binary {
    public static void main (String args[]) {
        int i = 0;
        int j = 10;
        while(i<j) {
            System.out.println(i+"\n");
            i++;
        }
    }
}
```

Here, the control statement while checks the values of i and j. While the statement i<j is true, it runs the code fragment that prints i and then increases it by one. As soon as i<j is false, the program drops out of the while loop and finishes. You will cover while loops in the section on control flow.

Operators on Boolean Types

The boolean type adds several new operators for logical computation. These operators are listed in Table 6.12.

Table 6.12 Boolean Operators

Operator	Operation
!	Boolean negation
&	Logical AND
|	Logical OR
^	Logical XOR
&&	Evaluation AND
||	Evaluation OR
==	Equal to
!=	Not equal to
&=	AND assignment
|=	OR assignment
^=	XOR assignment
?:	Ternary

If you consider the boolean value to be the equivalent of either a 1 for true, or 0 for false, the operators act the same as those for the integer operators if they are working on a single bit. Negation (!) is the equivalent of the integer bitwise complement (~) and is a unary operation. Table 6.13 lists the results of the operations.

Table 6.13 Results of Boolean Operations

AND			OR			XOR		
Op1	Op2	Result	Op1	Op2	Result	Op1	Op2	Result
true	true	true	true	true	true	true	true	false
true	false	false	true	false	true	true	false	true
false	true	false	false	true	true	false	true	true
false	false	false	false	false	false	false	false	false

The &, | and ^ operators evaluate both sides of the argument before deciding on the result. The && and || operators can be used to avoid evaluation of righthand operands if it is not needed.

The ?:, or ternary, operator works as shown here:

Operand1 ? *Statement1* : *Statement2*;

Operand1 is evaluated for its truth or falsity. If it is true, *Statement1* is completed; if it is false, *Statement2* is completed. The following code gives an example of this operation:

```
class TestTernary {
    public static void main (String args[]) {
        int i = 10, j = 10;
        boolean test = false;
        test ? (i = 0) : (j = 0);
        System.out.println(i+"\t"+j+"\n");
        test = true;
        test ? (i = 0): (j = 0);
        System.out.println(i+"\t"+j+"\n");
    }
}
```

Note the parenthesis. They are not needed in this example, but if you use more complicated statements, you might want to include them.

In addition to these operators, the &=, |=, and ^= work as assignment operators on boolean values just as for integer values.

Operators on Floating-Point Numbers

The traditional binary operations work on floating-point values (-, +, *, and /), in addition to the assignment operators (+=, -=, *=, and /=). Modulus (%) and the modulus assignment operator (%=) give the floating-point equivalent of an integer divide. Also, the increment and decrement (++, - -) work, increasing or decreasing the value of the variable by 1.0.

Similar to the integer variables, the result is placed in the largest denominator. If the operation includes two floats, the result will be a float type. If one or more of the operands is a double, the result will be a double. When you are using the relational operators (>, <, >=, <=, ==, and !=), note that floating-point variables do not behave like integers, and just because a==b is true does not mean that a<b || a>b is true! This is because floating-point values are not ordered like integers. Be careful when you are writing a program and making assumptions about floating-point values. Floating-point values also include Inf for infinity. Overflow produces an Inf (the floating point representation of an infinite number), underflow zero and divide-by-zero Inf.

Array Operators

Contrary to C or C++, the allocation for an array always uses the new operator to create the array and assign it to the variable. Here's an example:

```
int a[] = new int[10];
```

The preceding example creates an array of 10 ints and assigns it to a. You would refer to the individual variables by number: a[0], a[1], through a[8], a[9]. Note that the subscripts go from zero, the first element in the array, to the size of the array minus one. Arrays are used just like any other variable. The individual members of an array can be used anywhere that a variable of that type would be used. If x = 1; is valid, then x[3] = 1; is valid. Java also supports arrays of arrays:

```
char c[][] = new char[10][10];
float f[][] = new float[5][];
```

Notice in the second declaration that only one dimension is defined. Java requires that at least one dimension be defined at compile time (that is, explicitly in the source code). The remaining dimensions, however, can be allocated later.

Arrays are used where you would like to keep a lot of similar information in the same place and refer to it easily by number. Arrays are very powerful; they are discussed more in later chapters.

Strings

Strings can be concatenated using the + operator. If any of the operands are not Strings, they are converted to Strings before being concatenated. In addition, the += operator works by placing the concatenation of two Strings into the first. You used the + operator in the previous examples when you wanted to print several items on one line. Try using the System.out.println and the + operator to make different combinations of output with the interpreter.

As far as using Java for computations, you have covered all the basic operations that can be performed on variables. You should spend time with the information presented, and try experimenting with your own programs. Of course, even in the examples here, you broke down and used several control-flow statements to make the programs really do something. Control flow provides the basic engine for getting your calculations working. In the next section, you learn the control-flows available in Java.

Casting Types

The System method System.in.read() returns an integer value. Typically, however, you want to use it as a character. What happens when you have an int and need to place it into a char? You do what is called a cast. You cast the int into a char. The method for placing one type into another follows:

```
int a;
char b;
a = (int) b;
```

The parenthetical reference to int tells the compiler that you want to change the character into an integer and place it into a. On the other hand, if you need to go the other way, you would use:

```
b = (char) a;
```

It is important to remember how much space the ints and chars each take up. Because both ints and chars are 32 bits, you can move from one to the other without a loss of information. However, if you were to move from a long—64 bits—to an int, you might lose information because longs can hold numbers larger than 32 bits. Even if the two quantities are the same size, such as int and float (both hold 32 bits) you would loose information about fractional numbers. Java does now allow automatic casting like C or C++. Be careful when you explicitly cast something to make sure that it can hold the information you are casting. The casts that will not result in a loss of information are

➤ Byte to short, char, int, long, float, double

➤ Short to int, long, float, double

➤ Char to int, long, float, double

➤ Int to long, float, double

➤ Long to float, double

➤ Float to double

➤ Double can only be stored as a double without loss of information

Be sure to check the type of cast you want to perform. You might not always lose information if you perform a cast that is not listed here, but it would be dangerous to assume a cast of this nature will always work. For example, if you cast a long to an int, and the long number is less than the maximum storable in an int, there would not be any loss. This is because the leading zeros would be dropped, and wouldn't provide any information about the number. However, you have to be sure that the long is *always* less than the maximum allowable value for an int.

Control Flow

Control flow is the method used to make your program move through the steps needed in the correct order with the least amount of fuss. Java provides several control flow expressions, as shown in table 6.14. Control flow is the heart of the program, providing it with direction. Rarely does a program go through a single series of steps in order to produce its output. In order to have interaction, programs must be able to react to input and calculations, and make decisions about what code to execute next. In addition, if you need to repeat a code fragment several times in a row, it would be a waste of effort to keep repeating it, instead you can tell your program to repeat it. Java provides control flow methods for these and other situations.

Table 6.14	Control Flow Expressions
Type	**Expression**
if-else	if(boolean)statement
	else statement
switch	switch(expression1) {
	case expression2: statement
	...
	default: statement
break	break [label];
continue	continue [label];
return	return expression;
for	for(expression1 ; expression2 ; expression3)
	statement
while	while(boolean) statement
do-while	do statement while(boolean);
label	label:*statement*

The if-else Branch

The if-else branch is the basic control flow expression in the Java language. Simply put, *if* something is true, you execute the first statement; *else,* do the other statement. For example:

```
if(a < b) a = b;
else b = a;
```

Note

Note that the expression evaluated is a *boolean*, not a number. Unlike in C, you cannot place an integer here as a shortcut, in which 0 = false and any other number is true. You must make some relational statement in order for Java to evaluate the if statement.

If you don't want to do anything if the statement is not true, you can simply leave off the else. If you want to have your program do more than one thing for each statement, surround them with the curly brackets {}.

```
if(!lightOn) {
    wattage = 0;
    roomDark = true;
}
else {
    wattage = 60;
    roomDark = false;
}
```

In addition, if you want to string together a series of tests, you can do so as shown here:

```
if(boolean) statement
else if(boolean) statement
else if(boolean) statement
...
else statement
```

In this case, the boolean expressions at each stage are evaluated. If one is found to be true, it is executed; otherwise, the final else is executed.

Be sure to use the curly braces for your statements if it is unclear which order statements should be executed in. Here's an example:

```
if(x > 0)
    if(x == z) a = z;
else a = x;        //this else would be associated with the
                   //inner if.
```

The preceding example would produce the incorrect result if you wanted a to equal x only if x <= 0. Instead, the block notation should have been used to make it explicit:

```
if(x > 0) {
    if(x == z) a = z;
}
else a = x;
```

You now have enough pieces together to write a program that does something interesting. You will be introducing a new function—System.in.read(). This function enables us to read characters from the standard input, typically the keyboard. System.in.read() returns the character entered. If an end-of-input character is entered (Ctrl+D on Unix and Ctrl+Z on DOS and Windows systems) it will return a –1. Following is an example:

```
class Reply {
    public static void main (String args[]) {
        char a;
        System.out.println("Enter a number from 1-3:");
        a = (char)System.in.read();
        if(a == -1)
            System.out.println("\nno character entered");
        else if(a == '1')
            System.out.println("\nYou win a Car!");
        else if(a == '2')
            System.out.println("\nYou picked the goat");
        else if(a == '3')
            System.out.println("\nYou get to keep your
            100");
```

```
                else System.out.println("\nincorrect entry");
        }
}
```

Obviously, the program doesn't do that much, unless you are on a game show, but you can see the way in which you can use the if-else statement to control the flow of the program depending on the condition of certain variables.

The while and do-while Loop

The while loop checks to see whether an expression is true, and processes the given statement until the expression becomes false. On the other hand, the do-while loop will process a statement, and then evaluate the expression to see if the statement needs to be processed again. You used the while loop earlier to show the increment operator. You should remember that you must be changing whatever expression you are evaluating *in* the loop itself; otherwise, if it is true, you will enter an infinite loop because the statement will then always be true. Following is an example:

```
boolean test = true;
while(test) {
    System.out.println("Hey!, get me outta here!\n");
}
```

Try this code in one of the previous apps, but *don't* wait for it to finish (Ctrl+C breaks you out of the program). If you want to make sure that your statement executes at least once, even if the expression is false, use the do-while loop. Following is another example:

```
boolean test = false;
do {
    ...
} while (test);
```

This control is used much less frequently, but is sometimes necessary. Note the ending semicolon (;) after the while statement.

The switch Branch

The switch branch is a kind of if-else structure, but makes coding much easier than writing out if-else conditions, especially if there are several options. The control is executed by comparing the value of the variable in the switch parenthesis with the values listed for each case and executing the statement that occurs at each line. If none of the values match, the default: case is executed. After each case, you should use the break; statement. Otherwise, all the cases after the one found will execute. This is called drop-through. Try the following example with and without the break; statements:

```java
class SwitchTest {
    public static void main (String args[]) {
        char a;
        System.out.println("Enter a number from 1-3:");
        a = (char)System.in.read();
        switch(a) {
          case '1':
              System.out.println("\nYou win a Car!");
              break;
          case '2':
              System.out.println("\nYou picked the goat");
              break;
          case '3':
              System.out.println("\nYou get to keep your
              100");
              break;
          default:
              System.out.println("\nIncorrect entry");
        }
    }
}
```

Be sure to use the break statement, and if you do not need it, make sure that you will not be dropping down onto code you don't want to.

With the while and switch statements in hand, you can proceed to write a more substantial program. This program counts the number of digits, white spaces, and other characters entered from the terminal:

```java
class SwitchTest {
    public static void main (String args[]) {
        int numberOfWhite = 0, numberOfDigits = 0,
            numberOfOthers = 0;
        char c;
        while((c = (char)System.in.read()) != -1 && c !=
'\n') {
            switch(c) {
            case '0':
            case '1':    case '2':
            case '3':    case '4':
            case '5':    case '6':
            case '7':    case '8':
            case '9':    numberOfDigits++;
                            break;
                case ' ':        case '\n':
                case '\t':    numberOfWhite++;
                                break;
                default:        numberOfOthers++;
                                break;
            }
        }
        System.out.println("\nResults:\n");
        System.out.println("Number of digits = " +
        numberOfDigits + "\n");
        System.out.println("Number of white spaces = " +
        numberOfWhite + "\n");
        System.out.println("Number of others = " +
        numberOfOthers + "\n");
    }
}
}
```

The while loop at the beginning of the code grabs a character from the keyboard until the end-of-input flag is sent. Then, the switch statement takes the character and compares it to all the digits first, and then to the white spaces. When it finds one, it falls through and increments the relevant counter. When the number is incremented, the break statement ends the switch. If it cannot find any matches, it increases the "other" counter. The final switch in the default statement is not necessary, but is placed there for consistency and in case one day someone adds extra case statements to the end.

The for Loop

The for loop is a powerful tool for looping through a series until some limit has been reached. The format of the for statement uses a variable to compare with a certain limit. When the limit is reached, the loop is broken.

```
for( i=0 ; i<10 ; i++) ... ;
```

The format of the argument (*ex1* : *ex2* : *ex3*) is as explained next. The first expression tells the for loop where to start the variable. In this case i is set to zero. The second expression, i < 10, tells the for loop when it should stop. In this case, the statement is true (that is, the loop should continue) for all values 0–9. The last expression tells the loop what to do each time to the variable. In this example, the for loop runs i from 0 to 9. You could use a statement like this to address the members of an array in order:

```
int i, a[] = new int[10];
for( i=0 ; i<10 ; i++) a[i] = 0;
```

The preceding code would fill the array of integers with zeros.

You can declare your variable in the for loop header, and the last expression can be omitted; but be sure to do something with the variable in your statement.

```
for(int i = 10; i >= 0 ; ) i--;
```

An example of using the for loop would be to print a conversion from Celsius to Fahrenheit in five-degree increments:

```
class TempConversion {
    public static void main (String args[]) {
        int fahr, cels;
        System.out.println("Celsius  Fahrenheit\n");
        for(cels = 0; cels <= 100; cels += 5) {
            fahr = cels * 9 / 5 + 32;
            System.out.println(cels + "\t" + fahr);
        }
    }
}
```

for loops are used in many places—for array indexing, anywhere a series of numbers is needed, or any time something has to execute a specific number of times.

Labels

Labels provide a method for controlling loops when the simple break; method will not work. If a break is encountered in the execution of a loop statement, the loop ends, regardless of what the other control evaluations are. This is an example of how a simple break statement works.

```
boolean test = true;
int i = 0;
while(test) {
    i++
    if(i > 10) break;
}
```

The while loop runs only 10 times, despite the fact that the expression test always returns true.

What happens, though, when you are nested down several levels in statements and need to break out? The normal break will break out of only a single block. You can use labels to mark which statement you want to break out of.

```
char a;
outer:                  //this is the label for the outer loop
```

```
for(int i=0; i<10 ; i++) {
    for(int j=0; j<10; j++) {
        a = (char)System.in.read();
        if (a == 'b') {
            break outer;
        }
        if (a == 'c') {
            continue outer;
        }
    }
}
```

In this case, the loops accept 100 input characters from the keyboard, unless the b key is entered, at which time the break outer; statement ends both loops. Notice the continue outer; statement. This statement tells the computer to break out of the present loop and continue with the outer loop.

Java does not have a goto statement. To those C/C++ programmers who were accustomed to using goto—shame on you, you know better. gotos are confusing and end up causing more problems than they are worth. They are generally a quick solution to a dirty problem, but increase the amount of time needed later to figure out what a program is doing.

Note

Summary

You have learned quite a bit of material in a short amount of space. Java is a powerful programming language, and there are many ways to tackle the same problem. Learning what is the best way takes experience and much trial and error. This chapter mainly gave a general review of the fundamentals of the Java language. You learned the Java token set, Java types, operators, and control statements. This is a very long list for a single chapter. Do not worry if you feel as though there is too much to digest. As you work through problems in the following chapters, you will continually use the basic material you learned here. You will go through many programs before you become completely comfortable with all the elements of the language. Use this chapter as a reference if you are having syntactical problems with your code. You should be able to find the answers to your questions in this chapter.

To C/C++ programmers, it should be obvious that the Java language is a product of these languages. Be sure, though, to note the differences. Many programmers have come to rely on dangerous shortcuts involving the use of pointers and casting. Java does not allow this kind of coding. You might think that the advantages of being *close* to the system are more desirable; however, when you have no idea what system your code will be running, this kind of low-level programming is impossible. What Java gives up in this area, it gains in others. You will find that the ease of use, and naturally good performance of the Java environment, make giving up those old habits easy. True, you will never get the same speed from a Java application as from finely tuned C code—but you wouldn't be able to run that code over the Internet anyway.

By now you should be very comfortable with using the javac compiler and Java interpreter. You should be able to work through the examples and try out different combinations of your own. Seeing what doesn't work is just as useful as seeing what does work. In the following chapters you move on to the higher-level language elements, such as classes, interfaces, and packages. All of these elements are merely containers for the guts of the system you have just learned. These containers, however, provide powerful capabilities to our code. In the next chapter, you will see the way in which object orientation, and specifically its implementation in Java, brings ease of use, portability, reusability, and robustness to your costly investment of code.

Chapter 7

Getting It Together—Classes, Interfaces, and Packages

Using the Java programming language means learning object-oriented programming. So far the basics of classes have been discussed, and the examples provided have used the basic class structure to get you started. However, in order to utilize the full power of Java and object-oriented computing, you will need to learn how to create, import, and inherit your own and pre-built classes.

Quick Review

The topics covered up to this point focused on gaining an understanding of the Java environment, learning to use the Java run-time systems, providing interactive content over the Internet, and the beginnings of learning to program in the Java language. The Java environment fulfills a need in the Internet for distributed, secure, high-performance programs that will provide a level of interactivity unseen in traditional media, and provide the technology for the future of communications and information delivery. Object-oriented computing is the foundation and fundamental solution to many of these technological problems by providing the encapsulation and extensibility needed in the dynamic atmosphere expected in the future of the Internet.

The Java architecture is one based upon object-oriented methodologies. All but the most fundamental types, such as integers and floating point numbers, are objects, or classes. By encapsulating the language features in classes, Java can provide an extensible environment where programmers do not have to repeat the jobs other programmers have carried out. In addition, Java provides solutions for many of the problems of object-oriented approaches in languages such as C++ by providing run-time evaluation of the class structure to overcome the fragile superclass dilemma. This allows objects to be loaded from across the room or across the country just as easily—an important element when developing code for the Internet.

The HotJava browser and Java interpreter provide the run-time environment to load the developed classes in the form of Java bytecodes. This enables the end user to take full advantage of the object-oriented paradigm by simply removing the common hassles of more traditional approaches. The Java browser and interpreter enables the individual to load applications and applets seamlessly into their existing environment. In addition, the extensibility of the run-time environment through classes allows for new protocol and content handlers to be incorporated on an as-needed basis.

The previous chapters started to introduce the fundamentals of programming in the Java language. Chapter 5 introduced the compiler, browser, and interpreter as development tools, and showed you how to get a stand-alone application and applet coded, compiled, and running. Chapter 6 provided you with the foundations of the Java language in order to allow later examples to be more readable, and to get you started as soon as possible writing code that actually did something. By now you should be familiar with the Java tokens, identifiers, types, operators, and control flow statements. This sets you up for a more advanced understanding of Java's object-oriented approach—classes.

What This Chapter Covers

This chapter looks at two elements of the Java language:

➤ How classes are created and used

➤ The incorporation of interfaces and packages

Classes provide the Java equivalent of an object. You will look at the elements of a class—variables and methods—in addition to different methods of access. The creation and destruction of objects is covered, along with inheritance and other advanced topics. Next, interfaces and packages are discussed. These two elements of the language allow the incorporation of classes into existing code and are important in using classes to their full potential.

Objects in Java

Java's implementation of an object is called a class. The *class* declaration can be seen as a template for creating objects. After you have created a class declaration, you can reuse it to create as many objects of that type as you need. Some people say that classes add new fundamental types to a language, except the programmers provide all the functionality themselves, instead of the language. For example, you can create a Rectangle class that you can treat just like an Integer or String.

Java takes object-oriented computing to the extreme in making every executable an object. When you run a stand-alone application or applet in the browser or interpreter run-time environment, Java creates an instance of the class loaded. After the object that was constructed from the class template has been created, it controls its action by either executing its own methods, creating objects of other classes, or a combination of the two.

All classes in Java are inherited from a superclass, known as Object. A class does not, however, have to be an immediate subclass of Object. You can create your new class by inheriting another class. Figure 7.1 shows the relationship between a superclass and its derived subclasses.

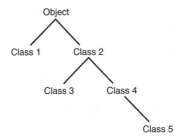

Figure 7.1
Inheritance from the Superclass Object.

In each case, the subclass inherits the properties of the superclass above it. In this way, a class can be several inheritances away from Object and still be said to be a subclass of Object. Object is the only class that does not have a superclass. In a way, it could be considered a fundamental type. If a class does not implicitly declare of which class it is an inheritance, Java assumes it is a subclass of Object.

Classes in Java

The basic declaration for a class is as follows:

```
class name {
     //class information
}
```

Note the beginning and ending curly braces, which designate the limits of the class definition. For example, perhaps you want to create a class of rectangles, and you have the following code:

```
class Rectangle {
    ...
}
```

In this case, the class Rectangle is a subclass of the class Object, because it doesn't specifically mention which class it is derived from. Later on, you will see how to designate which superclass to use instead of Object.

Instance Variables in Java Classes

After you have created your class, you need to be able to provide it with a means of storing its own information. You do this by declaring instance variables. If you recall from Chapter 6, "The Fundamentals—Types, Expressions, and Control Flow," you declare a variable by giving its type and then the identifier, or name, like in the following example.

```
type name;
```

In this case, you might want to store information about rectangles in the rectangle class:

```
int width, height;
```

Of course, you could hold other information, but for this simple rectangle, class width and height are enough. If you needed to, you could have instances of floats, arrays, or, as you will see later, classes themselves. Up to now, the class looks as follows:

```
class Rectangle {
    int width, height;
}
```

Of course, this object doesn't even do much; all it can do is hold its own width and height. If you want it to do anything, you have to provide it with methods.

Methods in Java Classes

A method is equivalent to a function in C or C++. You declare methods in Java with the following statement:

```
returnType name(parameters) {
    //function body
}
```

Again, note that you *do not* use the semicolon at the end of the method brackets as you would for normal declarations as mentioned in Chapter 6. Every method must return a value or be declared as void. Many times, methods are called to do specific calculations; in this case, they must return their result. The return type tells the compiler what kind of value to expect. In other cases, the method wants to indicate whether it has successfully completed its task. The parameters are a comma delimited list providing the method with information it needs. As an example of the return type and parameter list, perhaps your rectangle should be able to calculate its own area:

```
int getArea(int w, int h) {
    int a;
    a = w*h;
    return a;
}
```

When the method reaches the return statement, it sends this value back to where it was called from.

It should be noted that the variables the method is passed and uses, such as w and h, are merely copies. The method does not alter the originals. For example, the following code would in fact do nothing because it is only acting on copies of the variables:

```
int width, height;
swap(width,height);
void swap(int w, int h) {
    int temp = h;
    h = w;
    w = temp;
}
```

Additionally, if you declared this function, the rectangle variables width and height would be hidden by the new variable declarations (see Chapter 6 for a discussion of hidden variables):

```
void swap(int width, int height) { ...
```

If you wanted to actually swap the width and height, you would have to do so explicitly.

In the case of the rectangle, your class would now look like this:

```
class Rectangle {
    int width, height;
    int getArea(int w, int h) {
        int a;
        a = w*h;
        return a;
    }
}
```

In addition, the rectangle should also be able to draw itself. In this case, it will need another method:

```
class Rectangle {
    protected int width, height;
    protected int getArea(int w, int h) {
        int a;
        a = w*h;
        return a;
    }
    public void drawRect() {
        for(int i=width; i>0; i—) {
            System.out.print("#");
        }
        System.out.print("\n");
        for(int i=height-2; i>0; i—) {
            System.out.print("#");
            for(int j=width-2; i>0; i—) {
                System.out.print(" ");
            }
            System.out.print("#\n");
```

```
        }
        for(int i=width; i>0; i—) {
            System.out.print("#");
        }
        System.out.print("\n");
    }

}
```

Note

Notice that the final line of #'s is followed by `System.out.println("\n")`. This occurs because the print method does not actually output to the screen until the entire line is completed and the buffer is flushed. If you are not getting output, and you use the print method, make sure you have finished the output with a newline ("\n") character.

This new method is quite lengthy, but provides the class with a way in which to draw itself.

You should note the two additions to the method declarations: protected for getArea() and public for drawRect(). The protected modifier means that this method is only available to the Rectangle class and to any class that is derived from Rectangle. The public modifier means that drawRect() is available to any class that needs to tell the rectangle to draw itself. There is a third modifier, private, which means that only the class in which the modifier was declared can use the method; not even subclasses of the class can use those methods. These modifiers are also relevant for variables. If you do not want other classes to be able to see the instance variables, you can declare them as private. The following line of code shows the use of the private modifier.

```
private int secretVariable;
```

It is good practice to keep member variables and methods as restricted from outside use as possible. Of course, you also want the methods and variables that subclasses might need to be available. If you do not specify the access modifier, then it is assumed to be *friendly*, or only available to classes in the same package. Packages are discussed later in this chapter. Generally, you are safe if you use the protected modifier for everything other classes don't need to see, and public for those methods that other classes need to make your object work. Notice I said *methods*. It is not good practice to make any of your variables public. If someone might need to change a variable, make them do so through a method such as this:

```
public void setWidth(int w) width = w;
```

This way you can keep track of everything that goes on in your class.

Classes can also use the public modifier. If you do not use the public modifier in front of the class declaration, it will only be accessible to classes in the same package (see Understanding Packages in Java later in this chapter). Using the public modifier will allow all classes the ability to create instances of the class.

Overloaded Methods

What happens if you need to send the same method different kinds of information in different cases? You can *overload* the method by declaring more than one version. Essentially, you create a new method; you just give it a different parameter list, as in the following example:

```
void getArea(int w, int h);
void getArea(float w, float h);
```

In the second case, the method getArea() takes two float variables as its arguments. The compiler determines which method to call based upon how you call the method. If you provide the method with two ints, you get the first method. If you provide the methods with two floats, the second is used.

The Static Members

In addition to public, private, and protected, you can also declare members to be static. The *static* modifier indicates that a variable or method is the same for all classes. The rectangle might have a variable that you would want all rectangles to share, say the version number of the class. If you declare it as static, that variable will be the same for all instances of the class.

```
static int versionNumber = 1;
```

The benefit of static methods and variables is that they can be referenced without a specific instance of the class being created. For example, the drawRect() method uses the System.out.println method, even though you haven't created a System object. Out is a static variable, which enables you to reference the variable even though you haven't created an object from the variable's class— System. Additionally, there is a final modifier that tells the compiler that the variable or method cannot be changed by a subclass by overriding. Overriding methods are covered in a later section.

Object Creation and Destruction

Java provides methods and operators for creating instances of classes. After you have created the "template" for your objects using the class declaration, and if you want to use the new class, you must create it. To create an object, it must first have a creation method. After this is complete, another class can create a copy of the object by using the new operator.

When an object is about to be deleted because it has fallen out of scope, it first looks for a finalized method, and then proceeds to be garbage collected. The Java specification does not assure the programmer that the finalize method will be called as soon as the object falls out of scope, but it is good programming practice to always use the finalize method to finish off anything that the object might leave hanging. For example, if you have opened a file, it is wise to close it before the thread completely ends.

The Creation Method

The creation method in Java is a method with the same name as the class that does not return any value. Inside the creation method, you might want to initialize certain variables and get the object ready for use. The rectangle creation method is as follows:

```
public Rectangle(int w, int h) {
    width = w;
    height = h;
    area = getArea(w,h);
}
```

Note the use of the public modifier. Otherwise, later on, when you place Rectangle in a package, other classes won't be able to use the creation method.

You now have a completely usable class as follows:

```
class Rectangle {
    protected int width, height;
    protected int area;
    public Rectangle(int w, int h) {
        width = w;
        height = h;
        area = getArea(w,h);
    }
    protected int getArea(int w, int h) {
        int a;
        a = w*h;
        return a;
    }
    public void drawRect() {
        for(int i=width; i>0; i—) {
            System.out.print("#");
        }
        System.out.print("\n");
        for(int i=height-2; i>0; i—) {
            System.out.print("#");
            for(int j=width-2; i>0; i—) {
                System.out.print(" ");
            }
            System.out.print("#\n");
        }
        for(int i=width; i>0; i—) {
```

```
                System.out.print("#");
            }
            System.out.print("\n");
        }

    }
```

The new Operator

In order for a class to be able to use the Rectangle class, it must use the new operator to create an instance of it. You might, for example, have an application class that merely creates a 3×4 rectangle and draws it to the screen:

```
class doRect {
    public static void main(String args[]) {
        Rectangle rect = new Rectangle(3,4);
        rect.drawRect();
    }
}
```

Notice how the new operator is used in the previous example. Although you declare the variable as you do any other type (as in Rectangle Rect;), you must use the new operator to create a copy of the class which the new variable points to. Notice how the member method is invoked using the "." operator. The following is how you reference all class member variables and methods.

class.member

Of course, only those member variables and methods that are accessible according to the public, protected, friendly, and private modifiers are valid for referencing.

The finalize Method

In addition to the creation method, you can also provide a finalize method, like the following example.

```
void finalize() {
    //cleanup chores
}
```

This method enables you to close any files you might have open and generally makes sure that your object exits cleanly before the automatic garbage collection removes your object from memory. There is no guarantee that Java will invoke the finalize() method, so you should not depend upon the finalize method for your code to run correctly. Instead, you should think of it as an optimization of your code.

Command-Line Arguments

Now is a good time to cover command-line arguments in the interpreter environment. By now you have noticed the string args[] parameter which is in the main() method. This array of strings holds the command-line arguments entered when Java is run.

For C/C++ users, the command-line argument array does not include the call to Java or the class name itself. The array begins with the first argument after the class name.

Note

The doRect class can take those arguments and use them to enter the width and height of the Rectangle object to create. The following code sets the width and height variables to values entered at the command line.

```
class doRect {
    public static void main(String args[]) {
        int w = Integer.valueOf(args[0]).intValue();
        int h = Integer.valueOf(args[1]).intValue();
        Rectangle rect = new Rectangle(w,h);
        rect.drawRect();
    }
}
```

The Integer class is called a type wrapper, along with the Float, Long, and Double. The valueOf(String) method converts the

String number to the relevant type, and the intValue() method returns the int represented by the Integer class. Check out the class API for more information on type wrappers.

You now have the necessary pieces for creating an instance of the Rectangle class and having it draw itself. Create a file named doRect.java with the following contents:

```java
class Rectangle {
    protected int width, height;
    protected int area;
    public Rectangle(int w, int h) {
        width = w;
        height = h;
        area = getArea(w,h);
    }
    protected int getArea(int w, int h) {
        int a;
        a = w*h;
        return a;
    }
    public void drawRect() {
        for(int i=width; i>0; i—) {
            System.out.print("#");
        }
        System.out.print("\n");
        for(int i=height-2; i>0; i—) {
            System.out.print("#");
            for(int j=width-2; j>0; j—) {
                System.out.print(" ");
            }
            System.out.print("#\n");
        }
        for(int i=width; i>0; i—) {
            System.out.print("#");
        }
        System.out.print("\n");
    }
}
```

```
class doRect {
    public static void main(String args[]) {
        if(args.length = 2) {
            int w = Integer.valueOf(args[0]).intValue();
            int h = Integer.valueOf(args[1]).intValue();
            Rectangle rect = new Rectangle(w,h);
            rect.drawRect();
        }
        else {
            System.out.println("Wrong number of param
            eters");
        }
    }
}
```

Compile the file and run the application with the Java interpreter:

```
C:\> java doRect 20 15
```

You should see the output shown in figure 7.2.

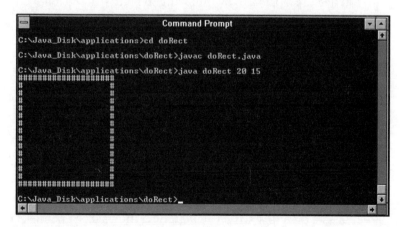

Figure 7.2

Output of the doRect application.

Understanding Packages in Java

Once you have created a class that you would like to use over and over again, it is useful to include it in a package. A *package* is a group of classes that all belong together. For example, Java provides packages, such as Java.io and Java.lang, which hold some of the basic classes used, such as System and String. You can create your own packages that bring together several classes that are related.

Your rectangle might be included in a general package known as Shapes. In addition to providing a simple way of referencing classes, packages also provide the scope for the friendly access modifier for variables and methods. Class members that you do not explicitly declare public, private, or protected can only be seen by classes in the same package. This allows for similar classes to have access to each other's methods, without compromising the encapsulation offered by object-oriented programming.

Declaring a Package

You declare a package by prefacing the file with the following declaration:

```
package name_of_package;
```

Typically, packages are grouped by relationships. In the case of the Rectangle class, it might be this:

```
package Shapes;
```

In this file, you might want to include classes for circles, triangles, and so forth. The package provides an easy way to associate these classes both for your own and other's benefit. The compiler creates a directory structure matching the package names. For example, javac creates the directory /Shapes/ in the /classes/ directory. You can nest packages by using the ".", as in the following example:

```
packages myclasses.Shapes;
```

This statement would create the directory structure /myclasses/ Shapes/ where it would place the Rectangle.class file.

In order for the compiler to know where to place the directory structure, indicate where you would like your packages placed with the following statement:

```
C:\> javac -d /your_path/ Rectangle.java
```

In this case, the Java compiler places the directory structure /Shapes/ Rectangle.class in the specified path. Be sure to include this path in your CLASSPATH environment variable.

Importing Other Packages

To use packages that have previously been compiled, you must import them into your source code with the import command. You can import classes in three ways:

1. By giving the full package reference before each class name:

    ```
    Shapes.Rectangle rect = new Shapes.Rectangle(10,20);
    ```

2. By importing the class itself:

    ```
    import Shapes.Rectangle;
        class doRect {
            Rectangle rect = new Rectangle(10,20);
            ...
        }
    ```

3. By importing the package that contains the class:

    ```
    import Shapes.*;
    class doRect {
        Rectangle rect = new Rectangle(10,20);
        ...
    }
    ```

Be sure that your CLASSPATH variable is set to the directory where the package bytecode file is located; otherwise, the Java compiler will not be able to link it in. In the case of the Rectangle.class file, it is in the /classes/ directory on the disk provided.

Creating and importing classes are important to utilizing the full functionality of Java. In later chapters, when you look at the different packages provided with Java, the use of importing classes becomes clear.

Using Inheritance in Java

Perhaps one of the most powerful tools in object-oriented programming is class inheritance. Class inheritance allows you to take an already existing class and build upon it. Say, for example, that you want to have a rectangle that would fill itself in when it was drawn on the screen. You could either start from scratch or use the old Rectangle class to build upon. The following sections will show you how to inherit the functionality of your Rectangle class, without rewriting the all of the code used in the Rectangle class.

The extends Modifier

The way in which Java enables programmers to inherit from already existing classes is with the extends keyword. To tell the compiler and run-time system that you are inheriting the existing class Rectangle, you must import the old class and refer to it in the new class declaration as follows:

```
import Shapes.Rectangle;

class fillRect extends Rectangle {
    //New code here
}
```

Overriding Methods

In the case of the fillRect class, there are two areas in which you can improve the Rectangle class: the drawRect method itself, and the addition of a filling capability.

You are going to create a private method so that you can shrink the size of the drawRect() method. If you notice, Rectangle has to draw a series of characters based upon the width and height of the rectangle. Instead of rewriting virtually the same code over, you can create a method for a rectangle to use when it needs to draw itself.

```
private String makeString(char ch, int num) {
    StringBuffer str = new StringBuffer();
    for(int i=num; i>0; i—)
        str.append(ch);
    return str.toString();
}
```

In this case, the for loop keeps adding additional characters to the end of the string until it is filled with the necessary number of characters. Then the method returns the string that has been built up. Notice the use of the StringBuffer class. Stringbuffer is used because String only creates a static type—it can't be changed, while StringBuffer creates a string type that can be added to.

Now, the code for the drawRect method can be rewritten as follows:

```
pubic void drawRect() {
    for(int i=height; i>0; i—) {
        System.out.println(makeString("#",width));
    }
}
```

The new class must create a solid rectangle. In order to draw a solid rectangle instead of just the outline the drawRect method is *overridden*. By using the same method name, you replace the old method with the new method. In its entirety, your class now looks as follows:

```
class fillRectangle extends Rectangle {
    public fillRectangle(int w, int h) {
        super(w,h);
    }
    private String makeString(char ch, int num) {
        StringBuffer str = new StringBuffer();
```

```
            for(int i=num; i>0; i—)
                str.append(ch);
            return str.toString();
        }
    pubic void drawRect() {
            for(int i=height; i>0; i—) {
                System.out.println(makeString("#",width));
            }
        }
    }
}
```

The size of the code has been shrunk, and the less code you have, the easier it is to keep bug-free. Notice that you no longer have to include all the code that is common between the two classes. Instead, just add the code that makes it do what you want. You do have to create a new constructor to differentiate between the two classes. In this case, the constructor is called for the superclass in order to initialize the instance variables. Notice, however, how the constructor is called with the super method name in the new constructor fillRectangle().

After you have begun creating your own set of reusable classes, the benefits of object-oriented programming becomes clear. You do not have to repeat many lines of code, and once you have debugged a class, you can inherit its features, knowing you only have to worry about implementing the new features you want to add.

Abstract Methods and Classes

There is a another way in which classes can be built. Java enables you to define what are known as *abstract* classes, which are made up of methods that have not been completed. It is up to the subclasses of the abstract class to override the methods. You create abstract methods with the keyword "abstract."

```
abstract returnType methodName(parameterList);
```

After you have included an abstract method in a class, the class itself is considered abstract and cannot be initialized. Only subclasses that override the abstract method can be created with the new operator. There are three kinds of methods that cannot be abstract:

- ✓ Constructors
- ✓ Static Methods
- ✓ Private Methods

Using Interfaces

Java provides a method for creating entirely abstract classes known as *interfaces*. You declare an interface as follows:

```
public interface interfaceName {
    //list of abstract methods
}
```

The default access is private. Variables in an interface are not expected to be changed, and are, therefore, always static and final. You do not use the abstract keyword when declaring the member methods.

You implement the interface in a class by using the implements keyword:

```
public class className extends superClass implements inter
        face [, optional interfaces] {
    //class body
}
```

Notice that a class can implement more than one interface.

What is the benefit of using interfaces? By creating an interface, you can define the protocols for an abstract class without worrying about the specific implementation, leaving that until later. In addition, you can share the same interface with several classes, without worrying about how the other class is handling the methods. If you inherit the properties of the interface, other users will automatically know what the method calls are for that class.

Say, for example, you want all your shapes to have a draw()
method. You could create an interface and name it Shape:

```
public interface Shape {
            void draw();
}
public class Triangle implements Shape {
    void draw() {
        //draw() implementation
    }
    ...
}
```

Now, any time you use a shape, you will know that it has a draw()
method, and what parameters it takes. You can also use the
Shape class as a type itself. This enables you to create methods
and member variables that can hold any of the objects that
implement Shape.

```
Shape sh;
void rotateShape(Shape rot) {
    ...
}
```

By using a class cast, you can give the function rotateShape an
instance of type Triangle.

```
Triangle tri = new Triangle();
rotateShape( (Shape)tri );
```

Casting Classes

Casting was covered in Chapter 6, but that was for the fundamental types such as Integers and Floats. The rules for casting classes
between subclasses and superclasses is as follows:

➤ You can cast from a superclass to a subclass implicitly,
without an explicit call for conversion, although explicit
casts to subclasses are not an error. The following code
shows this kind of casting.

```
Triangle tri = new Triangle();
Shape sh;
tri = sh;
```

or

```
tri = (Triangle)sh;
```

➤ You can cast a subclass into a superclass; however, references to instance variables may change, even though they are of the same name. You must explicitly perform the cast using the parenthetical reference. The following code shows an example of an implicit casting of classes.

```
Triangle tri = new Triangle();
Shape sh;
sh = (Shape)tri;
```

➤ Casting between sibling classes is not allowed. You could not for example, cast between the Rectangle and Triangle subclasses of Shape.

null, this and super Variables

There are three variables that all classes have: null, this and super. The *null* reference points to nothing and can be used in place of an actual object to indicate that there is no instance, as in the following example:

```
Rectangle rect = null;
```

This example creates the rectangle variable, but does not create an object to place in it. It is essentially like creating an empty box of the right shape to hold a rectangle. In addition, if a method expects an object, you can use the null reference instead, as in the following:

```
rotateShape(null);
```

The *this* reference is the actual object itself. What do you do, for example, if a class needs to pass a reference to itself or to another method? The class can refer to itself using this reference:

```
class Rectangle {
 void RectMethod() {
    newClass obj = new newClass();
    obj.Method(this);
    ...
 }
}
```

The rectangle object would send a reference of itself to the newClass' Method.

The *super* variable is a reference to the superclass type of the class. You might recall from earlier that this is how the constructor for the superclass of fillRectangle was called to initialize the instance variables.

Summary

The use of classes in Java is the foundation of its object-oriented approach. There is a lot of material in this chapter that is important to writing good Java code. Make sure that you are comfortable creating your own classes, importing already compiled classes, and inheritance. This will not only allow you to write cleaner, more efficient code, but it will be imperative to using many of the advanced features of Java later on.

The creation of a class is the fundamental job of a Java programmer. It is the class itself that the run-time environment executes. Instance variable and member methods all combine to encapsulate the behavior of the object into a user-friendly shell. It might seem like more work to create the class in the first place, but it will save time later when you want to reuse the class.

The reuse of classes through importing and inheritance is where object-oriented programming shows its true colors. As you saw with the fillRectangle example, by inheriting a class you had already created, adding new functionality was simply a matter of bringing in the new methods and overriding the relevant old methods. This will also become important in writing applets and using the class libraries. Much of the work in creating useful code has already been done for you. Learning classes now will allow you to take advantage of all that hard work.

The next chapter covers multithreading and exceptions. Both of these functions are encapsulated in classes, which means that adding threading and exception handling to your code is simply a matter of incorporating the right classes. In fact, the rest of the programming chapters deal with using specific classes in more detail, and how to add functionality to your Java programs and applets.

Chapter 8

Threads and Exceptions

Perhaps Java's next greatest strength behind its object-oriented foundation is its native multithreading capability. Multithreading—or the capability to maintain more than one concurrent execution path—is the major feature being incorporated into new releases of popular operating systems such as Windows 95 and the forthcoming Copeland MacOS. By providing native support for threads both in the language and in the class libraries, Java makes using this feature much easier.

Java also supports exception handling, a feature important for making robust programs. Whenever a run-time error occurs in a class method, it can throw an *exception*, which allows your code to either recover from the error or exit gracefully, without bringing down the entire system. This is important when your program is running at the same time as several other critical applications in a multitasking environment. Although the operating system might be able to close down your program without affecting others, this is not always assured. By being prepared to handle exceptions that might be thrown, you can create a more user-friendly program.

Quick Review

The Java environment provides both the end user and programmer with powerful features needed to use and develop advanced media and applications. Multithreading and exception handling are two important elements that form the cornerstone of modern applications. The Java architecture incorporates multithreading at more than one level, and exception handling is built in to many of the class libraries. The end user and content provider can benefit from these features through more responsive applications and interfaces. The programmer can benefit from the ease-of-use of the multithreading and exception handling elements of the language and class libraries by being able to quickly develop programs that incorporate these features.

The Java architecture supports multithreading at several levels, the least of which is the programming language itself, which has built-in modifiers for implementing threaded objects. In addition, the Java run-time environments in the browser and interpreter include a threaded automatic garbage collector, which cleans up unused objects after they are finished. Because Java provides all of the memory management, the programmer does not have to worry about conflicts with different threads and can concentrate on developing content in a secure, robust, and high-performance environment.

The browser and interpreter run-time environments also provide the end user and content provider with the security and performance necessary for distributed systems. The object-oriented and threaded paradigm enables the user to interact with multiple concurrent objects, each providing dynamic and extensible behavior. This functionality provides the user with a wider variety of resources over the Internet by removing the problems associated with platform-distributed software. The content provider can concentrate on content itself and not on worrying whether the potential users will have the means of dealing with it.

The previous chapters began to introduce the fundamentals of the Java language, both from a syntactical and organizational standpoint. By learning the fundamentals of the language, such as tokens, types, identifiers, operators, and control flow statements, you should be able to implement the computational side of the applications you want to develop. It is, however, the object-oriented paradigm that provides the Java programmer with the most functionality and power. By organizing your code along ideas of objects, you can create dynamic applications, free from the constraints of procedural code. It is important that you have a good grasp of how classes work, how to create your own, and how to implement already developed code.

What This Chapter Covers

This chapter covers the following subjects:

➤ How to implement multithreading capability into your own code

➤ How to use the exception class for handling errors

This chapter covers how to implement multithreading capability into your own code and use the exception class for handling errors. Multithreading is encapsulated in the Thread and Runnable classes. The Thread and Runnable classes enable you to make classes that can run concurrently with other processes on the system, and in your program, and detect and correct system and program errors. *Exceptions* are method calls made when Java encounters an error. You can handle these method calls in your own programs, allowing them either to recover from the error or close down gracefully. Threads and exceptions are the last major elements of a Java program that could be considered fundamental.

After You Finish This Chapter

After you have finished this chapter, you will have the framework and plumbing necessary to build your own Java applications. However, your program would look pretty sparse, and it may be difficult to do everything you would like to from scratch. Java provides the necessary class libraries for adding accessories and a pretty face to your applications. These include the class libraries for input/output, and other system functions, along with the windowing class library and network protocols. Later chapters discuss how to use these predesigned elements in your own code.

Understanding Multithreading

In all of the previous examples provided, the programs have been single-threaded applications. There was only one thing going on at any time in the program. In other words, you could follow what was happening with your finger (if it was fast enough). Of course, while your program was executing, everything else was waiting for it to finish. It had taken all the resources of the Java run-time system and used it to run only the single program.

Of course, this does not mean that your program is the only thing running on the whole system. In fact, Java includes its own garbage collection thread to manage memory for you, and the operating system was managing several tasks on the computer at the same time. To the Java run-time system, however, your program was the only thread running in the virtual machine.

Running a single-threaded program is fine when you only have to deal with small programs that have to do a single task, but what if you had a Web page with several applets that were all supposed to be running at the same time, or you wanted to run a calculation in the background while getting more user input? In this case, each of these applications would have to be multithreaded.

In Java there are two ways to create a class that can be multithreading:

➤ Create a class that extends the Thread class

➤ Create a class that implements the Runnable interface

The Thread Class and Runnable Interface

The implementation of a threaded class can be either an extension of the class Thread, or an implementation of the interface Runnable. Both ways are shown in the following example.

Creating Threads

You can create a thread by extending Thread with your own class, and overriding the run() method, which is similar to overriding the main() method for a standard application:

```
class className extends Thread {
    public void run() {
        //Thread body of execution
    }
}
```

For example, you might want to compute primes in the background.

```
class primeThread extends Thread {
    boolean keepRunning = true;
    public void run() {
        int number = 3;
        int mod = 0;
        boolean flag = true;
        while(keepRunning) {
            loop:
            for(int i=2; i<number; i++) {
                if((mod = number % i) == 0) {
                    flag = false;
                    break loop;
                }
            }
            if(flag) {
                System.out.println(number);
                flag = true;
            }
            number++;
            flag = true;
```

```
                }
        }
        public void stop() {
                keepRunning = false;
        }
}
```

In this case, the thread sets itself up in an infinite loop, printing out the prime numbers as it finds them. If you had this class and wanted to call the thread, you would create an instance of the class primeThread just like any other class:

```
primeThread getPrimes = new primeThread();
```

You would then call its start() method to cause it to run:

```
getPrimes.start();
```

The start() method causes the thread's run() method to be invoked. After the thread has been started with the start() method, the method immediately returns and the main thread of the program continues. The following example runs the prime thread, waiting for the user to press the Enter key.

```
class runPrimes {
        public static void main(String args[]) {
                primeThread getPrimes = new primeThread();
                getPrimes.start();
                char ch;
                while((ch = (char)System.in.read()) != '\n');
                getPrimes.stop();
        }
}
```

Note the call to the class' stop() method to exit execution of the thread. When the call to stop() is made, it changes the state of the variable keepRunning so that the while() loop in the primeThread class' run() method drops through.

In addition to extending the Thread class, you can have your class implement the Runnable interface:

```
class className implements Runnable {
    public void run() {
        ...
    }
}
```

A class that has implemented the Runnable interface can be run in a thread by passing the instance of the class to a new Thread object.

```
className instanceName = new className();
new Thread(instanceName).start();
```

The computation of primes using the runnable interface would be as follows:

```
class primeRunnable implements Runnable {
    boolean keepRunning = true;
    public void run() {
        int number = 10;
        int mod = 0;
        boolean flag = true;
        while(keepRunning) {
            loop:
            for(int i=2; i<number; i++) {
                if((mod = number % i) == 0) {
                    flag = false;
                    break loop;
                }
            }

            if(flag) {
                System.out.println(number);
                flag = true;
            }
            number++;
            flag = true;
        }
    }
    public void stop() {
        keepRunning = false;
```

```
        }
    }

class runPrimesRunnable {
    public static void main(String args[]) {
        primeRunnable getPrimes= new primeRunnable();
        new Thread(getPrimes).start();
        char ch;
        while((ch = (char)System.in.read()) != '\n');
        getPrimes.stop();
    }
}
```

Additional Thread Methods

In addition to the start() and stop() methods, the Thread class provides a number of additional methods and instance variables for controlling the execution of the thread.

There are three variables in the class Thread:

- ✗ MAX_PRIORITY

- ✗ MIN_PRIORITY

- ✗ NORM_PRIORITY

Note

Although it is said that threads run concurrently, they do not actually run at the same time. Instead, each thread gets a turn to run for a short time, then lets the other running threads have a chance to process. Because the times are so short and today's processors so fast, it appears as if all the threads are running at the same time.

To make sure the required threads have the time they need to run, they are given priorities. These essentially set the amount of time each has to run before it must give up control. Threads with low priority have less time, whereas threads with high priorities have more use of the processor.

MAX_PRIORITY is an integer holding the maximum allowable value for the thread's priority. MIN_PRIORITY holds the minimum priority value, and NORM_PRIORITY holds the default priority of a thread. You can set the thread's priority by using its setPriority(int) method. You pass the method an integer that indicates the priority of the thread. If you want to set a thread to its maximum priority, you would use the following:

```
Thread.setPriority(Thread.MAX_PRIORITY);
```

You can also see what a thread's priority is with the getPriority() method.

There are four constructors for the Thread class. The prime number example used two of them:

→ Thread()

→ Thread(Runnable)

In addition, you can give a thread a name when it is constructed by passing a string parameter:

→ Thread(String)

→ Thread(Runnable, String)

The Thread constructors create an instance of the Thread class, allowing the object to be run concurrently with other objects. When creating a thread, you can either create the thread by subclassing Thread itself; or, if you have a class that implements runnable, pass that class to the Thread constructor, which will then create a thread out of that class. The previous four constructors provide for both of these situations. Passing a String to the constructor allows you to create references to individual threads, which can then be used as symbolic references. For example, if you have created several instances of the same thread, you could give them each a distinctive name to keep track of them.

The getName() method returns a String holding the name of the thread, and setName(String) sets the thread's name.

The following are also useful methods for determining a thread's status and controlling the execution of a thread.

- ✓ currentThread() returns the currently executing thread.
- ✓ isAlive() checks to see if the thread is active.
- ✓ suspend() suspends the execution of the thread.
- ✓ resume() resumes execution of a suspended thread.
- ✓ sleep(*int*) causes the thread to sleep for *int* milliseconds.
- ✓ yield() causes the thread to give up execution to waiting threads.

There are additional modifiers, but these are the ones most used in controlling the execution of a threaded application. For more information on Thread methods, or for methods and variables of any of the class libraries provided with Java, check out the API reference on the accompanying disk.

Using Thread Modifiers in Classes

So far, only the class implementation of Threads has been discussed. Java also includes support for synchronization and optimization of classes, variables, and modifiers at the language level. One problem in dealing with multithreading applications is controlling their access to data. In single-threaded applications, you always know in what order the program will be accessing variables and data. However, when you have multiple threads running at once, there is no way to know when any thread might be reading or writing to a variable.

The Java run-time environment attempts to control thread access to data so that conflicts don't arise out of two or more threads attempting to modify or read the same data at once. This does not mean, however, that problems cannot arise. Your program might, for example, have two threads that are accessing the same object—one is changing data in the object, the other is printing data from the object. Imagine what would happen to the rectangle class if a function were added to change the width and height interactively.

```
public void setWH(int w, int h) {
    width = w;
    height = h;
    area = getArea(w,h);
}
```

Now, the doRect class might spin off two threads, one to print the rectangle, and another to get new information about the width and height from the user.

```
class drawRectangle implements Runnable {
    Rectangle rect = null;
    Thread kicker = null;
    public void run() {
        rect.drawRect();
    }
    public void start(Rectangle r) {
        rect = r;
        kicker = new Thread(this);
        kicker.start();
    }
}

class getWidthHeight implements Runnable {
    Rectangle rect = null;
    Thread kicker = null;
    public void run() {
        int w, h;
        char ch;
        StringBuffer str = new StringBuffer();
        System.out.println("Enter Width:");
        while((ch = System.in.read()) != '\n') {
            str.append(ch);
        }
        w = Integer.parseInt(str.toString()).intValue();
        System.out.println("Enter Height:");
        str = new StringBuffer();
        while((ch = System.in.read()) != '\n') {
```

```
                        str.append(ch);
                }
                h = Integer.parseInt(str.toString()).intValue();
                rect.setWH(w,h);
        }
        public void start(Rectangle r) {
                rect = r;
                kicker = new Thread(this);
                kicker.start();

        }
}
```

In the first thread class, drawRectangle, the call to rect.drawRect() would cause the rectangle to be printed out on the screen. At the same time, the second thread class, setWidthHeight, could be getting new width and height values. What happens if the setWidthHeight class started to change the values of width and height just as drawRectangle wanted to draw it? You might get some weird output on the screen—not the old rectangle or the new one, but a combination of both, depending on where each thread was. How can you make sure that each call to setWH() and drawRect() has completed before the other is able to run? You use the *synchronized* modifier.

The Synchronized Modifier

Imagine a relay race where runners have to be in possession of a baton to be able to run. Each team only has one baton, and after a runner has finished his portion of the race, he hands it off to the next so that he can begin. Each team only has one baton, so only one runner can be running at a time.

The Java equivalent to the baton is called a *lock*. Each class or object has a single lock that it can use to keep sections of code from running at the same time as others. By using the synchronized modifier, you are telling Java that the portion of code marked must have the lock in order to run.

In the rectangle class, the problem of the setWH() and drawRect() methods interfering with each other can be solved by setting them as synchronized.

```
public synchronized void drawRect() {
    ...
}

public synchronized void setWH(int w, int h) {
    ...
}
```

Now, the drawRect() and setWH() methods cannot be running at the same time. For each of them to run, they have to have the lock; however, there is only one lock per object, or class, so only one of them can be running at a time. This lock protocol ensures that each method has completed its work before the other can take over. Each method will wait until it can acquire the lock before executing.

In addition to setting the methods as synchronized, blocks of code can be synchronized with objects. If the methods were not synchronized themselves, but you still wanted to make sure that they were not called at the same time, you could indicate that they should be run synchronized when they are called. In the drawRectangle class, this would be the following:

```
synchronized (rect) {
    rect.drawRect();
}
```

For the setWidthHeight class, it would be the following:

```
synchronized (rect) {
    rect.setWH(w,h);
}
```

Notice the use of the object name in the parentheses. This use indicates which lock the block of code should wait to acquire. Both the drawRectangle and setWidthHeight classes should wait for the rect lock to be freed before calling the method. When the method has returned, and the block of code indicated as synchronized is exited, the lock for the object is freed, and any other code waiting for the lock can execute.

Although the second method for ensuring synchronization is adequate, the first is preferred for portability and ease of use. If you know that two methods could interfere with each other, you should mark them as synchronized in the class declaration itself. Programmers who later use your classes then won't have to worry about making sure the objects created can handle multiple threads. Also, while synchronizing called methods is one way to use the synchronized block, you can also use it to block out specific areas of code in a method, without necessarily causing the whole method to have to wait for the lock.

```
class className {
    void method1() {
        // non synchronized code
        synchronized (this) {
            // synchronized code
        }
        // non synchronized code
    }
}
```

Notice the use of the `this` object, referring to the class itself. By using the synchronized modifier this way, the method only requires the use of the lock for the minimum amount of time required, allowing it to be used by other threads.

The Threadsafe Modifier

If you know that a variable will never be changed by one thread while another is using it, you can mark it as *threadsafe*. Doing so enables the compiler to perform optimizations that would otherwise cause difficulty by masking changes that might occur to the variable in one thread from being seen in another. You might, for example, have a variable that is set when the class is created, but never changed by any methods.

```
threadsafe int variableName;
```

Make sure that any variables marked as threadsafe are actually free from alterations by methods that could be invoked from different threads. Typically, static and final variables will be threadsafe.

Using Exceptions in Java

Java code can detect errors and indicate to the run-time system what those errors were. When an error occurs, Java throws an exception. Normally, a thrown execution will cause the thread to terminate, and an error message will be printed. If you want to handle the exception yourself, you can include a `catch` statement to trap the exception.

Handling Exceptions

To handle exceptions, you must `try` the method that might throw an exception, and then catch any objects that could be thrown by the method.

```
try {
    // some code which might throw an exception
} catch (exceptionType name ) {
    // Handle the exception
 }
```

The code in the try block is executed and any exceptions generated are matched with the catch statement. You can, in fact, have several catch statements to cover different exceptions which might occur. Any code after an exception that is thrown in the try statement is ignored. If there is code you need executed even if an exception is thrown, use the "finally" block (covered in a later section). When an exception is thrown, the run-time system attempts to match the exception with the relevant catch statement in the following order:

1. The catch statement that matches the exception exactly executed.

2. The catch statement that matches the superclass of the exception.

3. The catch statement that is an interface that the exception implements.

For example, you could have the following code, which would catch several different exceptions:

```
class exceptionTest {
    void method1 {
        try {
            int i = 0;
            i = i / i;
            //any other code here will not be executed
        } catch (ArithmeticException e) {
            System.out.println("Attempt to divide by
zero");
        } catch (Exception e) {
            System.out.println("Some other error was
thrown");
        }
    }
}
```

After the attempt to divide by zero, the run-time system throws the exception. However, if for some reason another exception were to be thrown, it would be caught by the second catch statement.

Note

The exceptions thrown by the class libraries vary. You should check with the class library API for more information on the specific exceptions thrown by different errors. The section on run-time errors in this chapter lists the exceptions thrown by the Java interpreter.

Throwing Objects Around

You can also throw your own objects, which are either subclasses of the exception class, or any other object for that matter. To create your own exception, make a class that is a subclass of the exception class.

```
class newException extends Exception {
}
```

Now, you can throw this exception yourself:

```
void newMethod() {
    try {
        if(no error) {
            // run code
        }
        else {
            throw new newException();
        }
    } catch (newException e) {
        // handle exception
    } catch (Exception e) {
        // handle general errors
    } catch (Object e) {
        // catch anything thrown
    }
}
```

Notice that the final catch statement catches anything that is a subclass of Object. This is basically anything that can be thrown.

You also can have multiple levels of, or nested, exception handling. After you are finished with the exception at one level, you can throw it onto the next.

```
try {
    try {
        // Some code which generates an exception
    } catch (Exception e) {
        // Handle exception
        throw e;
    }
} catch (Exception e) {
    // Handle exception
}
```

The first time the exception is caught, it is handled and then thrown again, to be caught by the outer try statement.

Using The Finally Statement

You can use the finally statement to include code that should be executed even if an exception is thrown:

```
try {
    // code which might throw exception
} finally {
    //clean up after it
}
```

The finally block is executed no matter what happens in the try block. Even if there is a break, continue, return, or throw, the finally block will be executed.

Runtime Exceptions

The class library APIs list all the exceptions thrown by classes. In addition, the run-time system will throw the following exceptions:

➤ **ArithmeticException.** Dividing or taking the modulus of an integer by zero.

➤ **NullPointerException.** Attempt to access a variable or method in a null object.

➤ **IncompatibleClassChangeException.** A change to a class has been made that would affect references to methods or variables to that class in other objects, and those objects haven't been recompiled.

➤ **ClassCastException.** Incorrect casting of a class.

➤ **NegativeArraySizeException.** If an array is created with a negative size.

➤ **OutOfMemoryException.** New is called and there is no more memory available for objects.

➤ **NoClassDefFoundException.** A class is referenced, but the system cannot find it.

➤ **IncompatibleTypeException.** Thrown if an attempt to instantiate an interface is made.

➤ **ArrayIndexOutOfBoundsException.** Thrown if an attempt is made to reference an invalid element in an array.

➤ **UnsatisfiedLinkException.** Thrown if a native method cannot be linked at run-time (see Chapter 13, "Interfacing with C and Using the Java Tools," for information on native methods).

➤ **InternalException.** This exception should never be thrown, and indicates a problem with the run-time system itself.

Summary

The use of Thread and exception classes is an important feature of robust, high-performance Java programs. By using the multithreading and exception handling features, you are able to develop code that takes full advantage of the Java environment and modern operating systems. Multithreading enables you to use the full processing power available in today's computers, while exception handling provides the robust error detection and correction that is expected in modern applications. Java provides powerful and easy-to-use threading and exception tools for incorporating these features into your programs.

The Thread class and Java language synchronized and threadsafe elements provide the programmer with a full range of options for developing multithreading applications. You should be able to write your own classes that extend the Thread class or implement the Runnable interface. In addition, the synchronized and threadsafe modifiers will enable you to optimize your code for a multithreading environment. Because Java is a multithreading environment, it is important that you begin to think of your programs in the wider context of concurrent threads.

The exception class, and try, throw, catch, and finally statements, provide you with powerful tools for detecting, handling, and recovering from errors that occur in your program. Users expect robust applications and want programs that can take care of themselves without bringing down the rest of the system. Exception handling is the most important way to deal with any problems that arise.

By incorporating multithreading and exception handling capabilities into your Java programs, you provide a level of sophistication difficult to obtain with many other programming languages. Take advantage of the ease with which Java enables you to provide these features. In the following chapters, the class libraries and advanced features of Java are presented. Threads and exceptions are the last elements of the Java environment that could be considered fundamental to writing good Java code. In the next sections, the basic groundwork is extended to add functionality to your code by incorporating the class libraries of the Java environment.

Chapter 9

The Java and HotJava Class Libraries

The Java environment provides the programmer with a host of packages that contain class libraries for useful utilities often needed by programmers. Instead of having to write the classes for these utilities yourself, you can simply import the necessary packages into your program. Doing so makes writing sophisticated, functional programs much easier.

Almost all programming languages provide standard libraries that implement basic utilities beyond what the basic language can provide. These libraries typically include file input/output, system calls such as date and time, and classic functions for math and strings. Java provides these functions in its class libraries, collected in the form of packages.

Quick Review

Up to this point, you have learned the topics of using the Java run-time environments, providing Java content, and the fundamentals of programming in the Java language. The concept of providing useful functions through class encapsulation should be familiar to you by now. The encapsulation of classes allows plug-in functionality to the HotJava browser by incorporating distributed, portable applets and handlers. Content providers can take advantage of this extensibility by providing dynamic media over the Internet as never before. For the programmer, the object-oriented paradigm means more reusable code, and less repeated coding.

The user environment of Java provides for extensibility by allowing the incorporation of distributed code across heterogeneous hardware platforms. This means that classes can be loaded from across the Internet and incorporated into the browser or interpreter, allowing virtually unlimited modification of the user environment. By providing a powerful object-oriented paradigm that solves the fragile superclass problem, code can be ported safely without the worry that unknown updates might bring down earlier versions. In addition, the interpreter and just-in-time compiler provide a robust platform independent method for running downloaded code. Site administrators now don't have to worry about platform specific details when providing new, dynamic content.

In learning to program in the Java language, it is quite obvious that objects are everything. In the case of Java, the object is represented by the Java class. The fundamental programming skills learned in Chapter 6, "The Fundamentals—Types, Expressions, and Flow Control," are all encapsulated in the framework of classes. Anything you want to do in Java must be done in the form of a class. While it could be argued that object-oriented programming is more costly for the initial code creation, the encapsulation of classes allows for greater reusability in the long run. Once you have a grasp for programming with classes, the entire development process will fall together. By reusing classes that you, or others, have developed, programming time can be cut drastically. This is exactly what these later chapters are all about—using classes developed for the Java language that

provide utilities for getting solid Java programs out the door
quickly and effectively.

What This Chapter Covers

The goal of object-oriented programming is to allow the greatest
reusability of code as possible. In this light, Java includes class
libraries in the form of packages, which provide methods for
many basic functions of a Java program. These include file I/O,
System calls, graphical user interface classes, and network
protocol classes. By using these classes, you can quickly get up to
speed with your Java applications.

This chapter will provide:

➤ A brief overview of all the Java class libraries offered with the
  Java and HotJava run-time environments

➤ A study of the java.lang class library

The rest of this chapter and the next will be devoted to covering
the Java class libraries, comprised of the java.lang, java.util, and
java.io packages. Some of the classes have been seen in previous
examples, but most will be new. These classes are important no
matter what kind of Java code you are writing, be it applets,
stand-alone applications, or handlers.

After You Finish This Chapter

Once you have finished this chapter and the next, you will have
all the ingredients for making an advanced Java program. You
should pay careful attention to the lists of methods these classes
provide, because they can save you time and endless suffering
from attempting to code your own functions. Chances are, the
basic language class libraries have a class that can handle whatever you need.

With updates in the Java release, aspects of the Language
API might change. Be sure to check out the Appendix, "Further

Information," to find out where to find information on the latest state of the Java APIs. In addition, it is impossible to list all of the variables, methods, and exceptions of each class, or for that matter, even list all of the classes available. Check out the full hypertext version of the API that comes with the release of the Java environment.

Introduction to the Class Libraries

The class libraries provided with Java can be grouped into two broad categories—those for the general Java interpreter, and those for the HotJava browser. While the Java packages can be used by all Java programs, the browser classes are mainly intended for use in the environment of the HotJava browser.

Java Class Libraries

The Java class libraries provide three packages for utilization of low-level system methods. These packages are java.lang, java.util, and java.io. You can import all of these libraries at once as follows:

```
import java.*;
```

This will bring in all of the Java Class Library. Alternately, you can only import the packages you will specifically need.

The lang Package

The java.lang package provides the low-level classes used to encapsulate methods for basic program functionality. These include the following:

➤ Boolean, Character, and Number type wrapper classes

➤ Math classes for basic functions

➤ String and StringBuffer classes

➤ A System class for standard i/o and low-level system information

➤ Thread and ThreadDeath classes

➤ Abstract classes for the libraries

➤ The base Object class

These classes are used for the fundamental elements of a Java program, and provide useful methods for handling the basic objects. This package will be covered in the latter half of this chapter.

The util Package

The java.util package provides additional low-level utilities that enable the programmer to have greater control over program execution, and more advanced control and storage methods. These include the following:

➤ Lock and ConditionLock classes for synchronization

➤ Linker class for dynamic link libraries of native code

➤ Vector and StringTokenizer classes

➤ Stack and Hashtable classes

➤ Date class

The java.util package will be covered in the next chapter.

The io Package

The java.io package contains classes for implementing input/output with the Java language. Input/output can occur between several places, including the keyboard, screen, printer, disk file, or network. Utilities are included for the following:

➤ Files

➤ Data

➤ Buffers

➤ Filters

➤ Pipes

➤ Print Streams

➤ Random Access Files

➤ A Stream Tokenizer

If you plan on doing any input/output with your program, which is imperative for interactivity, you should pay careful attention to the java.io package. It provides useful classes for almost all necessary I/O needs.

HotJava Class Libraries

While their name—the HotJava Libraries—would indicate that they are to be used in the browser run-time environment, in actuality the HotJava classes can be used in the stand-alone environment also. The packages that fall under the HotJava category are the AWT, net, and browser packages. The AWT, or Another Window Toolkit, package provides classes for implementing a graphical user interface. The net package includes classes for Internet protocols. The browser package includes classes for applets, and other interfaces with HotJava. By using these packages, programmers can create powerful programs for distribution over the Internet.

The AWT Class Library

The AWT package provides classes for creating graphical user interface elements. By using these elements you can control the look and feel of your applet. Classes provided in the AWT package include methods for the following:

➤ Windows

➤ Buttons

➤ Menus

➤ Fonts

➤ Images

➤ Scrollbars

Almost all programs today rely on a graphical user interface. The days of text-based DOS and Unix interfaces are on their way out. By using the AWT class, you can impart a familiar and easy-to-use shell to your applications.

The net Class Library

The net package includes classes for extending the functionality of Java's I/O classes with interfaces to network protocols. Protocols that net will handle are the following:

➤ Sockets

➤ Telnet

➤ FTP

➤ NNTP

➤ WWW

By incorporating network protocols, a programmer can take advantage of the resources available across the Internet, extending the distributed nature of the Java language to the applications themselves.

The browser Class Library

The browser package includes classes for controlling the HotJava browser. You can control the formatting of HTML documents, in addition to including audio in your applications. In addition, the browser package includes the Applet class, which is used to create the applets included with HTML pages. Browser classes provide methods for:

➤ Applets

➤ Audio

➤ Links

➤ Style

➤ Properties

The browser class is the first level of classes extended by the programmer to develop code for applets executing in the HotJava run-time environment. For example, in order to create an applet that runs in a Web page, you extend the Applet class, which is a member of the browser package.

The Language Foundation Class Library

The language foundation class library provides the basic functionality required by programmers at the lowest level. At the top of the hierarchy of classes is the Object class, from which all other classes are descended. The Object class is included in the language class library. Additionally, the basic types are provided with *type wrappers*, defined later in this section, that encapsulate the fundamental types into classes that can provide methods for easier manipulation. The Math class provides the basic mathematical functions required beyond the classic operators handled at the language level. The library also provides classes for string manipulation. Finally, the language library provides a system class which included methods for low-level operating system interaction.

The java.lang package is automatically loaded with the compiler, so there is no need to import it explicitly. Many language classes also implement their methods as static members. Because static members can be accessed without a specific instance of the class itself, there is no need to create an instance of the class in order to use the function. For example, in order to determine the absolute value of an integer, you can use the Math class' abs() method:

```
int a = -1;
a = Math.abs(a);
// a now equals 1
```

The static member method abs() of the class Math has been used without creating a new instance. In earlier examples, the methods System.out.println() and System.in.read() were used in a similar manner.

The Object Class

The Object class is at the top of the class hierarchy. Whereas all classes have a superclass—Object is *the* superclass to everything. The methods implemented by the Object class apply to all classes, because they are all derived from Object. This means that you can use these methods with your own classes, or any class you import.

There are several useful Object methods you might want to use.

✓ **protected Object clone().** This method makes an exact copy of the Object, and returns the copy.

```
Rectangle rect = new Rectangle(10,20);
Rectangle rectCopy = rect.clone();
```

✓ **protected void copy(Object src).** This method copies the contents of the Object passed to the method into the current Object. Both Objects must be of the same type. The contents are considered the values of the instance variables of the Object being passed to the method.

```
Rectangle rect1 = new Rectangle(10,20);
Rectangle rect2 = new Rectangle(20,20);
rect1.copy(rect2);
// rect1 width and height are now both 20
```

✓ **public final Class getClass().** This method returns the class definition object Class. The Class object stores information about the class name, superclass name, implemented interfaces, and additional information. For example, Class has a method getName() that returns a String holding the name of the class.

```
Rectangle rect = new Rectangle(10,10);
System.out.println("class
name:"+rect.getClass().getName());
```

Notice how you can append methods to other methods. The order in which the methods work is left to right, and they act upon the return type of each previous method. In this case, the rect.getClass() method returns an object of type Class, which is then appended with getName() (Class.getName()). This is a useful and compact method for applying several methods to an object at once.

The Type Wrappers

The type wrappers are used to hold information about the fundamental types—boolean, character, int, long, double, and float—in addition to providing useful methods for comparison and string output. It is important to note that the type wrappers are classes, whereas the fundamental types are not. It is easy to get confused; for example, the Boolean wrapper differs from the fundamental type by only a capital B. The type wrappers and regular types are not interchangeable, so be sure to use the *type*Value() method provided with each of the wrappers to get the fundamental type from the wrapper. The classes implemented by wrappers are the following:

- Boolean
- Character
- Double
- Float
- Integer
- Long

While each of the type wrappers implements special methods for its specific type, there are several methods that are common to all of the wrappers.

✓ **public ClassType(type).** All of the wrapper constructors take a parameter that is the type they encapsulate. The following example creates wrappers for int, char, and float:

```
Integer i = new Integer(1);
Character ch = new Character('a');
Float flt = new Float(1.234);
```

✓ **public type typeValue().** This method will return the native type of the type wrapper created. The type wrappers are not equivalent to the native types, so you will need to use this method in order to process the value of the wrapper normally.

```
int x = i.intValue();
char y = ch.charValue();
float z = flt.floatValue();
```

✓ **public String toString().** This method will return the string representation of the type held in the wrapper. This function is useful for creating string representations of types for output.

```
System.out.println(i.toString());
System.out.println(ch.toString());
System.out.println(flt.toString());
```

✓ **public boolean equals(Object obj).** All wrappers except for the Character wrapper implement this method. Because the wrappers cannot be compared directly with the equals (=) sign, this method will return true if the two values are the same, and false if they are not.

```
Integer j = new Integer(2);
boolean bool = j.equals(i);
// bool is now false
```

The Boolean Type Wrapper

The Boolean wrapper does not implement any methods other than the standard methods mentioned previously. The Boolean class can have two states: TRUE or FALSE. You can change the state of the object by doing the following:

```
bool = Boolean.TRUE;
```

or

```
bool = Boolean.FALSE;
```

Notice that you cannot change them by using the bool = true; statement because these two types are not equivalent.

The Character Type Wrapper

The Character type wrapper implements several methods in addition to the methods for all of the wrappers. However, Character is the only wrapper class that does not provide an equals() method. The additional methods the Character wrapper provides are all static. This means that you can use them without creating an instance of the class.

```
public static boolean isLowerCase(char ch).
```

The isLowerCase() method returns a true if the character is lowercase, or false if it is not. You can use this method by referencing the Character class itself. With non-static methods, the only way to use the method is to create an instance of the class.

```
Character ch = new Character('a');
boolean LowerCase = ch.isLowerCase('b');
// LowerCase is now true
```

Notice that an instance of ch was created just to use the isLowerCase method. However, because it is static, the method can refer to the general Character class instead.

```
boolean LowerCase = Character.isLowerCase('b');
// LowerCase is now true
```

The following methods work the same way.

- ✓ **public static boolean isUpperCase(char ch).** This method returns true if the character is uppercase, or false otherwise.

- ✓ **public static int digit(char ch, int radix).** This method returns the integer value of the character ch. Radix is the base of the number (2 for binary, 8 for octal, 10 for decimal, and 16 for hexadecimal).

```
int x = Character.digit('a',16);
// x is equal to 10
```

✓ **public static boolean isDigit(char ch).** This method returns true if the character is a digit (0–9), or false otherwise.

✓ **public static char forDigit(int digit, int radix).** This method returns the character value for the digit in the specified radix.

✓ **public static char toLowerCase(char ch).** This method returns the lowercase equivalent of the character provided. If a lowercase character is given, it is returned the same.

✓ **public static char toUpperCase(char ch).** This method returns the uppercase equivalent to the character provided. Again, if an uppercase character is given, it is returned the same.

Type Wrappers for Numbers

In addition to the standard methods provided by the wrappers, the number wrappers Double, Float, Int, and Long provide several common methods. The instance methods provided are the following:

✓ public int intValue();

✓ public long longValue();

✓ public float floatValue();

✓ public double doubleValue();

These methods return the relevant values for each type. For example, if you have a Double instance, and you would like the int value for that Double, you could use:

```
Double d = new Double(1.234);
int x = d.intValue();
// note that there is a loss of precision in casting
   from
// double to int.
```

Of course, the methods that return the same types as those of their wrapper types are safe from casting loss mentioned in Chapter 6, "The Fundamentals—Types, Expressions, and Control Flow," but you should be aware of the precision you will lose if you use a different number type.

```
public int hashCode()
```

This method returns a hashcode value for the Double.

In addition to the previous instance methods, the number wrappers provide a static method for converting a string to the relevant wrapper type.

```
public static Type valueOf(String s)
```

This method converts the string and returns an instance of the wrapper type. The following code creates an instance of the class Long with the value 1234.

```
Long l = Long.valueOf("1234");
```

You could also convert a String to the basic type using the following:

```
int i = Integer.valueOf("1234").intValue();
```

Note

Remember that the valueOf() method returns an instance of the type wrapper referenced in the method call, *not* the basic type itself.

The number wrappers also provide two variables MAX_VALUE and MIN_VALUE that hold the maximum and minimum numbers for each type. You can use these numbers to ensure that your code does not exceed the boundaries and either cause an exception to be thrown, or a loss of data.

The Float Type Wrapper

The Float wrapper adds two final variables and two methods to the standard set of members implemented by the number wrappers. The two final variables are

✗   public final static float E   e = 2.718281...

✗   public final static float PI   π = 3.141592...

Notice that these numbers are regular floats. This means that you can use them directly with other types, unlike the Boolean variables TRUE and FALSE.

```
float f = Float.E;
```

Float also provides two methods for determining if Float numbers are either the special NaN or Inf. The public static boolean isNan(float f) method returns true if the float value is an NaN (not a number), or false otherwise.

The public static boolean isInfinite(float f) returns true if the float is an Inf (an infinitely large number), or false otherwise.

```
float f = 0, j = 1000;
j = j/f;
boolean bool = isInfinite(j);
// bool is true
```

Refer to the section on floating point numbers in Chapter 6, "The Fundamentals—Types, Expressions, and Flow Control," for more information on when a floating point operation might return either an Inf or a NaN.

The Integer Type Wrapper

The Integer wrapper adds both a new constructor, and several new methods to those provided by all number wrappers.

➜   **public Integer(String s).** This constructor creates an Integer instance from the string variable presented. This is different from the normal constructor, which would take an int. The radix is assumed to be 10. That is, the string is assumed to be a decimal number, rather than binary, octal, or hexadecimal.

✓   **public static String toString(int i, int radix).** This method is provided in addition to the standard toString() method. It allows you to specify the radix for the resulting string (2 for binary, 8 for octal, 10 for decimal, and 16 for hexadecimal).

✓ **public static int parseInt(String s, int radix).** This method returns the integer value of a String representation. The base of the representation is taken as radix. Notice that this is a static method, which you can use on any string, without creating an instance of the Integer object. If you do not include the radix (parseInt(String s)) then the base is assumed to be 10.

✓ **public static Integer valueOf(String s, int radix).** This method is similar to the standard valueOf() methods, except it takes radix as the base of the Integer representation.

Integers are used in almost every aspect of a computer program, and you will contsantly be using integers to keep track of control flow, mathematical equations, and user input/output. This means that you will be using the previous methods often, and it is worthwhile to play around with the Integer, and all wrapper classes.

The Long and Double Type Wrappers

The Long and Double type wrappers do not add any variables or methods other than the standard type wrapper and number members. They act as any other type wrapper, and can be used for extra precision, in the case of the Double wrapper, or for extremely large numbers, in the case of the Long wrapper.

The Math Class

The Math class provides several methods for implementing the standard mathematical functions. All of the Math member functions are static, so you do not have to create an instance of the Math class. Instead, append the method you want to use with the Math class reference.

```
Math.method(variable);
```

Be sure to note the return types and argument variables.

- ✓ public static double sin(double a)
- ✓ public static double cos(double a)
- ✓ public static double tan(double a)
- ✓ public static double asin(double a)
- ✓ public static double acos(double a)
- ✓ public static double atan(double a)
- ✓ public static double exp(double a)
- ✓ public static double log(double a)
- ✓ public static double sqrt(double a)
- ✓ public static double ceil(double a)
- ✓ public static double floor(double a)
- ✓ public static double rint(double a)
- ✓ public static double atan2(double a, double b)
- ✓ public static double annuity(double a, double b)
- ✓ public static double pow(double a, double b)
- ✓ public static int round(float a)
- ✓ public static int round(double a)
- ✓ public static void srandom(double a)
- ✓ public static double random()
- ✓ public static int abs(int a)
- ✓ public static long abs(long a)
- ✓ public static float abs(float a)
- ✓ public static double abs(double a)
- ✓ public static int max(int a, int b)
- ✓ public static long max(long a, long b)

✓ public static float max(float a, float b)

✓ public static double max(double a, double b)

✓ public static int min(int a, int b)

✓ public static long min(long a, long b)

✓ public static float min(float a, float b)

✓ public static double min(double a, double b)

Note that the srandom() method sets the seed for the random number generator method random(), which returns a random number between 0.0 and 1.0.

The String Classes

Java provides the programmer with two string classes—String and StringBuffer. The String class is for strings that are constant—they will not change. The StringBuffer class is for strings that are not constant and need to be altered. C and C++ do not provide any mechanism for strings at all; they are merely represented by null terminated arrays of characters. Using arrays for strings is wholly unsatisfactory in an environment like Java, where security and portability demand a much more robust approach. The danger of allowing strings to be represented by character arrays is that you always run the risk of overrunning the boundaries of the array. By encapsulating Strings in classes, the programmer does not have to worry about this problem.

Using Strings

The String class holds constant strings that cannot be changed once they are initialized. There are several constructors for Strings, depending upon how your String data is organized. The most basic constructor is that used for the string literals. When the Java compiler encounters a String literal, it actually creates an instance of the String class for that literal. Therefore, the easiest way to initialize a String object is to use the String literal

```
String s = "Hello, World!";
```

In addition, you can initialize the String in the traditional manner, by either including another String object, or a string literal.

```
String s = new String(someString);
```

You can also give the String constructor a character array for initialization. You can either pass the whole array,

public String(char value[])

or just a portion of the array, or subarray,

public String(char value[], int offset, int count)

Offset indicates where the subarray begins, and count indicates how long the subarray is.

Make sure that you do not alter the array after you use it to create the String. The array is not copied, and any alterations made to it will change the value of the characters in the String.

Additionally, you can use an array of bytes to initialize a String, in the same manner as an array of characters.

public String(byte ascii[], int hibyte)

public String(byte ascii[], int hibyte, int offset, int count)

In the case of an array of bytes, because Java uses the UNICODE character set, you need to indicate what the upper 8 bits of the 16-bit character are. You do this by using the hibyte argument. Typically the hibyte will be zero (0) for the Latin character set.

There are many methods provided for the String class. While this multitude of options can be confusing, there is undoubtedly a way to do something you want with this class. The following is a listing of some of the more important methods for the String class:

✓ **public int length().** This method returns the number of characters in the String.

✓ **public char charAt(int index).** This method returns the character at the position index.

✓ **public boolean equals(Object o).** This method compares two String objects, and returns true if their contents are the same, and false if otherwise.

✓ **public int compareTo(String s).** This method returns an integer based upon the lexical relationship of the two strings. If s is greater than this String, then a number less than zero is returned. If the two strings are equal then a zero is returned. If the String s is less than this String, then a number greater than zero is returned.

✓ **public boolean regionMatches(int toffset, String other, int ooffset, int len).** This method returns a boolean value based upon whether it can find a region starting at toffset in the String that matches a substring of other, beginning at ooffset, of length len. If a matching region is found, it returns true; otherwise, it returns false.

✓ **public boolean startsWith(String prefix).** This method is identical to the previous method except that it looks for the prefix at the beginning of the String.

✓ **public boolean endsWith(String suffix).** This method returns true if the String ends with the same String as suffix, false otherwise.

✓ **public int indexOf(String str).** This method returns the index of the first occurrence of str in the String. –1 returned if String not found.

✓ **public String substring(int beginIndex, int endIndex).** This method returns the substring that begins at beginIndex and ends at endIndex.

✓ **public String concat(String str).** This method returns the concatenation of the two Strings.

✓ **public String toLowerCase().** This method changes all the characters in the String to lowercase.

✓ **public String toUpperCase().** This method changes all the characters in the String to uppercase.

✓ **public char toCharArray().** This method creates a new array of characters from the String.

✓ **public static String valueOf(type variable).** This method creates a String from the variable argument. String provides a method for all of the basic types including boolean, int, long, float, double char[], and Object. This method implements the toString() method of the object passed as the argument.

It would be impossible to cover every single method of every single class Java provides. To cover any one class more than another would present an unbalanced impression of the Java class libraries. In addition, because the APIs will change, you should become familiar with how to use the online API guide that Sun provides with each release. While you will be able to do most of what you will need with the methods mentioned in this book, be sure to check out the API for a more comprehensive listing. You might just find a method that does exactly what you need.

The StringBuffer Class

The StringBuffer class provides methods for implementing a modifiable string. Whereas the String class dealt with strings that weren't meant to change, the StringBuffer class is essentially an expanding buffer for characters and other types to be used in creating Strings. This class provides methods for inserting and appending data to the String. Once you are finished creating your string, you can convert it with toString() to a String object that you can then manipulate with the String class methods.

Remember to use the StringBuffer class if you want to hold strings that you know will be changing.

Note

There are three constructors for the StringBuffer class:

→ **public StringBuffer().** This constructor creates an empty StringBuffer.

→ **public StringBuffer(int length).** This constructor creates a StringBuffer the size of length.

→ **public StringBuffer(String str).** This constructor creates a StringBuffer with the string str.

The methods implemented by the StringBuffer class are meant to allow you to create Strings from combinations of incoming types such as characters, integers, floats, and objects. The following example presents a use of the StringBuffer to build up a String from keyboard input:

```
StringBuffer str = new StringBuffer();
System.out.println("Enter Width:");
while((ch = System.in.read()) != '\n') {
    str.append(ch);
}
```

Notice that the StringBuffer was initialized as empty, and that the class automatically allocated space for new characters at the end. Here are a few of the more important methods. Again, check out the online API guide if you don't seem to find what you need in this list.

✓ **public int length().** This method returns the length of the String in the buffer (not the actual space of the buffer).

✓ **public int capacity().** This method returns the amount of space available in the buffer for new characters.

✓ **public synchronized StringBuffer append(type variable).** This method adds the variable type to the end of the StringBuffer. Valid types include Object, int, long, float, double, char[], and boolean.

✓ **public synchronized StringBuffer appendChar(char ch).** This method appends a single character to the end of the StringBuffer.

✓ **public synchronized StringBuffer insert(int offset, type variable).** This Method will insert the same types as append() in the location specified by offset.

✓ **public synchronized StringBuffer insertChar(int offset, char ch).** This method inserts a single character into the StringBuffer at the offset location.

✓ **public synchronized String toString().** This method converts the StringBuffer to a String.

Whenever you use the StringBuffer class, it automatically allocates more space for insertions. This way, you don't need to worry about overrunning your array of characters. You can explicitly allocate space in the buffer, and demand that a specific amount of space be set aside. Refer to the online API guide for more information on the StringBuffer class.

A Word on Arrays

Arrays in Java are a nebulous entity. They are classes, but they cannot be explicitly subclassed. As an object, the only instance variable that the array provides is length, which holds the length of the array. This is a useful variable for ensuring you are not exceeding the boundaries of the array. Even though Java will catch these mistakes, they will still throw exceptions, interrupting the execution of the program. If you catch boundary problems early, you can avoid the exceptions all together.

The System Class

The System class provides many functions for interacting with, and getting information about not only the Java run-time system, but the computer *outside* the Java environment. All of the System variables and methods are static. This means there is no need to create an instance of the System class at all. You merely reference the methods in the same way as the Math methods:

```
System.method
```

The System class includes three variables:

✗ public static InputStream in

✗ public static PrintStream out

✗ public static PrintStream err

These variables are instances of the Input and PrintStream classes, and provide the read(), print(), and println() methods used in the examples in this book to interact with stdin, stdout, and stderr. Typically stdin is the keyboard, while stdout is the terminal or monitor. Stderr is also sent to the screen by default in the interpreter; however, in the browser stderr is sent to the file weblog in the /.hotjava/ directory created from the HOMEPATH and HOMEDRIVE environment variables when HotJava loads.

For more information on the InputStream and PrintStream classes and their methods, see Chapter 10, "Using the Browser and AWT Class Library." For now, recall how the print(), println(), and read() methods were implemented:

```
System.in.read()
System.out.print(String)
System.out.println(String)
```

All of these methods were invoked from static member variables without creating an instance of System, InputStream, or PrintStream.

The methods provided by System enable interaction with both the Java interpreter and the Hardware platform itself. Here are a few of the more important methods. Check out the online API for a full listing.

✓ **public static void arraycopy(*type* src[], int srcpos, *type* dest[], int destpos, int length).** This method copies an array of type *type* from the source array src[] to the destination array dest[] starting at the srcpos index in the source array, of length length. The array is copied to the destpos index of the destination array. *Type* can be any one of boolean, byte, char, short, int, long, float, double, or Object.

✓ **public static int currentTime().** This method returns Greenwich Mean Time in milliseconds from some undefined epoch. This method is useful for comparing two timed events, but not for printed output.

✓ **public static int freeMemory().** This method returns the amount of free system memory in bytes. The API notes that this number is not always accurate.

✓ **public static int totalMemory().** This method returns the amount of system memory in bytes.

✓ **public static void exit(int status).** This method will cause the interpreter to exit with the exit code status.

✓ **public static InputStream execin (String command).** This method allows the program to execute a system command from within the interpreter, and send the output of the command to a FileInputStream. While this command will give you great power over the system, for obvious reasons the Java interpreter will not run this command if the code initiating it has come over a network.

✓ **public static OutputStream execin(String command).** This method will execute a system command from within the Java interpreter, and will return a FileOutputStream that is connected to the standard input of the command. Again, this will not run if loaded over the Internet.

✓ **public static void exec(String command).** This method executes a system command outside of the Java interpreter without redirecting standard input or output for the command.

✓ **public static String getenv(String var).** This method returns a String holding the value of the environment variable var. If the variable is not defined, the String is a null.

✓ **public static String getCWD().** This method returns the Current Working Directory.

✓ **public static String getOSName().** This method returns the name of the Operating System upon which the interpreter is running. While getting the operating system is useful for implementing OS dependent code, remember that Java's purpose is to be portable. Using code that is OS dependent should be for optimization only, and not a default solution. Otherwise, any other system your code might be used on would not be able to run your application.

While many of the System methods are useful for getting information about the platform and execution environment, in general, most of these methods will not need to be used, except for the in, out, and err variables.

If you do decide to place files on the client system, you should remember that Java, and the user, might severely restrict any file operations. Be sure to check the read and write path environment variables before attempting any file operations.

Summary

By now it is hoped that you have a clear understanding of the scope and depth of the Java language libraries. These libraries add functionality and ease of use beyond what the syntactical language structure can provide. The object-oriented paradigm allows the Java language to extend beyond mere language implementation and provide complex and powerful objects for the programmers use. It is this encapsulation of higher level programming elements that allows developers to implement difficult and error-prone code in an efficient and robust manner.

Unlike many object-oriented programming languages, which provide the means for object-oriented programming, but no content, Java comes with built-in classes for the basic objects and type wrappers, to more advanced system level classes that abstract the hardware layer. This provides a developer with a springboard for developing functional classes with more ease than before.

The next chapter will continue in the same vein as this chapter by presenting the Java I/O and utility packages. Like any good mechanic, you must know what is the right tool for each job. While it might seem tedious to go through the Java packages in such detail now, a couple hours of learning what is available will later save you days in coding. Take time to play around with the methods presented, and scan through the online API guide to see a full listing of the classes, methods, and variables. Once you have a grasp for the full range of Java packages, you will be able to tackle more complex projects with a full toolkit.

Chapter 10

The I/O and Utility Class Libraries

You probably will deal with the utility and i/o classes no matter what applications you are writing, unless you want to to repeat work that has already been done. The java.util and java.io packages provide useful classes and methods for controlling input and output, along with helper classes for string tokenization and vectors.

By encapsulating standard libraries into object-oriented packages, developers can more easily incorporate useful functionality into their programs without having to code it all themselves. In addition, the inheritance features of object-oriented computing enable the programmers to develop classes that build upon the standard library with their own ideas. A strong understanding of Java necessitates learning these standard classes.

Quick Review

Previous chapters have covered many aspects of the Java run-time and programming environments, including: using the Java browser and interpreter, providing content, and the fundamentals of programming in Java. The previous chapter extended the foundations of the Java language by introducing the language class library. For the programmer this means a more organized and efficient programming system. This environment is delivered by the object oriented paradigm implemented in the Java language, and provides the dynamic, extensible, robust, and high-performance functionality demanded for the next generation of the Internet.

The Java interpreter and HotJava browser provide the run-time environment for supporting the portable bytecode applications developed for distribution. Inside of each of these interpreters are several levels of authenitification, memory management and optimization blocks that all add to the overall Java system. Of particular significance to the object-oriented aim of Java is the run-time memory allocation and management, which allows objects to be brought in over the Internet, and seamlessly integrated. For the content providers this means less hassle in developing and distributing content, allowing them to focus on what they are delivering, rather than how they are delivering it.

Of course, developing content in Java means programming in Java, and all of the same benefits apply just as readily. For the programmer, a powerful set of libraries can mean the difference between an easy, low-bug experience, and a gigantic hassle in designing, programming, and debugging every single line of code needed to get the job done. By being an object-oriented language from the outset, Java ensures that if the classes exist for getting the job done, it will be possible to use them. In this light, Java comes with a feature-rich set of classes for getting programming jobs done as easily as possible. The previous chapter introduced the class libraries with the java.lang package, which provides additional basic language elements that would not be suited for inclusion at a language level, such as the String and Thread classes.

What This Chapter Covers

This chapter will continue where the previous chapter left off in covering the basic classes of the Java class libraries. These include the java.io and java.util package, include streams, input/output, date, vector, and tokenization classes among others. While it would be impossible to cover every class and method available in the API, it is hoped that this chapter will give the programmer a better feel for what classes are available, and make using the APIs easier and more useful.

After You Finish This Chapter

There is nothing more frustrating than trying to figure out how to code a problem, only to find out that a simple class from the standard library could have solved your problem with much less hassle. Once you finish this chapter, you will have a complete set of the basic tools needed to begin writing more complicated applications in Java. All of the programming elements up to this point could be considered the core of the Java language. In the next two chapters, the AWT, net, and browser packages will be presented. These classes provide the extra functionality to create graphical applications with connections to the wider world of the Internet. Next, general programming tips will be provided for developing different Java programs such as applets, stand-alone applications, and handlers. The last two chapters will present more advanced features of Java, including native code, the Java tools, and the Java Virtual Machine.

The I/O Class Library

The java.io package provides several classes for receiving and sending data to different input and output devices on a computer. The standard input device is the keyboard, while the standard output device is the terminal or monitor. These devices can be accessed using the InputStream and PrintStream classes, and have already been used in many of the examples presented in previous chapters. The most used input/output device after the keyboard and monitor is the file system. Java provides a RandomAccessFile class, which encapsulates the essential file access methods for getting data to and from disks.

Additionally, there are classes for buffered, filtered and piped streams, and string tokenization. The java.net packages use these abstract classes in order to interact with what could be considered the third class of input device—the network. By providing a range of classes with which to build input and output methods, it is simply a matter of opening the right stream, and using the predeveloped classes in order to read and write from the stream. Java also provides an AccessErrorHandler class for dealing with any problems that might arise from dealing with i/o methods.

Of course, what is presented here is a small number of the classes provided in the java.io package. Be sure to check out the online API for a comprehensive listing of all the classes and methods available. This section will cover the standard input and output classes, along with the RandomAccessFile class. These classes provide fast and easy access to the keyboard, monitor, and files on a system. They might not be the optimal classes in terms of performance, but will suffice for the majority of i/o jobs a program will need to handle.

The java.io library is not automatically loaded into the compiler as is the java.lang package. Therefore, you will need to explicitly load the package.

```
import java.io.*;
```

The * indicates that you want all of the classes in the io package to be loaded. You also can specify only the individual classes you want to load.

```
import java.io.RandomAccessFile;
```

stdin and stdout with InputStream and PrintStream

At the top of the java.io class hierarchy are two classes, InputStream and OutputStream, from which all classes in the java.io package are descended. Both of these classes are abstract, so cannot be initialized themselves, and must be extended for functionality. However, all classes that are subclasses of these two will have the same methods.

Interaction with the keyboard (stdin) and the monitor (stdout) are perhaps the most common streams programmers will have to deal with, and are encapsulated in the instance variables in and out of the System class. The instance variables in and out are of type InputStream and PrintStream, respectively. InputStream and PrintStream cannot be created with new directly. If you do not want to use System.in, or System.out, you can set your own stream objects equal to the System variables.

```
InputStream stdin = System.in;
PrintStream stdout = System.out;
```

You should try to use the System variables, because they will make your code easier for other programmers to understand. Other programmers will be familiar with the standard java.lang.System protocols.

The programs presented so far have already used three of the methods provided by the InputStream and PrintStream classes.

```
System.in.read();
System.out.print();
System.out.Println();
```

The next two sections will take a more detailed look at the methods provided by the InputStream and PrintStream classes.

InputStream

The basic job of the InputStream class is to read bytes from whatever stream it is attached to, be it the keyboard, a disk, or the Internet. There are two important attributes of the InputStream class:

1. When a call for information is made to InputStream the method employed will wait until input is available. This is known as blocking. For example, if you invoke the following, the method will wait until a byte can be processed (the user has typed something from the keyboard and pressed return) before returning:

```
System.in.read();
```

2. The InputStream class works with bytes, not characters. While the old ASCII format was only an 8-bit character set, the same as a byte, the newer Unicode character set is 16 bits long. This means that when receiving characters from stdin, you will not be receiving the hibyte of the Unicode character set.

Using the Read Method

The main method of the InputStream is read(). You are probably familiar with this method because it has been used in previous examples to read in characters from the keyboard.

```
StringBuffer buf = new StringBuffer();
int ch;
while((ch = System.in.read()) != -1) {
    buf.append(ch);
}
```

There are actually three overloaded methods with the name read. They are the following:

✓ **public abstract in read().** This method reads in a single byte from the input stream, and returns it as an integer. You will typically receive an error if you try to put the integer directly into a character, because an integer type is 16 bits larger than the character type. Notice the abstract modifier. This method is always implemented in a subclass. It is the method invoked with the `System.in.read()` call.

✓ **public int read(byte b[]).** This method takes a byte array as its argument, and places the incoming bytes into this array beginning at index 0. You can use this method to grab several characters at once from stdin. Be sure that the byte array is large enough to hold the information that the read method sends it, otherwise you will end up with an IOException being generated.

```
class input {
    public static void main(String args[]) {
        byte buf[] = new byte[50];
        System.in.read(buf);
        String str = new String(buf,0);
        System.out.println(str);
    }
}
```

Notice the statement String str = new String(buf,0). The String constructor takes a byte array, and appends the hibyte specified as the second argument to each of the bytes in the array in order to generate the Unicode character set. In almost all cases, the hibyte will be zero (0), which maps the same ASCII characters to Unicode characters.

✓ **public int read(byte b[], int off, int len).** This method is similar to the previous read() method, except that you can specify where in the byte array you would like for the input to be placed. off determines how far from the beginning of the array the method will begin to place data, and len indicates how many bytes to fill.

```
class input {
    public static void main(String args[]) {
        byte buf[] = new byte[50];
        System.in.read(buf, 5, 20);
        String str = new String(buf,0);
        System.out.println(str);
    }
}
```

The previous method is good for ensuring that you do not run out of array before the input is finished. By setting the offset as zero (0) and the length as the length of the array, the method will only fill the specified blocks in the array.

```
System.in.read(buf, 0, 50);
```

Note An important note to remember when using the read() method: You should use an integer to store the value of the returning input. This allows you to catch the end of file indicator, which is a –1. If you were to use a character, which is an *unsigned* number, you would not be able to tell when the end of the input had been reached.

The System.in.read() method is useful when dealing with stand-alone programs only using stdin and stdout. However, if you want to use keyboard input in a graphical program, you have to implement a different method. This technique is covered in Chapter 11, "Using the Browser and AWT Class Library." In the mean time, for basic stand-alone programs, the System.in.read() method will suffice.

PrintStream

The PrintStream class provides two methods for sending output to the screen: print() and println(). Both of these methods are overloaded with several argument parameters. The print method sends the characters to a buffer where they are stored until the buffer is flushed by a newline '\n' character. This means that characters will not appear on the display immediately, but rather, only after a newline is sent out with print(), or a println() call is made. The standard format for the print() method is

```
public void print(type variableName)
```

where *type* can be any one of the following:

➤ Object

➤ integer

➤ long

➤ float

➤ double

➤ boolean

In addition to the previous overloaded methods for print(), there are two overloaded synchronized versions of print, where type is either String or char[].

```
public synchronized print(type variableName)
```

All of the overloaded println methods are synchronized and allow for any of the previously listed types.

```
public synchronized println(type variableName)
```

In addition, a println() with no arguments will print a newline character.

Accessing Files

In addition to accessing the screen and keyboard, the most important i/o device is the file system. The java.io package provides a file input/output class known as RandomAccessFile. This class allows you to read and write information from a file in all of the Java fundamental types. In addition, there is a File class that holds information about a specific file name and methods for getting the status of the file.

The File Class

The File class provides a system-independent method for storing information about a file, its directories, and how it can be accessed. In addition to information about files, you can create instances of the File class that represent directories. Unix file systems access everything as files, including directories. For this reason, the File class is designed to not only deal with files, but directories as well. You can create an instance of the File class in three ways:

➔ **public File(String path).** This constructor creates a File object based upon the directory structure in path. This constructor creates an object based upon the final directory. The following examples are for a file text that exists in the following directory structure:

```
c:\users\Ritchey\text\input.txt
```

If you passed the string text, the File object could be said to be the directory \text\. Note that you can either pass the directory as an absolute reference:

```
File dir = new File("c:\users\Ritchey\text");
```

or as a directory relative to the directory of the executable

```
File dir = new File("text");
```

The machine specific implementation of the File class will determine how your slashes go (/ for Unix and \ for NT).

➔ **public File(String path, String name).** This constructor is used to create an instance of the File class for a specific file—not the whole directory.

```
File input = new File("text","input.txt");
```

➔ **public File(File dir, String name).** This constructor is identical to the previous constructor, except that instead of passing the directory as a String, you pass it as an instance of a File class, which has been created for the directory.

```
File input = new File(dir,"input.txt");
```

It is important to realize that by creating the File class, you don't actually create a file on the system. You only create an object that holds references to a file or directory. The methods in table 10.1 allow you to find out more about how the file relates to the actual system.

Table 10.1　File Class Methods

Method	Information Returned
public String getName()	The name of the file in a String. This does not include the directory structure where the file is located.
public String getPath()	The path of the file in the File class.
public String getAbsolutePath()	The file name, with the path of the executable appended to the front.
public String getParent()	The name of the parent directory if there is one, and null if it doesn't exist.
public boolean exists()	True if the file actually exists on the system, and false if the method cannot find it.
public boolean isFile()	True if the File instance is a valid and normal file, otherwise it returns false.
public boolean canWrite()	True if the file exists and is writable, and false otherwise.
public boolean canRead()	True if the file exists and is readable, and false otherwise.
public int lastModified()	The last time the file was modified. This should only be used for comparing modification time, and not printing out a time.
public boolean renameTo(File dest)	Renames the actual file with the file name in the dest File class. The method returns true if the renaming was successful, false otherwise.
public boolean mkdir()	Creates the directory in the File class relative to the current directory. This can be used if the directory does not actually exist. The method returns true if the directory was successfully made, false otherwise.
public boolean mkdirs()	Same as the previous method, except it will create the entire directory structure.
public String[] list()	Lists the contents of the directory in the File class. It returns an array of file names except for the "." and ".." equivalents. This method only works with instances of the File class which are directories.

Example of Using the File Class

The following code accepts a directory and file name, and then outputs information about the file and directory:

```java
import java.io.*;
class input {
    public static void main(String args[]) {
        System.out.println("Enter Directory:");
        char ch;
        StringBuffer dirBuf = new StringBuffer();
        while((ch=(char)System.in.read()) != '\n')
            dirBuf.appendChar(ch);
        File dir = new File(dirBuf.toString());
        System.out.println("Enter Filename:");
        StringBuffer fileBuf = new StringBuffer();
        while((ch=(char)System.in.read()) != '\n')
            fileBuf.appendChar(ch);
        File input = new File(dir,fileBuf.toString());
        if(input.exists()) {
                System.out.println("\nFile Found");
                System.out.println("File Name:
                "+input.getName());
                System.out.println("File Path:
                "+input.getPath());
                System.out.println("Abs. Path: " +
                input.getAbsolutePath());
                System.out.println("Readable?:
                "+input.canRead());
                System.out.println("Writable?:
                "+input.canWrite());
                System.out.println("\nDirectory listing:");
                String listing[] = dir.list();
                for(int i=0; i<listing.length; i++)
                    System.out.println(listing[i]);
            } else {
                System.out.println("File Not Found");
            }
        }
    }
```

The RandomAccessFile Class

The RandomAccessFile Class provides the programmer with a wealth of methods for interacting with a file. While there are more basic file accessor classes such as FileInputStream, and FileOutputStream, the RandomAccessFile class provides all the functionality of these classes combined, with the additional functionality of a file that can be accessed anywhere. With the standard FileInputStream and FileOutputStream classes, the file is accessed sequentially from beginning to end. With the RandomAccessFile class, you can determine exactly where in the file you want to retrieve data.

It is important that you are familiar with the following constructors:

→ **public RandomAccessFile(String name, String mode).**
This constructor takes the file name provided by name and opens a file for either read only or read-write. The mode depends upon the mode String, which is either r for read only or rw for read-write. When the file is accessed it can throw an IOException if the application does not have permission to access the file in the specified manner. Note that the file name is very system dependent; therefore, it would be better to create a File class instance, check for the existence of the file and the read-write permissions, and use a second constructor.

→ **public RandomAccessFile(File file, String mode).** This constructor takes the file described by the File class instance file and opens it in the access mode.

Once you have created the instance of RandomAccessFile, there are several methods for retrieving information from the file. The RandomAccessFile class allows you to access the file anywhere. You are not constrained to accept the bytes as they stream in. You do this by positioning a file pointer where you want to start taking data from, or writing to. When you first open the file, the file pointer will be at the beginning of the file. Before you can start moving the pointer along, you need to know how big the file is. You can do this with the length() method. This method returns the length of the file in bytes (8-bit intervals).

public int length().

Once you know the range of where you can move the file pointer, you can do so by using the seek() method. If you need to find out where the pointer is, you can use the getFilePointer() method. The seek() method moves the file pointer to the specified position in the file. The getFilePointer() method returns the position of the file pointer in bytes (8-bit intervals).

public void seek(int pos).

public int getFilePointer().

It is important that once you have finished with a file that you close it down with the close() method. You can either close it immediately, or implement a finalize method which would close the file when garbage collection occurs. This method closes the file stream.

public void close().

```
finalize {
    fileName.close();
}
```

Once you have opened the file, and determined where the file pointer is, you can begin to read data from the file. The RandomAccessClass provides several methods for reading different types of data from a file. These include the methods in table 10.2.

Table 10.2 Integer and String Methods for the RandomAccessFile Class	
Method	Description
public int read()	Reads a single byte, and moves the pointer forward 8 bits.
public int read(byte b[])	Reads and fills a byte array from the file, moving the pointer as many bytes as the size of the array.
public int read(byte b[], int off, int len)	Reads an array of bytes of length len and places them in the array at off. The pointer is moved len bytes.
public final String readLine()	Returns the entire line terminated by a '\n' or EOF (end of file) in a String.
public final String readUTF()	Return a string from a UTF formatted file.

The following methods all return a value of the type specified, and move the file pointer forward the same amount.

✓ public final boolean readBoolean()

✓ public final byte readByte()

✓ public final short readShort()

✓ public final char readChar()

✓ public final int readInt()

✓ public final long readLong()

The following code will read in a text file, and print its contents out on the screen:

```
import java.io.*;
class input {
   public static void main(String args[]) {
      System.out.println("Enter Directory:");
      int ch;
      StringBuffer dirBuf = new StringBuffer();
      while((ch=(char)System.in.read()) != '\n')
         dirBuf.appendChar(ch);
      File dir = new File(dirBuf.toString());
```

```
        System.out.println("Enter Filename:");
        StringBuffer fileBuf = new StringBuffer();
        while((ch=System.in.read()) != -1)
            fileBuf.appendChar(ch);
        File input = new File(dir,fileBuf.toString());
        if(input.isFile() && input.canWrite() &&
        input.canRead()) {
                RandomAccessFile file = new
                RandomAccessFile(input,"rw");
                System.out.println("File length: " +
                file.length());
                System.out.println("Pointer pos: " +
                file.getFilePointer());
                while(file.getFilePointer() < file.length())
                        System.out.println(file.readLine());
                file.close();
        } else {
                System.out.println("Can't read file");
        }
    }
}
```

In addition to reading a file, you can also write data to a file. Essentially, all of the read methods have a corresponding write method. It should be noted that when you write to a file, you do not insert the data. Instead, the method will write over any information already in the file with the new data. Be aware of what you are sending to a file. Additionally, you should know where you can and can't read and write files. It is not good practice to expect to be able to read or write files on a client machine over the Internet. If you do need to read or write files in a client machine, typically the /temp/ directory is set aside as the write path. Here is a listing of all the write methods:

✓ public void write()

✓ public void write(byte b[])

✓ public void write(byte b[], int off, int len)

✓ public final void writeLine(String line)

✓ public final void writeUTF(String utf)

✓ public final void writeBoolean(boolean b)

✓ public final void writeByte(byte b)

✓ public final void writeShort(short s)

✓ public final void writeChar(char c)

✓ public final void writeInt(int i)

✓ public final void writeLong(long l)

In addition, the following method is used for taking a String, and outputting it as 8-bit bytes so that the resulting file will be in ASCII, not Unicode:

public final void writeBytes(String s)

You will find that the RandomAccessFile class provides all of the functionality needed to read and write files in your Java programs. Try writing and reading your own file, and playing around with the different read and write types. You should be aware that Unix and DOS systems differ widely in their formatting of text files. Be sure to check how your system creates a text file. Typically Unix will only have a newline at the end of a line of text, while DOS text files have a carriage-return/newline combination. The following code writes lines entered from the keyboard to a DOS type file (which must already exist). You end inputting by typing an end of file character (Ctrl + Z for Windows NT and Ctrl + D for Solaris).

```java
import java.io.*;
class output {
   public static void main(String args[]) {
      System.out.println("Enter Directory:");
      int ch;
      StringBuffer dirBuf = new StringBuffer();
      while((ch=System.in.read()) != '\n')
         dirBuf.appendChar(ch);
      File dir = new File(dirBuf.toString());
```

```
System.out.println("Enter Filename:");
StringBuffer fileBuf = new StringBuffer();
while((ch=System.in.read()) != '\n')
    fileBuf.appendChar(ch);
File input = new File(dir,fileBuf.toString());
if(input.isFile() && input.canWrite() &&
input.canRead()) {
        RandomAccessFile file = new
        RandomAccessFile(input,"rw");
        System.out.println("File length:
        "+file.length());
        System.out.println("Pointer pos:
        "+file.getFilePointer());
        StringBuffer line = new StringBuffer();
        while(ch != -1) {
            line.setLength(0);
            while((ch=System.in.read()) != -1)
            line.appendChar(ch);
            line.append("\r\n");
            file.writeBytes(line.toString());
        }
        file.close();
} else {
        System.out.println("Can't read file");
    }
  }
}
```

The Utility Class Library

The java.util package has many classes for special functions.
These include dates, hashtables, vectors, locks, and stacks. This
section covers the use of the Date and Stack class. Check out the
API for more information on the other utility classes available in
the java.util package.

The Date Class

The Date class provides methods for retrieving the current date
and time, and also for computing days of the week and month.

You can create an instance of the Date class in several ways.

→ **public Date().** This constructor places the current date and time in an instance of Date.

→ **public Date(int year, int month, int date).** This constructor creates an instance of the Date class with the month, day, and year specified.

→ **public Date(int year, int month, int date, int hrs, int min).** This constructor creates an instance of the Date class with the year, month, day, hours, and minutes specified.

→ **public Date(int year, int month, int date, int hrs, int min).** This constructor creates an instance of the Date class with the year, month, day, hours, minutes, and seconds specified.

The conventions for the argument values are the following:

➤ Year—post-1900

➤ Month—0-11

➤ Date—1-31

➤ Hours—0-23

➤ Minutes—0-59

➤ Seconds—0-59

Once you have created the class instance, you can use it to retrieve information about the date, as shown in table 10.3.

Table 10.3   The Date Class Methods

Method	Information Returned
public int getYear()	the Year.
public int getMonth()	the Month.
public int getDate()	the Date (1-31).
public int getDay()	the Day of the week (0-6).

continues

Table 10.3 Continued	
Method	**Information Returned**
public int getHours()	the Hour.
public int getMinutes()	the Minute.
public int getSeconds()	the Second.
public boolean before(Date when)	Checks the instance date against the date when. Return true if the instance date is earlier than the when date, false otherwise.
public boolean after(Date when)	Checks the instance date against the date when. Return true if the instance date is later than the when date, false otherwise.
public boolean equals(Object obj)	Compares the two objects, and returns true if they are equal, false otherwise.
public String toString()	This method returns a string formatted with the date convention of the host system.

Using the Date class is quite straightforward. You can generate the current date simply by creating an instance without any arguments.

```
Date today = new Date();
System.out.println(today.toString());
```

or

```
System.out.println(today);
```

Notice that the println method automatically invokes the toString method without the need to explicitly call it.

The Stack Class

The Stack class is an additional class provided by the java.util package. You could develop your own stack, but it is much easier to use the stack provided by Java. This stack allows you to store any object you need to on a first in, last out (FILO) basis. You can imagine a first in, last out stack like one of those spring-loaded cafeteria tray despensers. The base of the stack makes sure that the top tray is always at the same level. It lowers as more trays are placed on top, and raises as they are taken off the top (see fig. 10.1). The FILO stack works the same way. If you place an object on the stack, it is placed on the very top, and if there is any other information on the stack, it moves down one level. Then, when you need the item, you simple pop it off. However, if items have been placed on the stack after the object you need, you need to pop off all of the elements that are on top of the one you need.

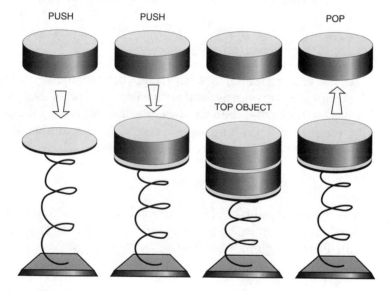

Figure 10.1

A representation of a FILO stack.

To create an instance of the Stack class, there is only a single constructor:

public Stack()

You can push Objects onto the stack using the push method, just as you can pop items off the stack.

public Object push(Object item)

public Object pop()

When you pop() an Object off the top of the stack, it is gone from the stack. If you only want to look at what is on the stack without removing it you can peek at the stack with this method:

public Object peek()

You also can test to see if the stack is empty with the empty() method. This method returns true if the Stack is empty, and false otherwise.

public boolean empty()

Finally, you can search for a particular object on the stack. The search() method returns the distance from the top of the first object that matches the search criteria. If an object is not found, a –1 is returned. The return value is essentially the number of pops necessary to bring the Object to the top of the stack.

public int search(Object o)

The following code uses two date Objects to demonstrate a Stack. Note the order in which the objects come off the stack when you run the application.

```java
import java.util.*;
class stack {
    public static void main(String args[]) {
        Stack s = new Stack();
        Date today = new Date();
        Date kristinBDay = new Date(1972,7,24);
        System.out.println(today);
        s.push(today);
        System.out.println(kristinBDay);
        s.push(kristinBDay);
        System.out.println(s.peek());
        while(!s.empty())
            System.out.println(s.pop());
    }
}
```

Summary

This chapter has been a quick review of some of the highlights of the java.io and java.util packages. This chapter, combined with the previous chapter, should give you a good idea of the basic classes and methods available in the Java programming environment. These chapters do not cover every class and every method in the Java packages, and to do so would have been unwieldy. A conscious decision was therefore made to focus on the classes and methods that would give the beginning Java programmer the widest view of what is possible with the class libraries. These chapters are not intended to serve as reference guides, even though the majority of the time the classes and methods you need will be found here. For a more complete listing, check out the online API guide for all the classes and method listings for the class libraries.

By now you should have in your toolkit a wide range of classes to tackle your programming problems with. With the fundamentals of the language, presented in Chapters 6, 7, and 8, the class libraries should fill out the basic groundwork for programming in Java. You now have the pieces for writing your own programs. However, you would still be writing programs that only took input from the keyboard, and placed output on a text display. The next chapters look at the AWT, or Another Window Toolkit, class library. These classes will allow you to develop a graphical user interface for your applets and applications. After that, the browser and net classes for interfacing with the HotJava browser and the wider Internet will be covered. Then, for the C and C++ programmers out there sitting on all that code you've written over the years, interfacing with native code will be discussed, in addition to using some of the more advanced Java Tools. Finally, the last chapter will cover the Java Virtual Machine in more detail.

Chapter 11

Using the Browser and AWT Class Library

Up to this point, the examples and focus of the programming chapters has been on stand-alone applications; and while those elements are applicable to creating applets and handlers for the browser environment, the applet itself has not been looked at since the HelloWorld program in Chapter 5, "Getting Started on Your Own Java Code." This chapter will begin to look more closely at the browser and AWT packages that provide encapsulation of the methods required to develop applets and graphical programs.

Quick Review

The majority of the book has been focused on getting the Java environment up and running, in addition to learning the basics of programming in the Java language. The first chapters looked at the features and capabilities of the Java specification with respect to portability, performance and ease of use. The interpreter and browser environments have been discussed both from the end user and server sides, and the dynamic and extensible nature of the Java language has been covered in the programming sections. It is this extensible, or object-oriented, nature that allows Java programmers to take advantage of the powerful class libraries provided with the Java environment.

By allowing the incorporation of distributed code across diverse platforms, Java creates an extensible user environment. This means that classes can be loaded across the Internet and used in the browser or interpreter, allowing potentially unlimited modification possibilities for the user environment. Of course, to be able to do this, Java had to solve several problems inherent in traditional compiled object-oriented languages, in particular the fragile superclass problem. Solving this problem means that programmers now know they can use a class library and it will work on the client's machine. For the site administrator, the solving of the superclass problem means that distributing code can be done without the hassles of scripting or other workarounds. For the end user, it means the availability of consistent and powerful applications delivered over the Internet.

In order to develop these programs as quickly and easily as possible, Java provides several class libraries. The first of these is of course the java.lang package, which encapsulates many of the basic language elements such as Type Wrappers, Strings, and Threads. The java.io package provides several useful classes for input and output streams. The java.util package provides classes for additional functionality such as Date and Stack. The classes presented so far provide for the basic functionality expected from any programming language, and once you have a firm understanding of them, you can go out and write full-featured programs. However, in today's application environment, the user has come to expect fully functional graphical interfaces, with full connectivity with the Internet. Java provides this functionality in the browser, AWT, and net packages.

The browser package provides the classes necessary for creating applets that run under the browser environment such as HotJava. The AWT provides a fully functional window toolkit that includes many features for images, controls, and resources. The net package, and the other packages under the net designation, provide easy connectivity to the wider Internet.

What This Chapter Covers

This chapter introduces the use of the AWT and browser packages for creating applets that run under the browser environment. More so than with the java.lang, java.io, and java.util packages, it would be impossible to cover every aspect of the AWT and browser classes and methods. The APIs themselves cover hundreds of pages of material, and provide numerous methods for different functions. Therefore, this chapter focuses on a limited number of applet programming problems in order to get you up and running as quickly as possible, and to give you an idea of where to go if you want to use the full functionality of the window and browser packages.

➤ **Browser class library.** The browser section covers the Applet class, and the functions it provides (and you must override) in order to interact with the graphic environment and the user.

➤ **Another window toolkit (AWT) class library.** The AWT section covers some of the basic elements of the window toolkit, and shows how they are incorporated into an applet.

After You Finish This Chapter

Once you have completed this chapter, you should have a good idea of how to use some of the classes and methods provided by the graphical packages. While every class and method will not be covered, understanding the rudiments will allow you to go on to a more comprehensive study of the APIs for the AWT and browser packages. The following chapter will discuss how to interact with the Internet in your application using the net packages, in addition to hints and tips on developing handler applications for dealing with new media types. The last two chapters will cover more advanced topics such as interfacing with C code and the Java Virtual Machine.

The Browser Class Library

The browser class library contains over 40 classes and interfaces for developing programs for the browser environment. The basic function of the classes is to provide methods for controlling the appearance of the browser environment as well as any applications in the environment. Classes such as BasicStyle, Document, and WRFormatter help to control the look of HTML documents and any applets that are referenced. Of course, the primary class of the browser package is Applet. As you might recall from Chapter 5, "Getting Started on Your Own Java Code," the Applet class is the superclass for all applets to be used in the browser. By extending the Applet class, the programmer is given a host of methods for running a program in the browser environment.

Extending the Applet Class

In order to create your own applet, you must extend the Applet class:

```
import browser.Applet;
class ClickAnimation extends Applet Implements Runnable{
Thread animationThread = null;
...
}
```

Notice that the class also implements Runnable. This is not a requirement for an applet, but if you do not want your applet to interrupt other applications running, it is good practice for it to be able to execute as a thread. For the example in this chapter, our applet will be running an animation whenever there is a mouse click on the applet. Because it is bad practice to have everything stop when the applet runs, it also implements the Runnable interface.

When an applet is loaded into the browser, its init() method is called. The format for the init() method you must override is the following:

```
protected void init() {
   resize(100,100);
   ...
}
```

Notice that the first method called is resize. This allows the applet to adjust its size so that the formatting of the document will be correct. It is important that you call the resize method from within the init() method. Otherwise, if you call resize() somewhere else, it can cause the entire document to be reformatted at an inopportune time. It is always good practice to set the amount of screen real-estate you want to use in the beginning. Because HTML formats the pages linearly, anything you change in one portion of the page, could alter formatting in the rest of the page. The ClickAnimation class loads a 25×25-pixel image, so the applet is resized to those dimensions.

Getting Attributes

The init method is also the perfect place to load any attributes specified in the HTML <APP> tag. If you recall from Chapter 3, "Using the Java Environment," the HTML tag for loading an applet can include programmer-defined attributes. In the case of the ClickAnimation class, the applet should be able to control how many times it runs through the sequence of frames. This attribute can be called CYCLES. In order to get the attribute from the HTML tag, you use the getAttribute() method, which returns the string held in the attributes tag.

```
class ClickAnimation extends Applet Implements Runnable{
Thread animationThread = null;
protected int cycles = 0;         // create an instance vari
         able
                              //"cycles"
protected void init() {
   resize(25,25);
   String cyclesTemp = getAttribute("CYCLES");
   if (cyclesTemp != null)
      cycles = Integer.valueOf(cyclesTemp).intValue();
}
```

The Integer wrapper is used to get the integer value of the cycles string. First, if the attribute exists, the String returned by getAttribute is converted to an Integer object by valueOf(), which is then in turn converted to an integer by intValue(). The attribute is included in the tag as follows:

```
<APP CLASS="ClickAnimation" CYCLES="3">
```

Loading Images

At the same time that the applet sets the number of cycles to run through, it should load the images it needs for the animation. Images are encapsulated in an AWT class called Images. In the case of the ClickAnimation applet, it needs to hold 10 pictures for the animation; therefore, it needs an array 10 items long. The choice of 10 frames is purely arbitrary.

```
protected Image frame[] = new Image[10];
```

The Applet class has a method that loads an image given its filename.

```
public Image getImage(String name)
```

The ClickAnimation applet needs to load 10 images, so it can be done with a for loop.

```
... init() {
   ...
   for(int i = 0; i < 10; i++)
       frame[i] = getImage("frame"+i+".gif");
```

The method is given a series of file names, which should reside in the same directory as the HTML file calling the class. The frames of the animation are held in the GIF images frame0.gif through frame9.gif.

Once the applet has been created and the init() method called, the next method to be run by the browser is start(). The ClickAnimation class runs the animation the first time the class is loaded, and then only from user input. The start() method needs to spawn the animationThread in order for the animation to run the first time.

```
protected void start() {
   animationThread = new Thread(this);
   animationThread.start();
}
```

When the animationThread is started, it calls the run() method. Note the use of this designator to refer the instance of the class to itself.

Painting Images

The run() method cycles through the animation frames, telling the applet to redraw itself with each new frame.

```
int cur = 0;
...
public void run() {
   for(int i = 0; i < cycles; i++) {
      for(cur = 1; cur < 10; cur++) {
         repaint();
         for(int j = 0; j < 50000; j++);
      }
      cur = 0;
      repaint();
   }
}
```

The for loop cycles instance variable *cur* through the frames of the animation, each time calling the repaint() method. When repaint is called, it causes the applet to be updated. When the browser wants the applet to draw itself, it uses the paint() method. By calling repaint(), the thread is causing the applet to cycle through the frames of the animation. The cycle starts with frame 1 and ends with frame 0, so that the picture in the applet when not in use is frame 0. The outer for loop causes the animation to run the number of times specified in cycles, while the innermost loop places a small delay to give time for the frame to be seen before the next is drawn.

```
public void paint(Graphics g) {
    g.drawImage(frame[cur], 0, 0);
}
```

The paint() method takes an argument that is an AWT object known as Graphics. This class has functions for drawing all of the basic graphics types, such as lines, characters, strings, and rectangles; as well as methods for clipping regions and scaling. When the browser calls paint() it sends it the applet's graphics context to draw in.

The class is now to the point where it runs. Here is the complete code:

```
import browser.Applet
import AWT.Graphics;
import AWT.Image;
class ClickAnimation extends Applet implements Runnable {
    Thread animationThread = null;
    protected int cycles = 0;
    Image frame[] = new Image[10];
    int cur = 0;
    protected void init() {
        resize(25,25) ;
        String cyclesTemp = getAttribute( "CYCLES" );
        if (cyclesTemp != null)
            cycles = Integer.valueOf(cyclesTemp).intValue();
        for(int i = 0; i < 10; i++)
            frame[i] = getImage("frame"+i+".gif");
    }
    protected void start() {
        animationThread = new Thread(this);
        animationThread.start();
    }
    public void run() {
        for(int i = 0; i < cycles; i++) {
```

```
        for(cur = 1; cur < 10; cur++) {
            repaint();
            for(int j = 0; j <50000; j++);
        }
        cur = 0;
        repaint();
    }
}
public void paint(Graphics g) {
    g.drawImage(frame[cur], 0, 0);
}
}
```

Create an HTML file to include the applet, and place it in a directory with the .class file in a subdirectory classes. You can either use some frames that were created to test the animation, or create your own. The applet should look like figure 11.1.

Figure 11.1

The ClickAnimation class in HotJava.

Handling Mouse Events

Of course, the animation only runs through the first time the applet is loaded, and it is supposed to run every time the cursor is clicked on it. Whenever events like the mouse entering the applet's area, or a button being pressed while the cursor is on the applet occur, the browser invokes the necessary method. If you have overridden the method for the specific event, you can specify what should happen.

```
public void mouseDown(int x, int y) {
    animationThread = new Thread(this);
    animationThread.start();
}
```

Now, each time the mouse is clicked on the applet, it plays the animation. There are several mouse events you can deal with, so be sure to check out the API for the full list of calls the browser can send to your applet.

Dealing With Keystrokes

If you want to intercept keystrokes, you must first get the focus. When you enter keys on a keyboard, it is difficult for the computer to know where to send the keystrokes. In order to send the keys to the right applet, the system requires that the applet be *in focus*—essentially indicating that it is the current applet recieving keystrokes. You can call the getFocus() method in the mouseDown() method. This way, when you click on a mouse in the applet, it gains the focus. The browser then issues a gotFocus() call. Once the applet has the focus, the browser sends keystrokes to it through the keyDown(int key) method. By overriding this method, you can deal with keystrokes however you want; for example, by appending them to a StringBuffer object.

```
public void mouseDown(int x, int y) {
    getFocus();
}
public void keyDown(int key) {
    SomeBuffer.appendChar(key);
}
```

Playing Sounds

Of course, now that the applet plays an animation, it is only proper that it also be able to play a sound. This is easily accomplished because the Applet class has methods for getting and playing .au files.

The AU file format is popular on Unix machines. However, there are several players available for creating AU files for Windows machines. There are typically AU helper apps available for different browsers, so check out your browser documentation for information on AU helper apps.

In order to load an audio file, use the getAudioData() method, which returns an object of type AudioData. Once the class has the AudioData object, it can use the play() method to run the file every time the animation is run.

```
import browser.Applet;
import AWT.Graphics;
import AWT.Image;
import browser.audio.AudioData;
class ClickAnimation extends Applet implements Runnable {
    Thread animationThread = null;
    protected int cycles = 0;
    Image frame[] = new Image[10];
    int cur = 0;
    AudioData sound = null;
    protected void init() {
        resize(25,25);
        String cyclesTemp = getAttribute("CYCLES");
        if (cyclesTemp != null)
            cycles = Integer.valueOf(cyclesTemp).intValue();
        for(int i = 0; i < 10; i++)
            frame[i] = getImage("frame"+i+".gif");
        sound = getAudioData("sound.au");
    }
    protected void start() {
        animationThread = new Thread(this);
        animationThread.start();
    }
    public void run() {
        for(int i = 0; i < cycles; i++) {
            play(sound);
            for(cur = 1; cur < 10; cur++) {
                repaint();
                for(int j = 0; j <50000; j++);
            }
```

```
            cur = 0;
            repaint();
        }
    }
    public void paint(Graphics g) {
        g.drawImage(frame[cur], 0, 0);
    }
}
```

Now, every time the animation cycles through it plays the associated sound.

These are only samples of the different methods available in the Applet class, and only samples of the classes in the browser package. Be sure to check out the API for a comprehensive listing of the classes and methods available.

The Another Window Toolkit (AWT) Class Library

The AWT, or Another Window Toolkit, provided by the Java environment includes over sixty classes and interfaces for creating graphical user interfaces. As with the browser, and all of the APIs, it is impossible to cover every method in every class, and they in fact deserve a book in their own right. This section presents a few of the methods from a sample of classes in order to give you a flavor of what using the AWT class is like.

The Graphics Class

The Graphics class is perhaps the most important of the AWT classes. It provides several drawing and clipping routines that can be used to either draw on the screen, or control how the drawing looks on the screen. You have already seen the drawImage() method in the ClickAnimation class, there are also several other methods for drawing objects on the screen.

✓ **public void drawRect(int X, int Y, int W, int H).** This method draws the outline of a rectangle of the given dimensions (relative to the applet region) in the foreground color.

✓ **public void drawRect(int X, int Y, int W, int H).** Same as previous method, except the entire rectangle is filled with the foreground color.

✓ **drawString(String str, int x, int y).** This method draws the String str at x, y in the current font.

✓ **public void drawLine(int x1, int y1, int x2, int y2).** This method draws a line in the foreground color from x1, y1 to x2, y2, relative to the application region.

✓ **public void copyArea(int X, int Y, int W, int H, int dx, int dy).** This method copies the region specified by the first four coordinates, and copies to the point dx, dy.

In addition to drawing methods, the Graphics class also implements several methods for changing the preferences for drawing.

✓ **public void setForeground(Color c).** This method takes an object of type Color, and uses it as the foreground (drawing) color.

✓ **public void setFont(Font f).** This method takes an object of type Font, and uses it for all text output through Graphics. Fonts available on all platforms are Helvetica, TimesRoman, ZapfDingbats, Dialog, DialogInput, and Courier in point sizes 8, 10, 12, 14, 24, and 36.

An important method for animation is the clipRect() method. Because the normal call to repaint causes the entire applet to be repainted, flashing can become quite obvious for larger images in which only a small section changes. Flashing refers to when the entire image blinks on and off because the video system cannot repaint the image fast enough to fool the eyes into believeing they are seeing a continuous image. In order to overcome this problem, you can clip the region in which you want painting to occur, then the rest of the image will be left alone, and only the clipping region will be changed.

In order to use the clipRect() method, you can override the update() method in the Applet class. The update method is called on a repaint() method invocation. The following is an example of an update method that clips a region of the applet area for painting.

```
public void update(Graphics g) {
    if(animating?)
        g.clipRect(x, y, W, H);   // clip to changing area
    else g.clipRect(0,0,appletWidth, appletHeight); // if
    // not animating, allow entire applet to be repainted
    paint(g); //call the paint() method with g
}
```

Color

The Color class allows you to specify a color for use by the Graphics, or another class. For example, you could set the foreground color for Graphics output. You can either create a new color object by passing the red, green, and blue values of the color, or using the static variable colors provided with the class.

```
Color MyColor = new Color(g.wServer,12,156,87);
g.setForeground(Color.lightGray);
```

The g.wServer is an instance variable held by the Graphics class of the windows server for the drawing area. The following is a list of all static colors:

black	green	pink
blue	lightGray	red
cyan	magenta	white
darkGray	orange	yellow
gray		

Controls

In addition to drawing lines, rectangles, and Strings on the screen, you can also include control items with which the user can interact. The AWT package includes classes for dialog boxes, scroll bars, text fields, radio buttons, menus, and the common button. Controls allow you to create a familiar interface for the user. Traditionally, implementing controls was a difficult process, and it is still not the easiest thing to do even with today's "visual" compilers and libraries, although it is worlds better than it was even a few years ago.

While Java doesn't support the drag-and-drop style interface creation that many of the modern development environments do, it is still simply a matter of subclassing the provided classes with the functionality you need. The next example shows you how to include a button in a stand-alone application.

Buttons

The Button class in the AWT package provides the necessary methods for creating a button that responds to being pressed. In order to create the button, you must create a subclass that handles the selection of the button for you. In this case, the subclass will be the following:

```java
import AWT.*;
interface buttonReturn {
   public void buttonPressed(String s);
}
class NewButton extends Button {
     buttonReturn obj = null;
     String n = null;

   public NewButton(String label, String name, Window w) {
     super(label,name,w);
     n = name;
     obj = (buttonReturn)w;
   }
   public void selected(Component c, int pos) {
     obj.buttonPressed(n);
   }
}
```

The class is derived from Button, and adds two variables and overrides the selected() method. When a NewButton is created, it expects to receive a subclass of the Window class, which implements the buttonReturn interface. This way it can keep track of which class created it and tell the class when it is pressed, because all classes that implement buttonReturn must implement a buttonPressed class. After storing information about its name and the creating class, it waits for the window server to call its selected() method. The class can then call the buttonPressed method in order to tell the parent class what button was pressed.

The following code creates a window server, frame, and window. It then places text, and two buttons in the window. When the "Try Me!" button is pressed, it switches an image on and off. When the "Quit" button is pressed, the application exits.

```
class StandAloneGraphics extends DisplayItemWindow
                        implements buttonReturn {
    static WServer ws;
    static Frame frame;
    static Graphics graphic;
    static DisplayItemWindow window;
    static NewButton quit;
    static NewButton imgB;
    static Image img = null;
    static boolean displayImg = false;
    public StandAloneGraphics (Frame frame) {
        super(frame,"new");
    }
    public static void main(String argv[]) {

        ws = new AWT.WServer();
        ws.start();
        frame = new Frame(ws, true, null, 200, 200,
        Color.lightGray);
        frame.setTitle("StandAloneGraphics");
        window = new StandAloneGraphics(frame);
        graphic = new Graphics(window);
        quit = new NewButton("Quit","quit",window);
```

```
        quit.move(100,10);
        quit.map();
        imgB = new NewButton("Try Me!","imgB",window);
        imgB.move(10,50);
        imgB.map();
        img = window.createImage(new GifImage("image.gif"));
        frame.map();
    }
```

When the program is loaded, the main() method is called. The window server is first created and started, and then the application frame is created, and its title set. Using this frame, a window can be created, and then a Graphics object for drawing in the window. When the window is created, it has its own constructor that it calls the super constructor. The next several lines create the buttons for the application. The button is created with its label, name, and parent window, then moved to the proper location and told to display itself. Finally, an image is loaded into the img variable, and the frame is told to display itself.

```
public void update() {
    paint(graphic);
}
```

Because the program should be able to update itself whenever the image needs to be updated, an update method is needed that calls the paint() method with the graphic variable as its argument.

```
public void paint(Graphics g) {
    g.drawString("Hello There", 10, 10);
    if(displayImg)
        g.drawImage(img,100,50);
    else g.clearRect(100, 50, 100+img.width,
    50+img.height);
}
```

The paint() method draws a String into the window, and then tests whether to paint the image or to clear the area where the image is, based upon the displayImg flag.

```
public void buttonPressed(String s) {
    if(s.equals("imgB")) {
        displayImg = (displayImg)?false:true;
        update();
    }
    else if(s.equals("quit")) {
        stop();
    }
}
```

The buttonPressed method is the implementation of the buttonReturn interface, and allows the buttons created to send back a message when they are pressed. The buttonPressed() method checks to see which button was pressed, and then takes action accordingly. If the Try Me! button was pressed, it changes the state of the displayImg flag, and calls the update() method. If the Quit button was pressed, it calls the stop()method.

```
public void stop() {
        frame.dispose();
        System.exit(0);
    }
}
```

The stop() method disposes of the frame, and then calls the system exit function with a 0 for success.

The entire code for the program, and the final output (see fig. 11.2) of the program is as follows:

```
import awt.*;
interface buttonReturn {
    public void buttonPressed(String s);
}
class NewButton extends Button {
    buttonReturn obj = null;
    String n = null;

    public NewButton(String label, String name, Window w) {
        super(label,name,w);
```

```
        n = name;
        obj = (buttonReturn)w;
    }
    public void selected(Component c, int pos) {
        obj.buttonPressed(n);
    }
}
class StandAloneGraphics extends DisplayItemWindow
                        implements buttonReturn {
    static WServer ws;
    static Frame frame;
    static Graphics graphic;
    static DisplayItemWindow window;
    static NewButton quit;
    static NewButton imgB;
    static Image img = null;
    static boolean displayImg = false;
    public StandAloneGraphics (Frame frame) {
        super(frame,"new");
    }
    public static void main(String argv[]) {

        ws = new awt.WServer();
        ws.start();
        frame = new Frame(ws, true, null, 200, 200,
        Color.lightGray);
        frame.setTitle("StandAloneGraphics");
        window = new StandAloneGraphics(frame);
        graphic = new Graphics(window);
        quit = new NewButton("Quit","quit",window);
        quit.move(100,10);
        quit.map();
        imgB = new NewButton("Try Me!","imgB",window);
        imgB.move(10,50);
        imgB.map();
        img = window.createImage(new GifImage("image.gif"));
        frame.map();
    }
    public void update() {
        paint(graphic);
    }
```

```
public void paint(Graphics g) {
    g.drawString("Hello There", 10, 10);
    if(displayImg)
        g.drawImage(img,100,50);
    else g.clearRect(100, 50, 100+img.width,
    50+img.height);
}
public void buttonPressed(String s) {
    if(s.equals("imgB")) {
        displayImg = (displayImg)?false:true;
        update();
    }
    else if(s.equals("quit")) {
        stop();
    }
}
public void stop() {
    frame.dispose();
    System.exit(0);
}
}
```

Figure 11.2

The application before and after the Try Me! button is pressed.

Summary

This chapter has given you a short introduction to developing applets, and, in general, graphical applications for the browser and interpreter environments. You should be able to write your own simple animation applets and begin to deal with mouse and keyboard events. While this is only the simplest form of interaction an applet can have, it is the best place to start for learning the fundamentals of the browser and AWT packages. Of course, there are hundreds of other classes and methods provided by these packages that are not covered in this chapter. The full API would require the devotion of an entire book to the subject. Hopefully this introduction gives you the necessary tools to begin studying the API, and incorporating them into your own programs.

The primary use of Java is to interact with the Internet. The next chapter looks at how to include network methods to your classes, and how to develop programs with specific purposes in mind, such as applets or handlers. The final two chapters will cover implementing native C methods, the Java tools, and the Java Virtual Machine. You have now passed the threshold from the basic functionality of the Java language, to the advanced features meant to provide complex interaction in the new graphical world of the Internet. This is not an easy topic to learn, and you shouldn't expect to build mammoth applications from the outset. Study the APIs, check out example programs on the Web, and start trying your own hand at small applications. Soon, you will have the pieces together for completing more challenging projects.

Chapter 12

Java for the Internet

The implementations of Java discussed so far, and covered in examples, used the existing Internet HTML protocol to deliver portable applets that run under the browser environment. In the main, this is the primary use of Java—advanced dynamic content for HTML pages. However, this only breaks the surface of what Java can actually do. The Java net packages and the Java architecture allow it to be used as a dynamically extensible architecture that can actively use the Internet as a source for code, data, and input. By incorporating Java packages, programmers can quickly get their programs up to speed and on line with Telnet, FTP, NNTP, and WWW protocols. Additionally, Java applications can dynamically load classes needed for execution over the Internet, providing a virtually limitless array of functionality for both the end user and developer.

Quick Review

Up to now, the Java applications covered in this book have passively used the Internet for distribution. Java can also interact with the Internet on its own, drawing data in the form of bytecode files for classes, content files such as images or audio, or input for interaction with other users. The main interface for this functionality is through the Java browser environment; although, the interpreter can also deal with network connections. In order to be both extensible and portable, the Java language needed to provide an object-oriented architecture free from the constraints of precompiled implementations. In addition, to meet client demands, Java had to be a high-performance, robust, and secure environment.

In many ways, the robust, secure, portable, and extensible qualities of the Java language are solved by the interpreted design. By compiling to a virtual machine, and creating memory layout at run-time, rather than compile-time, Java is able to assess the condition of the code before it is run on a client machine. This includes the following:

➤ Verifying bytecodes for compliance with the Java language

➤ Separate memory spaces for network loaded classes

➤ The lack of pointers and a predefined memory layout that could aid in the programming of Trojan horses or viruses.

All of these security measures come at the cost of performance. However, Java overcomes much of the performance penalty by coding to intermediate bytecodes for efficient interpretation or just-in-time compilation, and providing multithreading, especially in terms of memory management

Of course, providing all of this functionality does not aid the programmer in creating the modern GUI interfaces demanded by today's users. Java provides this functionality in two packages: browser and AWT. The browser package provides classes and methods for creating applets for inclusion in Web pages, while the AWT class provides a more general windowing toolkit that can be used either for creating applets or stand-alone programs.

Having pretty interfaces is not the purpose of a Java program— providing dynamic content and connectivity through the

Internet is. Java has the capability to both use standard Internet protocols, and define its own. This capability is not only a function of the Java architecture, but the encapsulation of network methods in the net packages.

What This Chapter Covers

This chapter introduces the use of the net packages that come with Java, along with ways of implementing the four basic Java programs:

➤ Applets

➤ Stand-Alone Applications

➤ Content Handlers

➤ Protocol Handlers

The Java net packages are actually divided into six separate packages, which can be imported into your applications:

➤ net

➤ net.ftp

➤ net.nntp

➤ net.www.content.image

➤ net.www.html

➤ net.www.http

These packages each provide separate classes and methods for dealing with Internet protocols.

The second section in this chapter covers the different types of Java programs you can write. The applet is primarily used for inclusion in HTML pages, similar to inline images. The application is meant as a stand-alone program to be run inside the Java interpreter. The handlers are similar to applets in that they are typically used in a browser environment. However, instead of directly providing the content themselves, handlers can be used to process any content of a particular type.

After You Finish This Chapter

This chapter completes the overview of the class libraries that are provided with the Java environment. All together, each level of the class libraries provides additional functionality to the Java programming environment, allowing the programmer the flexibility to develop powerful applications quickly and easily. The remaining two chapters are for more advanced programming and architectural detail. The next chapter covers the importing of native methods and the Java tools, while the last chapter covers the Java Virtual Machine in more detail.

Networking Your Applications

Networking your applications is perhaps the most important of all the Java functions to implement. In order to make this process as easy as possible, Java has provided several packages for quick access to the standard Internet protocols. In many cases, there is a minimal amount of code needed to connect your application with the Internet.

The packages provided by Java implement several protocols, including Telnet, FTP, NNTP, and WWW.

The Telnet Stream Classes

The net package provides several classes for the basic network functions needed by all protocols. Following are four of the classes:

- ➤ InetAddress
- ➤ Socket
- ➤ TelnetInputStream
- ➤ TelnetOutputStream

These classes provide the basic functionality needed to create socket connections and handle data streams to and from host computers once connections have been made. Many of the other net packages and classes use these classes.

The net group of packages, as listed at the beginning of the chapter, are each separate packages. You cannot import all of the packages by importing net.*. What you are actually doing is importing all of the classes in the net package. Instead, you must import all of the packages individually.

The InetAddress class includes several variables and functions for storing information about an Internet host address.

✗ **public String hostName.** This variable holds the name of the host, (newriders.mcp.com).

✗ **public int address.** This variable holds the numerical address of the host, (131.68.10.33).

✗ **public static String localHostName.** This variable holds the name of the local host (the computer the application is running on).

The constructor can be used along with static methods to retrieve the address and port of a word address. For example, if you have the host name newriders.mcp.com, you can acquire its complete address information by using the following getAddress class:

```
import net.*;

class getAddress {
   public static void main(String args[]) {
      if(args.length == 1) {
         InetAddress a = InetAddress.getByName(args[0]);
         System.out.println("Host name:    " + a.hostName);
         System.out.println("Host address: " + a.toString());
         System.out.println("Local host:   " +
         a.localHostName);
```

```
    }
    else System.out.println("Enter:java getAddress
                                        <hostname>");

    }
}
```

When the code is run, it probes the network for the address of the host name given and prints out all of the relevant information. Notice the use of the toString() method to output the numerical address in a readable format. Figure 12.1 shows the output of the getAddress class.

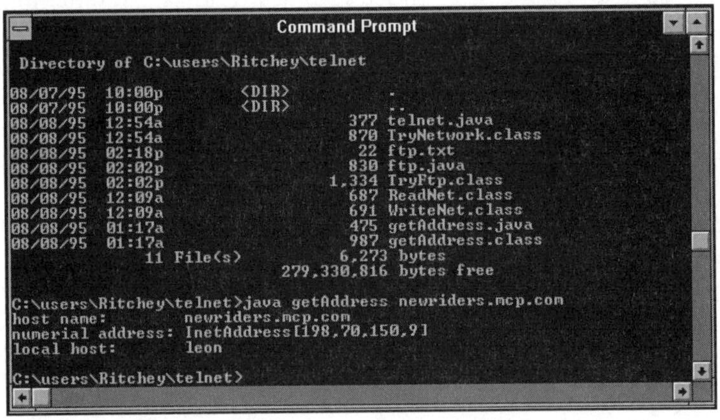

Figure 12.1

Output of the getAddress class.

The getAddress class is a useful example of how Java packages can make a programmer's task simple. In 14 lines of code, the class was able to get the information from the network it needed, and present it to the user.

In addition to the InetAddress class, the net package also provides a TelnetInputStream and TelnetOutputStream in order to process streams for telnet clients. Because of the way in which different systems implement carriage returns and line feeds at the end of lines, it is necessary to handle a certain amount of processing to make sure that telnet clients are receiving the correct character sequence. The TelnetInputStream and TelnetOutputStream provide this functionality, and are used by many of the other packages, such as net.ftp, as you shall see in the next section.

The read and write functions provided by the classes are similar to other streams implemented in java.io. In fact, they are sub-classes of the FilterInputStream and FilterOutputStream classes.

1. TelnetInputStream

    public int read(). This method returns a single byte from the stream.

    public int read(byte bytes[]). This method places the data into the byte array bytes[], begining at index 0.

    public int read(byte bytes[], int off, int len). This method places the data into the bytes[] array, beginning at index off-1 for len bytes.

2. TelnetOutputStream

    public void write(int c). This method writes the int c to the output stream, and does any carriage return, line feed formatting required.

    public void write(byte bytes[], int off, int len). This method writes the bytes in the array from index off-1 for len bytes to the output stream.

Implementing a Simple FTP Application

The Java net.ftp package provides classes for making FTP connections, and methods for logging on, listing directories, setting the transfer protocol, and sending files to and from the FTP server. The main class is the FtpClient class, which encapsulates almost all FTP functionality.

The variables for FtpClient hold information about the use of a proxy. A *proxy* is a server that stands in between a computer and the rest of the Internet, caching recently accessed data in case computers using the proxy call for it.

✗ **public static boolean useFtpProxy.** This variable is a flag for whether to use a proxy for FTP transfers. If the variable is true, then the proxy host is used.

✗ **public static String ftpProxyHost.** This variable holds the name of the proxy host to be used if useFtpProxy is true.

✗ **public static int ftpProxyPort.** This variable holds the port of the proxy host to use if useFtpProxy is true.

There are three constructors for FtpClient. You can either make a connection with a host name and port, or just a host name. Also, you can create the FtpClient object without making a connection.

➜ **public FtpClient(String host).** This constructor creates an FTP connection using only the host name.

➜ **public FtpClient(String host, int port).** This constructor creates an FTP connection using the host name and port number.

➜ **public FtpClient().** This constructor creates an instance of the FtpClient class, without opening an FTP connection. The openServer method can be used to open a connection later.

After the class has been created, it provides several methods for interacting with the FTP server.

✓ **public void openServer(String host).** This method opens a connection to the host FTP server.

✓ **public void openServer(String host, int port).** This is an overloaded version of the previous method that opens a connection to the FTP server with both a host name and port number.

Once the port is open, you need to log in to the server itself.

✓ **public void login(String user, String password).** This method logs in to the FTP server using the user and password arguments. In case of anonymous logins, an e-mail address can be given for the password.

Once the connection to the server is open, and you have logged in with a user name and password (or alternatively with anonymous/ftp and e-mail address), you can begin to send commands to the FTP server. The FtpClient class provides several control commands.

✓ **public void cd(String remoteDirectory).** This method changes the directory on the remote system to that indicated in the string remoteDirectory.

✓ **public void binary().** This method sets the transfer protocol to binary format. You should use this format for any executable, compressed, or special formatted files not suitable for ASCII.

✓ **public void ascii().** This method sets the transfer protocol to ASCII format. This format is suitable for plain text files and any other non-formatted files.

In addition to the command methods, the FtpClient class also provides methods for sending and retrieving directory listings and files. These methods return input and output streams, which can then be read or written to.

✓ **public TelnetInputStream list().** This method returns an input stream of the current directory on the remote machine.

✓ **public TelnetInputStream get(String filename).** This method gets the file name on the remote machine and transfers it using the TelnetInputStream.

✓ **public TelnetOutputStream put(String filename).** This method opens up an output stream for writing and sends it to the remote computer as filename.

In each of these methods, it is up to the programmer to take the relevant stream and either read the incoming data, or write the outgoing data. The following code opens an FTP connection with a host provided as the first command-line argument. It then lists the first directory and allows you to enter a file for viewing.

```
import net.ftp.*;
import net.*;

import net.*;
class TryFtp {
    static FtpClient ftp;
    public static void main(String args[]) {
        StringBuffer buf = new StringBuffer();
        int ch;
        ftp = new FtpClient(args[0]);
        ftp.login("ftp","tdr20@cus.cam.ac.uk");
        ftp.ascii();
        TelnetInputStream t = ftp.list();
        while((ch = t.read()) >= 0)
            buf.appendChar((char)ch);
        t.close();
        System.out.println(buf.toString());
        System.out.println("\nEnter File To Download:\n");
        buf.setLength(0);
        while((ch = System.in.read()) != '\n')
            buf.appendChar((char)ch);
        t = ftp.get(buf.toString());
        buf.setLength(0);
        while((ch = t.read()) >= 0)
            buf.appendChar((char)ch);
        t.close();
        System.out.println(buf.toString());
    }
\
```

Figure 12.2 shows an example of the output from the getFile class.

In 19 lines, the getFile class makes an FTP connection with a remote computer, downloads an ASCII file, and prints the 1000 characters of it to the screen. This is quite an accomplishment that shows the power of using an object-oriented language, and Java in particular.

Figure 12.2
Example output from the getFile class.

Additional Protocols

Besides the FTP and Telnet protocols, Java provides classes for implementing NNTP and WWW protocols. These protocols build upon the net package of classes, and provide additional functionality for connecting to network news servers, and handling documents and content from HTTP servers. These two protocols are perhaps the most widely used protocols for interacting with others on the Internet outside of e-mail.

The NNTP Protocol

The NNTP, or network news transport protocol, is used to deliver messages for newsgroups around the Internet. The newsgroups are a structured listing of topics to which people can read and post messages. The net.nntp package is much the same as the net.ftp package in its behavior. The primary class in the net.nntp package is the NntpClient class.

As with the FtpClient class, the NntpClient has constructors and methods for connecting to a newsgroup server and retrieving and sending information. Here is an abbreviated list of methods provided by the NntpClient class:

- ✓ public NntpClient(String host)
- ✓ public NewsgroupInfo getGroup(String name)
- ✓ public setGroup(String name)
- ✓ public InputStream getArticle()
- ✓ public PrintStream startPost()
- ✓ public boolean finishPost()

These methods can be used to implement your own newsgroup reader within a Java applet or stand-alone application. For example, you could add functionality to a browser that already supports limited newsgroup functionality by adding an applet to download separate uuencoded files, concatenate them together, and extract the whole binary file.

The WWW Protocol

The WWW protocol package is divided up into several different packages, each providing a different functionality for dealing with WWW pages and HTTP servers. The packages are separated as follows:

- ➤ net.www.content.image
- ➤ net.www.html
- ➤ net.www.http

The net.www.content.image package provides the classes necessary to deal with the different images that HotJava can handle automatically. These include gif, xbitmap, and xpixmap.

Essentially, these are the MIME types and subtypes that HTTP servers send to the browser as inlined files for eventual display.

The net.www.html package provides several important classes for dealing with HTML documents and content. The ContentHandler class is the superclass of all classes that are used to handle inline content. This class is looked at in more detail in the section on creating content handlers.

The net.www.html package provides Tag and TagRef classes to provide encapsulation of HTML directives included in documents. The Tag class stores the actual information in an HTML tag, while the TagRef holds a reference to a Tag object and its position in the document.

The Document class stores an HTML page in an internal format so that it can be accessed by standard methods. The Document class splits off the HTML tags and places them in a vector array. The class then places the remaining text in a byte array, and, additionally, an optional source text array can hold the original raw HTML file.

- ✗ protected String htmlSource
- ✗ protected byte text[]
- ✗ protected Vector tags
- ✗ protected String title

In addition to storing the contents of an HTML file, the Document class includes several methods for accessing the tag vector and creating new entries in an HTML document.

- ✓ public Vector getTags()
- ✓ public byte getText()
- ✓ public String getTitle()
- ✓ public void setText(byte text[])

✓ public final void setSource(String source)

✓ protected final TagRef addTagRef(TagRef ref, int offset)

The net.www.html package also provides a Parser class to take an HTML file and create an instance of the Document class. The Parser constructor takes the data from an input stream and places it in the provided Document object.

public Parser(InputStream is, Document html)

In addition to encapsulating HTML directives and documents, the net.www.html package provides a class for encapsulating URLs. The URL class takes an URL in several formats and stores the necessary information, which can then later be used by class methods to access information on the Internet. The URL class provides several methods for interacting with Objects referenced by the URL. The constructors for an URL Object are as follows:

→ **public URL(String protocol, String host, String file)**. This constructor creates an URL given the protocol, host, and file name to use.

→ **public URL(URL context, String spec)**. This constructor creates an URL object based upon the context and spec. If spec is an absolute URL (it includes protocol, host and filename), then the URL is parsed in the same manner as the following constructor. Otherwise, the spec is considered to be a relative URL, and it is parsed in relationship to the URL context. For example, many times URLs refer to a fil e name only. It is assumed in these situations that the file name exists in the same directory on the same computer as the HTML file itself.

→ **public URL(String spec)**. This constructor parses the String spec, which holds an absolute URL (protocol, host, and file name), and generates an URL object.

Once the URL has been created, the URL class includes several methods for opening and retrieving the file associated with the URL.

✓ **public Object getContent()**. This method returns the object referenced by the URL.

✓ **public Object getContent(InputStream is, Observer o)**. This method returns the object referenced by the URL. In this case, if there is no handler for the object, the Input-Stream passed to the method is used to deliver the object.

In addition to pulling over the object referenced by the URL itself, you can open a stream to the object.

✓ **public InputStream openStream()**. This method opens a stream to the object referenced in the URL and invokes the proper protocol handler.

✓ **public InputStream openStreamInteractively()**. This method acts the same as the previous method, except that it allows the stream handler to interact with the user in cases of problems that openStream would merely toss an exception on. For example, the HTTP handler can ask for a username and password in order to gain authentication.

net.www.html provides an URLStreamHandler class that can be overridden to provide new protocol handlers for the Browser. The class provides an openStream and openStreamInteractively method that can be overridden by the programmer to deal with new protocols. Developing protocol handlers is dealt with in more detail in the next section.

By using these, and other standard classes, you can create applications that extend the functionality of a browser extensibly by incorporating your classes into the structure of the overall interface. The next section covers how to create a simple content or protocol handler.

The www.http package can be used to handle the HTTP protocol by dealing with authentication requests, header fields, and InputStreams. The main class is the HttpClient class, which encapsulates authentication, proxy, and stream status information.

All of these packages together constitute Java's encapsulation of the network functionality necessary for creating dynamic, network-aware content. The present state of how Java is implemented is still in flux. Remember that the technology is still in the Alpha stage at the time of this writing. It is important that you check out the most recent information available.

The Different Java Program Types

Java is a language and environment that supports several different kinds of applications. The traditional division of Java programs is the following:

➤ Applets

➤ Stand-Alone Applications

➤ Content Handlers

➤ Protocol Handlers

The main difference between the programs in the previous group is a development strategy that divides applications from handlers. The application side of programming in Java is covered by applets and applications—the front line between the user and the underlying system and network. The handlers, both in terms of content and protocol, provide an encapsulation of the underlying system and network calls, providing the applications with a consistent interface in a constantly changing environment.

Applets versus Stand-Alone Programs

The application side of Java programming is what this book has been mainly concerned with. The applications, whether executed in the interpreter or browser environment, are typically perceived as the actual program being run by the user. In fact, once the Application class has been loaded, any number of supporting classes can be invoked to actually provide the eventual output. In a sense, the Application class marshals the execution of different pieces of code. The class might use the System class in order to handle input/output, it could then use the Graphics class to draw images or controls on the screen. The overall interaction can be seen in figure 12.3.

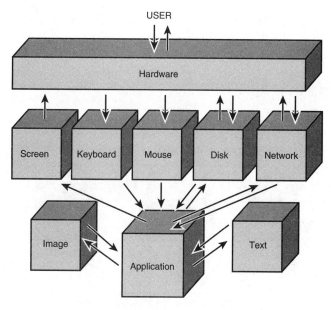

Figure 12.3

The interactions of an application.

The difference between a stand-alone application and an applet consists essentially of what services the program expects to find. These services can be provided in either the interpreter or browser environments. When an instance of a subclass of Applet is created inside a browser, the browser itself provides the class with information about the display context, mouse and keyboard events, and so on. Applets are always derived from the Applet class itself, and automatically inherit all of the class's functionality. In the stand-alone environment, none of this is provided, and the programmer has to create all of the functionality assumed by the browser. This means creating a window server, frame, and so on. The example in the previous chapter of awt control objects is an example of what must be done in order to get a stand-alone application to interact in a graphical environment. The Applet class doesn't need to worry about any of those details.

Protocol and Content Handlers

The protocol and content handlers are classes that can be perceived as filters of data. They take information from either the network or system, and give your Java class an object it can deal with in a standard way. In effect, the handlers sit between your application and the hardware classes that interact directly with the system, changing raw streams of data into objects (see fig. 12.4). Java comes with several content and protocol handlers for gifs, bitmaps, ftp, and nntp.

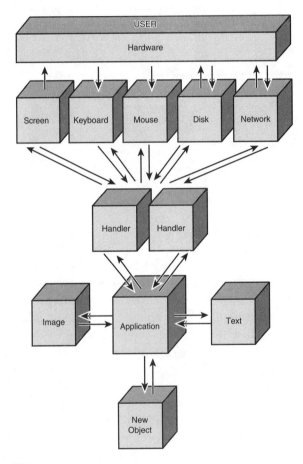

Figure 12.4

Content handlers and a Java application.

To add handler functionality to your system, you must place the new handler class in a specific directory structure. All handlers are placed in the classes/net/www/ directory, under subdirectories that indicate what types of data they deal with. Content handlers are in the subclass /content/ in their own directory that is named after the type they handle. For example, a handler for the text/plain MIME type would be called plain.class, and exist in the classes/net/www/content/text/ directory of the HotJava install path. Protocol handlers are stored in much the same way. They are in the classes/net/www/protocol directory. Each protocol class is called Handler.class, and is in a subdirectory named after the specific protocol it handles. For example, the `file:` protocol class is in the /classes/net/www/protocol/file/ directory with the name Handler.class.

Creating a Content Handler

If you take a look at the text handler that comes with Java, you will notice that it simply takes an input stream of bytes, and turns it into a String, which is then returned. This handler is used as an example of how to implement a content handler within the confines of the existing Java architecture.

Perhaps you feel that plain text should be shown in a particular manner, so you want to alter how the String returned from the handler looks. The traditional code for the handler simply changes the byte stream directly into a String. However, you could perform some formatting to the stream as it goes into the string. For example, you could make all of the letters uppercase.

```
public class plain extends ContentHandler {
    public Object getContent(InputStream is, URL u) {
        StringBuffer buf = new StringBuffer();
        int ch;
        while((ch = is.read()) >= 0)
            buf.appendChar(Character.toUpperCase((char)ch));
        is.close();
        return sb.toString();
    }
}
```

If you compile this class and replace the old plain.class in the /classes/net/www/content/text/ directory (be sure to rename the old class, not write over it), you should see all of your plain text files in uppercase, as in figure 12.5.

Figure 12.5

The results of the new plain text content handler.

It should be noted that the content handler is based upon the MIME type sent by the HTTP server. This is not the only way to provide content. Another way being used by many programmers is to create an applet that loads the special file itself, and then does all of the display work in the Applet. In the case of the ContentHandler class, the Browser then takes over the stream to display the image. Instead, you can create an applet that displays the file in its own area. Examples of these kinds of handlers can be found in the "Latest Cool Applets" link on Java's home page at java.sun.com. Two good examples are the chemical and 3D modellers that can handle xyz and wavefront file types.

Summary

Using the Internet is difficult, even when you have the proper tools. Creating those tools yourself is even more difficult still. Java provides powerful packages for connecting your applications through the various protocols. By using the network API, you should be able to develop networked programs quickly and effectively with the least amount of hassle.

The previous chapters on the Java packages provided a brief overview of a large and complex set of classes, variables, and methods for getting what you want out of the Java environment. Because the main focus of this book is learning to program in Java, and not necessarily the learning of any single API, breadth of information was consciously selected over depth. In this way, you hopefully have a better view of the entire Java API structure, from which you can begin to look more closely at the specific implementation of each class. Take time to glance through the API, even if it does seem wildly complex. Check out the sample applets on the Net, and stay tuned to the latest information about programming on Java's home page: java.sun.com.

Chapter 13

Interfacing with C and Using the Java Tools

This is the final chapter on developing Java applications. The previous chapters have covered the basics of the Java language semantics, the object-oriented and multithreading features of the language, and the class libraries. This chapter covers how to implement native C code into your Java programs. This chapter also includes a reference to the Java tools, rounding out this book's coverage of the different elements of the Java programming environment.

Quick Review

Up to this point, this book has covered the main features of the Java architecture, run-time environments, programming language, and class libraries. The Java architecture, in order to be portable across heterogeneous platforms, was necessarily designed to eschew the specifics of any single hardware implementation. The run-time environment, embodied in the browser and interpreter programs, is the interface between the Java

Virtual Machine bytecodes and the specific platform it is being run on. The Java language is the tool that enables programmers to create Java applications easily and effectively. The Java class libraries help make programming easier by providing an encapsulated set of useful classes for common programming problems such as input/output, graphics, and network connectivity.

Java creates an extensible run-time environment by allowing the incorporation of distributed code across a heterogeneous platform for networked computers. Because classes can be executed from anywhere on the Net, the need for portability is of paramount importance. Java's creators knew, however, that people would not want to give up the advantages their powerful hardware gave them, such as faster processors and better displays. If you are using a DEC Alpha 275 with Windows NT, you certainly don't want it acting like a 486/33. The Java architecture makes sure that the interpreted nature of the language exacts the minimum amount of overhead, while at the same time providing the flexibility to load native code to squeeze out every last ounce of performance.

Java's flexibility comes from its object-oriented paradigm and interpreted nature. Instead of taking an existing language and attempting to make it both backward compatible and forward thinking, Java started from scratch. This means that Java has none of the leftover problems of older, procedural style programs, and can implement object-oriented behaviour at the most basic levels. While overcoming the problems associated with upgrading an existing language to OOP (object-oriented programming), Java also had to deal with the problem of unpredictable changes in code that might come over the network. With traditional compiled languages, changing code in a any one library can bring down any classes inherited from that code. The problem of the fragile superclass, as it is known, is created from the compile time layout of memory. The fragile superclass is covered in Chapter 2, "An Introduction to Java." Because it is an interpreted environment, Java is able to retain the symbolic nature of class until run-time. At run-time, Java can lay out the memory of the classes, independent of any changes that might have occurred.

Java's features mean programmers have the full benefit of an object-oriented language, in addition to the cross-platform compatibility demanded by today's users. The object-oriented nature of the language means that programmers can begin to develop powerful applications quickly by reusing code provided in the form of packages. The reusability of code essentially means that programmers can take advantage of all the programming time used to develop the class libraries in their own applications. A programmer can inherit an entire class and add a single new method. At the same time, many programmers already have large amount of legacy code—code that is written in another language, which is typically of a specialized purpose and difficult to port to other languages. Java allows programmers to import C code, for instance, for both compatibility and performance purposes.

What This Chapter Covers

This chapter covers the process of importing C code into Java classes, and the Java tools provided with the release of the Java environment. In order for Java programs to be able to call C libraries, and vice versa, you need to create header files for your C code, which indicate how your C code is to interact with the Java classes. In addition, you must also create C stub files, which act as intermediaries between the C code and Java code.

The last section in the chapter provides a reference to the full set of Java tools provided with the Java environment. These tools include the following:

➤ HotJava

➤ Java

➤ Javac programs

➤ Profiling tools

➤ Disassembler

After You Finish This Chapter

After you finish this chapter, you will have completed all of the sections on programming in the Java language provided in this book. In addition, you should be able to use the command line options and additional tools provided in the Java release. This hopefully puts you at the point where you are comfortable writing, compiling, and running your own code, along with studying code others have developed on the Net. The next chapter takes a more advanced look at the run-time environment and Java Virtual Machine to give you a better understanding and appreciation of Java's underlying architecture.

Interfacing with C

Importing native C code has both its ups and downs. You might or might not want to import native C code, depending on what your particular problems are. There are several reasons why a programmer might want to interface native C code into a Java program. The following is a list of these reasons:

➤ Hardware compatibility

➤ Speed

➤ Legacy code

Any of these reasons is good enough to warrant the implementation of native methods in Java; however, you face a compromise when you choose to use native C code. The compromise is the fact that you *are* using native C code, which defeats almost all of the positive features of Java:

➤ Portability

➤ Security

➤ Robustness

Using native methods means that for your code to be portable, you have to port it to every platform you want it to run on.

Linking C code to a Java program does not instantly make your C code as portable as Java bytecodes. If your main purpose is, however, to provide hardware compatibility, then you don't need to worry about portability anyway—your Java program is only going to run on one platform, and that is the platform you need hardware compatibility with.

Using native methods also introduces all of the old problems of security and robustness. C does not provide the bytecode verifiers, automatic garbage collection, or run-time memory layout features of Java. While site administrators might be leery about allowing Java applets to run wild on their machines, you might have a decidedly more difficult time convincing them that your native code, which can in essence take advantage of every systemic weakness in the hardware and operating system, is safe to download and run on their computers. Of course, if you are distributing your Java code as a package, and not over the Internet, it would be perfectly acceptable to include native code, because you are distributing native code anyway with any other language environment such as C or C++.

Of course, there are also advantages to implementing native code.

Hardware Compatibility

Implementing native code into Java makes hardware compatibility easier and more complete than just using Java alone.

Native code can be used to implement functions that are not normally available in the Java environment, or that exist as dearly bought legacy code. Due to Java's portable nature, it abstracts somewhat from the underlying hardware platform. Therefore, particular functions of a specific platform (if these functions are not common to most hardware) won't be implemented in the Java language or classes. For example, perhaps you have a special piece of hardware, like a 3D input device, that is not available as a standard configuration or on any other platform. You have created C programs that interface with the hardware, and now want to be able to use it from Java.

Speed

Implementing native code into Java provides the program with the full power of the hardware it will be executing on.

If you have extremely intense code that taxes a system to its limits, the interpreter environment does not give you the same speed as native code. One example of a situation where you might need such performance is in 3D visualization, which is always one step beyond the present hardware platforms on people's desks. Including native C functions in Java means that they run at the full speed of the system. You can implement the majority of the code in Java, weed out the methods that require the most processor time, and then implement only those in native code. In many programs, there is a small amount of code that does most of the work. By converting only that code, you gain the benefits of speed where it is needed, and portability where it is not.

Legacy Code

Implementing native code into Java provides the programmer with the ability to reuse code already developed.

A good example of how well implementing legacy code works is the PowerPC platform and MacOS operating system. When Apple converted from the 68 K Macintosh to the PowerPC platform, they needed to port the operating system to the new RISC-based architecture—a difficult and time-consuming process. However, Apple noticed that 20 percent of the operating system code was taking up 80 percent of the processing time. By only converting that 20 percent, Apple was able to create a completely satisfactory operating system—even though eighty percent of the code was for the 68 KB chipset, and was being run in emulation mode, which is a notoriously slow process. By choosing carefully which portions of code to leave as Java bytecodes, and which to implement natively, you can reduce the effort needed to port the native sections to a minimum.

Importing Native Code

Once you have decided it is necessary to import native code into your Java application, there are several steps you must make to create the dynamic libraries needed. The actual implementation of each of these steps is highly platform- and compiler-specific. Therefore, this section presents the general steps used to link in native C code, rather than presenting a specific procedure for any one compiler. Check with your specific compiler setup for the exact methods necessary for creating dynamic libraries out of C code.

The steps for importing C code into your Java program are as follows:

1. Create Java code that refers to native methods

2. Generate the C header files and stub files from the Java compiled code for the C functions.

3. Create the C Code, C stub file, then compile and link them as a dynamic library.

4. Link the new library into your Java program.

The compiler-specific step is the third—compiling and linking the dynamic library. Otherwise, all of the steps are the same no matter what platform you are on.

Creating Native Methods in Java

In order to use native C code, you must include native methods that match the C methods you want to include. The modifier for a method is native:

```
public native returnvalue methodName(arguments);
```

Notice that the method does not have a body, and is finished off by a semicolon. The declaration indicates to the Java compiler that the run-time system loads the necessary classes for these methods.

The Java run-time environment loads the classes using the Linker class provided in the java.util package. You import this class at the beginning of the file and include a static function call at the beginning of the class that tells the Linker which library to load.

```
import java.util.Linker
public class LoadNative {
    static {
        Linker.loadLibrary("library");
    }
    ...
}
```

The following code is a hypothetical class that might need to perform a complicated calculation on a float. To speed up the calculation, the class could use a native method.

```
import java.util.Linker;
public class figureNumber {
    static {
        Linker.loadLibrary("calculate");
    }
    float Number;
    public figureNumber(float f) {
        Number = calc(f);
    }
    public native float calc(float f);
    public float getNumber() {
        return Number;
    }
}
```

The previous class would take a float in its constructor, do a calculation on it, and allow the parent class to retrieve the new number.

Generating the C Header Files and Stub Files

Once you have created your class and compiled it using the javac compiler, you need to generate the C header and stub files so that the C code and Java know how to interact. The header file created gives the C code information about the Java class that it needs to access data in the class and return the proper data when called. You can generate the header file by invoking the javah command using the class name of the class implementing the native methods:

```
C:\> javah figureNumber
```

The javah program creates a subdirectory CClassHeaders where it stores the resulting file figureNumber.h. The following is a listing of the generated C header file.

```
/* Header for class figureNumber */
#ifndef _Included_figureNumber
#define _Included_figureNumber
typedef struct ClassfigureNumber {
    float Number;
} ClassfigureNumber;
HandleTo(figureNumber);
#ifdef __cplusplus
extern "C" __declspec(dllexport)
#endif
float figureNumber_calc(struct HfigureNumber *,float);
#endif
```

Notice that the javah program has generated a C structure and function declaration that map the relevant methods and variables into C.

In addition to the C header file, you must create a stub file from the Java class that will be used in the creation of a C file that connects the structure defining the Java object and the object data itself. In order to create the stubs file, you must compile a C file that includes a standard java include file, and the stubs file generated by invoking:

```
C:\> javah -stubs figureNumber
```

This command creates a subdirectory stubs, which holds the file figureNumber.stubs. The file generated for the figureNumber class looks like this:

```
/* Stubs for class figureNumber */
/* DO NOT EDIT THIS FILE - it is machine generated */
/* SYMBOL: "figureNumber\calc(F)F", figureNumber_calc_stub,
*/
_declspec(dllexport) stack_item
*figureNumber_calc_stub(stack_item *_P_,struct execenv *_EE_)
{
    extern float figureNumber_calc(void *,float);
    _P_[0].f = figureNumber_calc(_P_[0].p,((_P_[1].f)));
    return _P_ + 1;
}
```

You then need to take this file, with the following at the beginning, and compile it with your C compiler, to be included in the dynamically loadable module.

```
#include "stubsPreamble.h"
```

The include file can be found in the /hotjava/include/ directory, along with additional header files needed for implementing native methods.

Creating the C Code, and Compiling the Dynamic Library

Once you have created the header files and stub interface, it is time to code the C functions. The C code needs to include several Java header files, and the header file created by the javah program, then you can include your own header files, and finally the C functions. The C functions you write must be in the form designated by the header Java header file created for the Java class. In the case of the figureNumber class, the C library must implement the following function:

```
float figureNumber_calc(struct HfigureNumber *,float)
A sample file might be:
#include "StubPreamble.h"
```

```
#include "javaString.h"
#include "figureNumber.h"
#include <math.h>
float figureNumber_calc(struct HfigureNumber *this, float
number)
{
    float temp;
    temp = sin(number);
    return temp;
}
```

Of course, there would probably be no need to actually use the sin function natively; this is meant simply as an example.

Because building the library is compiler specific, you should check out the documentation that comes with each compiler for how to create a dynamically loadable library. In any case, you need to compile the C implementation of the Java native method, such as the previous code, and link it with the stubs file compiled earlier into a dynamically loadable library.

Linking in the New Code

The new library created can then be linked into the Java class at run-time by implementing the dynamic linker class Linker, provided in the java.util package. The following example shows how to cause the compiler to link in the new code:

```
import java.util.Linker;
public class figureNumber {
    static {
        Linker.loadLibrary("calculate");
    }
```

This code tells the run-time environment that the library calculate must be loaded for this class to be runnable. If the linker is unable to load the library for any reason, it throws an UnsatisfiedLinkException. The library loaded by the linker is produced from the name given, and is system dependent. For example, on Solaris, the compiler will look for a libcalculate.so file.

One option for giving yourself optimum flexibility in creating a class is to have the linker attempt to bring in a native library based upon the known operating system (for example, with the System.getOSName() method). The class can then catch the UnsatisfiedLinkException and handle the functions in Java itself. This procedure provides the best combination of native speed for implemented platforms while still providing a truly portable application.

Including native code in your classes is perhaps the most difficult task to perform in Java, especially because you have to deal with two separate compilers, linkers, and execution environments. It is important that you understand the workings of both compiler environments. However, the effort is well worth the reward if you truly need to use the C language to get a job done. Remember to always keep the native methods to a minimum by using C code only when absolutely necessary.

Using the Java Tools

This section presents a comprehensive list of the Java tools included with the release of the Java environment. These tools include the following:

- ➤ HotJava browser
- ➤ Java interpreter
- ➤ Javac compiler
- ➤ javah C header and stubs file generator
- ➤ javap class file disassembler
- ➤ javaprof profiling data prettyprinter

These files reside in the /hotjava/bin/ directory, and run from any directory if you set the PATH statement when you set up the system for programming.

The HotJava Browser

The HotJava browser provides both the traditional services of a World Wide Web browser along with a run-time environment for Java applications. The executable itself can either be invoked from the command line, or an icon can be created for it in Windows NT or Solaris. If it is being loaded from the command line, it can accept a URL as a command line option.

```
C:\> hotjava URL
```

The URL argument is the first document loaded as soon as the application has started.

HotJava does not have any other command-line options; however, it does have an extensive number of environment variables. Table 13.1 lists the environment variables HotJava uses.

Table 13.1   The Java Environment Variables

Variable	Function
HOTJAVA_HOME	This is the directory where HotJava looks for the resources necessary to run. The default is the directory in which it was installed.
WWW_HOME	This variable tells HotJava what URL to use as the home page.
HOTJAVA_READ_PATH	This variable tells HotJava where applets can read files from. The default is *<install-dir>*:$HOME/public_html/
HOTJAVA_WRITE_PATH	This variable tells HotJava where applets can write files to. The default is /tmp/:/devices/:/dev/:~/.hotjava/
CLASSPATH	This variable tells Java where classes can be imported from. The directories are separated by semicolons.
NNTPSERVER	Set this variable to your news server for HotJava to be able to read newsgroups.

When HotJava must use the HOTJAVA_READ_PATH and HOTJAVA_WRITE_PATH to determine whether an applet has permission to perform a file operation, HotJava gives applets permission if the following apply:

➤ The file name the applets are attempting to read or write is in a directory of the environment variables.

➤ The file name the applets are attempting to read or write is in a subdirectory of the environment variables.

➤ The exact file name is specified in the environment variables.

You can disable all checks for reads or writes by specifying "*" in as the value for either the HOTJAVA_READ_PATH and HOTJAVA_WRITE_PATH. Note that the * is in quotes. Unix shells incorrectly handle the *.

It is important that you set the HOTJAVA_READ_PATH and HOTJAVA_WRITE_PATH to the correct values for security purposes. The environment variable for HotJava determines how the run-time environment and the applications it is running see your system. By setting these variables, you can create your first line of defense against Java programs that either intentionally or unintentionally attempt to invade the client system.

The Java Interpreter

The Java interpreter allows the execution of Java bytecodes without the incorporation of the World Wide Web browser implemented in HotJava. The command-line options for Java are as follows:

```
C:\> java options className arguments
```

The className must include all packaging information as well as the classname itself. Also, the Java interpreter expects the name of the class, not the file name of the Java bytecodes. All classes to be executed under the interpreter environment must include a main method that the interpreter first calls, passing any arguments from the command line.

```
public static void main(String args[]) {
    ...
}
```

Table 13.2 includes all of the options the Java interpreter accepts.

Table 13.2 The Java Interpreter Command-Line Options

Option	Function
-cs, -checksource	This option tells the interpreter to recompile any class whose .java source file is later than its .class file—in effect, recompiling any class that has been updated since its last compile.
-classpath *path*	This option overrides the CLASSPATH environment variable and tells Java where it can look for classes. More than one directory can be included if all are separated by colons.
-ms *x*	This option sets the size of the memory allocation pool to *x* bytes. The specified pool must be larger than 1,000 bytes. In addition, a "k" or "m" can be appended to the number to indicate that it refers to kilobytes or megabytes respectively. The default value is 3 megabytes.
-noasyncgc	This option turns off the asynchronous garbage collection. The only time garbage collection occurs is when the program calls for it, or runs out of memory.
-prof	This option causes Java to generate a profile file java.prof in the current directory that holds information about the execution of a class. This is the file used in the javaprof program.
-ss *x*	This option sets the maximum stack size for C threads to *x*. *x* must be greater than 1,000 bytes, and is indicated in the same manner as -ms.
-oss *x*	This option sets the maximum stack size for Java threads to *x*.
-v, -verbose	This option tells Java to print a message to stdout whenever a class is loaded.
-verify	This option tells Java to use the verifier on all code.
-verifyremote	This option tells Java to use the verifier only on classes loaded with the classloader.
-noverify	This option tells Java to not use the verifier.
-verbosegc	This option tells Java to have the garbage collector print out a message whenever it frees memory.

The Javac Compiler

The Javac compiler takes Java source code and produces the bytecodes for the Java Virtual Machine. The command-line call for Javac is as follows:

```
C:\> javac options filename.java
```

Notice that, unlike the interpreter, Javac expects to find an extension on the file it is compiling. That extension is .java. The command-line options are listed in Table 13.3.

Table 13.3   The Command-Line Options for the Javac Compiler

Option	Function
-classpath *path*	This option sets the path where Javac looks for classes that it needs to load. This is a colon delimited list of directories.
-d *directory*	This option specifies the root directory to be used when creating a directory tree for a hierarchy of packages.
-g	This option turns on debugging tables in code generation for later debugging of the bytecodes generated.
-ng	This option turns off debugging tables and shrinks the size of the code; however, you are not be able to use debuggers later on with the bytecodes produced.
-nowarn	This option suppresses the generation of warnings that the compiler produces.
-O	This option tells Javac to optimize the code produced by inlining static, final, and private methods.
-verbose	This option tells Javac to print out messages about the source file being compiled, and any classes being loaded.

javah

The javah program creates the C header and stubs files needed to include native C methods in a Java class. The command line for calling javah is the following:

```
C:\> javah options classname additionalClasses
```

The javah program works like the Java interpreter in that it expects the classname without the .class extension. The javah program can accept several class names for producing header and stubs files. Table 13.4 lists the command-line options for the javah program.

Table 13.4   The Command-Line Options for the javah Header File Generator

Options	Function
-o *outputfile*	This option tells javah to place all of the resulting class header or stubs files into a single file *output*.
-d *directory*	This option tells javah to place the resulting class header or stubs files into the given directory.
-td *directory*	This option tells the javah program to place temporary file in *directory* instead of /tmp.
-stubs	This option tells javah to produce the stubs files instead of header files.
-verbose	This options tells javah to print the status of generated files to stdout.
-classpath *path*	This options tells javah to use the *path* directory to look for Java class files. Multiple directories should be separated by colons.

The javap Disassembler

The javap command disassembles a Java bytecode file, and returns information about the member variables and methods. The command-line invocation is the following:

```
C:\> javap options classname additionalClasses
```

The standard output for javap are the public variables and methods of a class. For example, the output from the class TryFtp created in the previous chapter is

```
Compiled from C:\users\Ritchey\telnet\ftp.java
private class TryFtp extends java/lang/Object {
    static net/ftp/FtpClient ftp;
    public static void main(java/lang/String []);
    public TryFtp();
}
```

Table 13.5 includes the available command-line options.

Table 13.5	The Command-Line Options for the javap Disassembler
Option	Function
-p	This option tells javap to print out private methods and variables as well as public ones.
-c	This option tells javap to print out the actual compiled bytecodes for the methods.
-classpath *path*	This option tells javap to search for the classes in *path*.

The javaprof Profiling Tool

This command takes the java.prof file created when the Java interpreter is run using the -prof option and sends to stdout a formatted version of the information provided in the file. The command-line invocation is the following:

```
C:\> javaprof options java.prof
```

The only command-line option for javaprof is -v, which causes the output to include additional information about the profile of the class execution. The default output of the command returns the following information:

➤ The time, and number of calls per method

➤ The time, and number of calls per class

➤ The memory usage per data type

You can use the output of javaprof to find out where resources are going in your executing programs.

Summary

The Java tools section is the last topic to be presented on programming in the Java language in this book. This does not mean that you are finished learning Java; because in many cases, only overviews, or simple examples could be included in this book. Java is a complex and powerful programming environment, and to cover every element or to give programming examples of every feature would not be possible. However, rather than eliminate an one section in favor of a another, a small sample of all the Java elements was included.

It is hoped that based on a firm understanding of the underlying basics provided in the chapters on the language, classes, multithreading, and foundation classes will give you enough information to begin programming your own Java code. Additionally, the overview of the advanced class libraries such as io, util, awt, browser, and netshould allow you to understand other programs you find on the Internet, and read through the APIs provided by Sun.

The final chapter covers more advanced material on the run-time environment and Java Virtual Machine. Understanding these topics will not only give you a greater appreciation for the underlying complexity and advanced features of the language, but will allow you to fit your own work into the context of the overall Java architecture.

Chapter 14

Advanced Topics: The Java Virtual Machine

This chapter deals with more advanced topics in the Java environment—particularly those dealing with the run-time system and virtual machine specification. Java provides a robust system for interpreting its bytecodes. Although the bytecode verifier was referred to early on, it is worthwhile to cover this aspect of the architecture more carefully before moving on to the Java Virtual Machine. The Java Virtual Machine is a hypothetical machine for which all Java programs are compiled. By porting an interpreter for this machine specification to a computer system, you are assured that all code compiled for it will run on that system. It is the basis for Java's portability.

Quick Review

You have covered the majority of Java's main features and been through the ins and outs of using it as both an end user and developer. You have looked at Java, where it came from, what it can be used for now, and where it might be going in the future. Moving on, the user end of Java was covered, as well as looking at the browser and interpreter as tools for running Java stand-alone applications and applets. Next, the server side of Java delivery was considered, looking at the new burdens a system administrator will have to bear in implementing Java on the network. It was then time to start programming in Java itself. This occupied the rest of the book and then some. Hopefully, you have worked through the code examples and played with some of your own. By the time you read this chapter, you should be comfortable with the language and programs in the Java toolkit. It is in closing that we should cover the very foundations of the system in the run-time environment.

What This Chapter Covers

The Java system begins with the Java code developed by a programmer. This code is fed to a compiler which generates the Java bytecode for the virtual machine. When a system loads the bytecodes, it takes the bytecodes through several stages including the class loader, bytecode verifier, interpreter, run-time block, and code generator before reaching hardware. This material is covered to give you an idea of the process a bytecode undergoes before execution.

The bytecode itself which is executed is compiled for the Java Virtual Machine. In the next section we will cover the specifications for this hypothetical silicon, and look at how it provides a bridge between easily ported interpretable code, and high-performance, native-like code. These are almost mutually exclusive traits, and we shall look at how Java attempts to overcome this barrier.

After You Finish This Chapter

After you have finished this chapter, you should have a firm understanding of both the process of creating and executing the Java bytecode. This chapter is by no means a requirement for using Java, but many might find it an interesting study of the problems facing computer programmers in this age of heterogeneous networked platforms. Knowing what happens with your code after it leaves your compiler gives you a greater appreciation for the hard work that goes into providing the ease of use, functionality, and speedy performance demanded by today's programmers.

From Class File to Execution

What happens when you finish writing your program and run it through the compiler? What happens when you hit a Web page with an applet in it? How is it executed? You will find answers to these and other questions in this section.

The first step in the Java application life-cycle is the compilation of code. Although this is pretty straightforward, there are several things that a Java compiler does which are different from a C or C++ compiler. Mainly, this has to do with the computation of numeric references. This chapter looks at this difference, why it exists, and how it affects the run-time environment.

Once the Java code has been compiled, and an end user downloads it, it must then be interpreted. For security reasons, the Java interpreter contains many safeguards against faulty code. It is not all right, but at least a step above intolerable when software you personally install crashes your system. It would be inexcusable, however, for code you happened to run across while surfing the Net to bring down the whole ball of wax. Pretty soon, no one would trust *anyone's* code, and Java would become the scourge of the Internet. Well, Java has placed many safety nets between the code and the system in order to ensure against this inevitability, and this is a major portion of the run-time engine.

The Compilation of Code

The Java compiler acts like any other compiler. It creates the machine code (essentially assembler code) for execution out of a higher level language. This enables the programmer to write in a somewhat intelligible way what he or she wants done, while the compiler converts it into a format that a specific machine can run. The only difference between the Java compiler and other compilers is that the specific machine that would normally run the compiled code doesn't exist in Java. It is the Java Virtual Machine for which the Java compiler compiles the source code. There are, however, several key differences from other languages in the way the compiler resolves references in the code.

As mentioned in Chapter 2, "An Introduction to Java," The Java compiler does not reduce the references in a program to numbers, nor does it create the memory layout the program will use. The reason for this implementation is portability, both in terms of neutrality and security. When a C compiler produces the object code, it can expect to be run on a specific hardware platform. Because the executable, even while running under an operating system, must be self supporting in terms of addressing, the compiler can reduce the overhead by referring to exact memory offsets instead of to a symbolic reference which would then have to be looked up.

Java Opcodes and Operands

Imagine you are a computer executing a piece of code. For you, code consists of two types:

➤ *opcode*— a specific and recognizable command

➤ *operand*—the data needed to complete the opcode

All of these opcodes and operands exist as a stream that you, the computer, execute sequentially. You might, for example, take a number from memory and place it on the stack, kind of a local pigeonhole for keeping data you will use immediately. You might then take another number, place it on the stack, and add the two numbers together, placing the result back into memory. In the Java Virtual Machine Instruction Set, it would look as it does in table 14.1. The specifics of the opcodes are not important unless you are planning on writing your own compiler, but it is interesting to see how it all works.

Table 14.1 Adding Together Two Long Integers	
Opcode	Numerical Representation
lload address	22 xxxx
lload address	22 xxxx
ladd	97
lstore address	55 xxxx

Each command (lload, lstore) is an 8-bit number that tells the machine which instruction to execute. The address variable is a number telling the machine where to look in memory for the variable. Each address reference is a 32-bit number. Therefore, the above code would take up 16 bytes or 128 bits. Now, imagine that this little piece of code was a member method of a class. It would be embedded in all the other methods for the class when the compiler produced the code. So, how would the compiler find this piece of code when the program called the function? Because the compiler knows the exact length of all the code, and has laid them out in memory, it can simply tell the machine to jump to the exact address at the start of a method needed for it to execute. In order to call a method, you should use the following command, which jumps (jsr) to the 16-bit address (*xx*):

jsr *address*   168 *xx*

Memory Layout in Java

If you know the memory layout of the program from the compiler and the memory layout of the system the program will be running on, what can stop you from placing the *wrong* address in your code for the placement of this method? Nothing.

The Java compiler does not allow this kind of memory addressing because it does not reduce references to numeric values that are based upon the memory layout of the code. Instead, the compiler leaves the symbolic reference to the method in the code, and when it is run, the interpreter, after creating the memory layout at run-time, looks up where it placed the specific method. The new way to call a class method would be

invokevirtual *index bytes*   182 *xx*

This command references an index of method *signatures* which exist in the program. If it is the first time the reference is used, the interpreter takes the method signature and looks up from the method table where it placed it in memory when loading the class at run-time. This lookup only occurs the first time a reference is encountered. From then on, the method signature will include the proper address, and the call will not need to use the lookup table. This method retains the protection afforded run-time memory layout, without the steep overhead of lookup table calls every time a method is invoked.

The reason for going to all of this overhead is twofold. First, as mentioned before, is the fragile superclass problem. If classes are laid out in memory at compile-time and updating changes this memory layout, if a programmer inherited one of these classes, and then tried to call a method after the superclass had been updated, as he or she had before, its placement in the memory layout may have changed, and the program could be jumping anywhere in the code. By allowing the interpreter to set the memory scheme at run-time, the new subclass can call methods from the superclass symbolically and be assured of invoking the right code. Second, is for security. If a programmer cannot directly control the addressing of memory, he or she cannot intentionally try to send the program into the operating system to wreak havoc. This ensures that the code you receive will be free from errant memory calls and is sure to be able to use imported classes, even if they are being loaded from across the Internet from sources that might have updated them since the original compile.

The Running of Code

The job of running the code compiled for the Java Virtual Machine falls to the interpreter. The interpreter process can be divided into three steps: loading of code, verification, and execution. The loading of code is done by the Class Loader. This section of the interpreter brings in not only the Java file which is referenced, but also any inherited or referenced classes that the code will need. After this is complete, all the code is sent through the bytecode verifier to ensure that the code sticks to the Java standard and does not violate system integrity. After this has been completed, the code is passed to the run-time system for execution on the hardware (see fig. 14.1). These three steps in the interpreter process are discussed in greater detail in the next section.

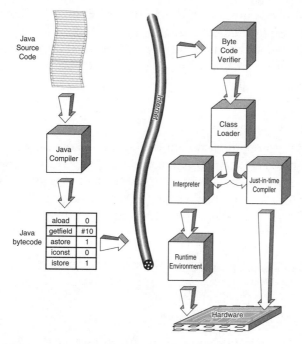

Figure 14.1

The Java Run-Time System.

Class Loader

The class loader brings together all the code needed for execution of an application, including classes you have inherited from, and any classes you call. When the class loader brings in a class, it places it in its own namespace. This is similar to the virtual machines within which applications run in an operating system. Without explicit calls to classes outside their namespace, which are referenced symbolically, classes cannot interfere with each other. The classes local to the machine are all given one address space, and all classes imported are each given their own namespace. This allows local classes the added performance benefit of sharing a namespace, while still protecting them from imported classes, and vice versa.

After all of the classes have been imported, the memory layout for the total executable can be determined. Symbolic references can have specific memory spaces attached, and the lookup table can be created. By creating the memory layout at this late stage, the interpreter protects against fragile superclasses and illegal addressing in the code.

Bytecode Verifier

The interpreter does not, however, start assuming at this point that the code is safe. Instead, the code passes through a bytecode verifier which checks each line for consistency with the Java specification and the program itself. By using a theorem prover, the bytecode verifier can trap several of the following problems with code:

➤   no forged pointers

➤   no access restriction violations

➤   no object mismatching

➤   no operand stack over- or underflows

➤   parameters for bytecodes are all correct

➤   no illegal data conversion

The use of the bytecode verifier serves two purposes. First, because all these conditions are known, the interpreter can be sure that the executable will not crash the system through errant procedures. Second, the interpreter can execute the code as quickly as possible, knowing that it will not run into problems which it might otherwise have to stop and check for during the run. In both cases, the code is subject to the procedure once and then can run unimpeded for its duration.

Code Execution

After the code has been collected and laid out in memory by the loader and checked by the verifier, it is then passed on to be executed. The execution of the code consists of converting it to operations that the client system can perform. This can happen in two ways:

➤ The interpreter can compile native code at run-time, then allow this native code to run at full speed, or

➤ The interpreter can handle all the operations, thunking the code to the correct configuration for the platform a piece at a time.

Typically, it is the second method that is used. The virtual machine specification is flexible enough to be converted to the client machine without copious amounts of overhead. All the methods used in this book rely on the interpreter to execute the bytecodes directly. For the most computationally intensive problems, the interpreter provides a just-in-time compiler which will convert the intermediate Java bytecode into the machine code of the client system. This allows the code to be both portable and high-performance.

The stages of the run-time system are a balance between three issues: portability, security, and performance. The portability issue is dealt with by using an intermediate bytecode format that is easily converted to specific machine code form. In addition, the interpreter determines memory layout at run-time to ensure that imported classes remain useable. The security issue is addressed at every stage of the run-time system. Specifically, though, the bytecode verifier ensures that the program will execute correctly according to the Java specification. Finally, the performance issue is dealt with by making sure that all overhead is either performed at the beginning of the load-execute cycle or runs as a background thread, such as the garbage collector. In these ways, Java takes modest performance hits to ensure a portable, secure environment, while still ensuring that performance is available when needed most.

The Java Virtual Machine

The *Java Virtual Machine* (JVM) is an attempt to provide an abstract specification to which builders can design their interpreter without forcing a specific implementation, while ensuring that all programs written in Java will be executable on any system that follows the design. The JVM provides concrete definitions for several aspects of an implementation, specifically in the distribution of Java code through an interchange specification. This specification includes the opcode and operand syntax, along with their values, the values of any identifiers, the layout of structures such as the constant pool, and the layout of the Java object format as implemented in the class file. These definitions provide the needed information for other developers to implement their own JVM interpreters, making the Java specification open for outside development. The hopes of the designers were to free Java from the restrictions of a proprietary language and allow developers to use it as they desire.

Why a New Machine Code Specification?

The JVM provides the hardware platform specification to which all Java code is compiled. All computers have a specific processor known as the CPU, or central processing unit. There are a whole host of different CPU's out there which give each machine its computing power. Intel's *x*86, Apple/IBM/Motorola's PowerPC, DEC's Alpha, Mips R series, Sun's Sparc chips, and a whole host of others. Each of these chips has a different way of doing things, so software must be written for each individual machine type to run properly. For Java to overcome this problem of portability, the developers picked a single machine to compile for, and then it would be interpreted on all the others. So, which chip did they choose to write Java for? None.

The Java Virtual Machine is a hypothetical CPU which can be easily implemented on a host of computers without being too close to any of them. The virtual machine must overcome differences in many CPUs. For example, the Intel CPUs are all CISC, or *Complex Instruction Set Computing*. They provide a whole host of instructions which the CPU can perform, the idea being that by providing many functions in microcode (essentially small software inside a chip), the shorter the code the chip needs to execute can be. Providing many functions, however, costs the CPU in performance because executing microcode is slower than if all the functions were hardwired.

RISC chips, or *Reduced Instruction Set Computing*, take the opposite philosophy. Instead of providing a whole host of instructions, the RISC computer only provides the very basics needed to execute a program. This means that a program may be larger in order to do the same thing a CISC program would do because it must perform the instructions it has many more times in order to duplicate the functionality found in a single instruction of CISC. All these instructions on a RISC processor, however, are hard wired into silicon, allowing them to run at incredible speeds, thus overcoming the longer pieces of code.

To pick one design over the other would make it difficult for whatever system wasn't chosen to interpret the commands effectively. Instead, the Java designers came up with their own specification for a chip's instruction set. These opcodes are closely related to the Java language and can be considered an intermediate step between leaving the files as uncompiled source code, which would be the ultimate in portability, and compiling for each individual hardware system, which would provide the best possible speed. By providing a neutral intermediate specification, the Java Virtual Machine attempts to make a compromise between these two important aspects of distributed systems: portability and performance.

The Java Virtual Machine Description

The JVM consists of the following five specifications which control the implementation and interpretation of Java code.

- ➤ The Instruction Set
- ➤ The Register Set
- ➤ The Stack
- ➤ The Garbage Collected Heap
- ➤ The Memory Area

It does not matter how you want to implement each of these features, as long as they follow the specifications laid out by the designers for running all Java code. This means you could choose to interpret the Java bytecodes, creating a system similar to the Java, or HotJava executables. Or, you could recompile the incoming Java code into native machine format to benefit from native code performance. If you really need to produce the best possible speed, you could even implement the JVM in silicon—of course, it then wouldn't be a JVM, but rather a JM.

The Instruction Set

The instruction set for the JVM is exactly equivalent to the instruction set for a CPU. When you compile Java source code into binary, you are in essence creating an assembly language program just as in C. Each instruction in Java consists of an *opcode* followed by an optional *operand*. Example opcodes include instructions for loading integers from memory (iload, load an integer), managing arrays (anewarray, allocate a new array), logical operators (iand, logically and two integers), and flow control (ret, return from a method call). Each opcode is represented by an 8-bit number, followed by varying length operands. These operands give the needed data for each opcode such as where to jump or what number to use in a computation. Many opcodes do not have any operands.

It is typical in computing to align all opcodes and operands to 32- or 64-bit words. This allows the machine to move through the code in constant jumps, knowing exactly where each next instruction will be. However, because the opcodes are only 8 bits and the operands vary in size, aligning to anything larger than 8 bits would waste space (see fig. 14.2). The wasted space would be a function of the average operand size, and how much larger the byte code alignment was. Deciding that compactness was more important than the performance hit incurred, the Java designers specifically chose this method.

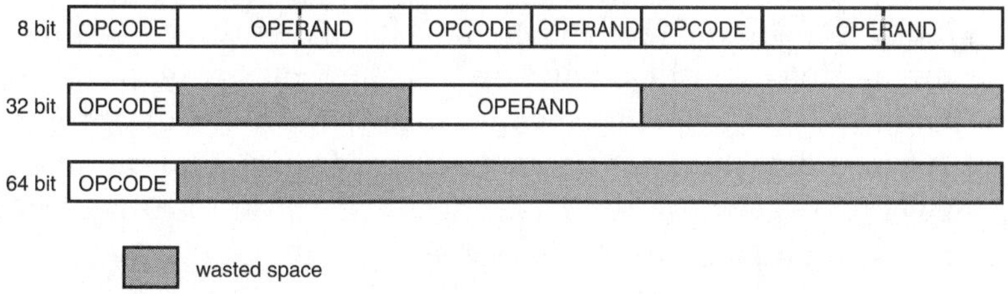

Figure 14.2

An 8-bit byte alignment versus a 32- or 64-bit byte alignment.

Operands are often more than 8 bits long and need to be divided into two or more bytes. The JVM uses the *big endian* encoding scheme, where the larger order bits are stored in the lower ordered memory spaces. This is the standard for Motorola and other RISC chips. Intel chips, however, use *little endian* encoding, placing the least significant bits in the lowest memory address. The two methods are compared in table 14.2.

Table 14.2	Big versus Little Endian Encoding
Memory Address 0	Memory Address 1
Big Endian	
Byte 1 * 256	Byte 2
Little Endian	
Byte 1	Byte 2 * 256

The differences can be confusing when trying to move data between two opposing systems that expect larger than 8-bit fragments to be encoded their way. Make sure you know which method your system uses.

The instruction set provides a host of functionality to the JVM and is specifically designed as an implementation of the Java language. This includes instructions for invoking methods and monitoring multithreading systems. The 8-bit size of the opcode limits the number of instructions to 256, and there are already 160 opcodes which can be used. It is unlikely that this number will ever rise, unless future advances in hardware are unable to be dealt with under the current JVM specification.

The Registers

All processors have what are called *registers*, which hold information that the processor uses to store the current state of the system. Each processor type will have different numbers of registers. The more registers a processor has, the more items it can deal with quickly, without having to refer to the stack, or global memory, which would result in a reduction in performance. Because of the wide difference in register variables, it was decided that Java would not have that many. Otherwise, if it had more than any processor it was being ported to, those CPUs would take enormous performance penalties attempting to mimic the register states in regular memory. Therefore, the register set was limited to the following four registers:

➤ **pc.** Program counter

➤ **optop.** Pointer to top of the operand stack

➤ **frame.** Pointer to current execution environment

➤ **vars.** Pointer to the first (0th) local variable of the current execution environment

Each of these registers is 32 bits wide, and some of them might not need to be used in a specific implementation.

The program counter (pc) keeps track of where the program is in execution. This register does not need to be used if recompiling into native code. The optop, frame, and vars registers hold pointers to areas in the Java stack, which is discussed in the next section.

The Java Stack

The Java stack is the principle storage method for the Java Virtual Machine, which is considered a stack-based machine. When the JVM is given the bytecodes of a Java application, it creates a stack *frame* for each method of a class that holds information about its state. Each frame hold three kinds of information:

➤ Local variables

➤ Execution environment

➤ Operand stack

Local Variables

The local variables in a Java stack frame are an array of 32-bit variables whose beginning is marked by the vars register. This effectively is a large store for method variables. When they are needed in the computation of an instruction, they can be loaded onto and stored from the operand stack. When a variable is longer than 32 bits, such as double precision floats and long ints which are 64 bits, it must be spread across two of these local variables. However, it is still addressed at only the first location.

Execution Environment

The execution environment provides information about the current state of the Java Stack in reference to the current method. Information stored in the execution environment include the following:

➤ Previous method invoked

➤ Pointer to the local variables

➤ Pointers to the top and bottom of the operand stack

The execution environment is the control center for an executing method and makes sure that the interpreter or recompiler can find the necessary information that pertains to the current method. If the interpreter were asked to execute an iadd, for example, it would need to know where to find the two numbers it needed to do the arithmetic. First, it would look to the frame register to find the current execution environment, then it would look to the execution environment to find the pointer to the top of the operand stack where it would remove the two required numbers, add them, and then place them back onto the stack.

Operand Stack

The Operand Stack is a FIFO, or *first in, first out*, 32-bit wide stack that holds the arguments necessary for the opcodes in the JVM instruction set. It is used both for gathering the operands necessary for completion and for the storage of the results. In Java parlance, "The Stack" is generally a reference to this area in the Java Stack.

The Java Stack is the primary area for storage of current status information for the execution of the Java bytecode. It is equivalent to the stack frame in standard programming languages. It provides method implementations of the local variables, the execution environment and the operand stack.

In addition to the instruction set, registers, and Java stack, there are two remaining elements to the JVM specification: the garbage collected heap and memory areas.

The Garbage Collected Heap

The heap is the store of memory from which class instances are allocated. It is the job of the interpreter to provide handles for the memory needed by a class for execution. After this memory has been allocated to a specific class instance, it is the job of the interpreter to keep track of this memory usage, and, when the object is finished with it, return it to the heap.

The Java specification does not enable a programmer to control the memory allocation or deallocation of objects, except in the new statement. The reason the designers chose to implement Java in this manner is for portability and security reasons which were mentioned before. Because of this, the job of memory deallocation and garbage collection is the responsibility of the run-time environment. It is up to the implementor to decide how this garbage collection is carried out. In Sun's Java and HotJava environments, the Garbage collection is run as a background thread. This provides the best possible performance environment while still freeing the programmer from the dangers of explicit memory usage.

The Memory Area

The JVM has two other important memory areas: the method area and the constant pool area. The *method* area is the region in memory where the bytecode for the Java methods are stored. The *constant pool* is a memory area where the class name, method and field names, and string constants are stored. There are no limitations where any of these memory areas must actually exist, for two main reasons. First, for a portable system, making demands on the memory layout would create difficulties on porting to systems which could not handle the specific layout chosen. Second, if there is a specific memory layout, it would be easier for someone wanting to break a system to do so by knowing where their code might be in relation to the rest of memory. This way, memory layout is not only left until run-time, but is specific to any implementation.

The Java Virtual Machine is a platform-independent specification for the execution of the Java bytecode program. To provide a balance between portability and performance, an intermediate stage between the source code language files and compiled native code was chosen. This choice, however, is a compromise, and although you have primarily been reading about the positive side of the implementation, it would be useful to look at the problems with the Java implementation.

Limitations

The limitations with the Java implementation are its limits on operand and stack sizes. These limits mean that the JVM can only address a certain number of address spaces before it runs out of numbers to use.

The JVM's internal addressing is limited to 4 GB because the stack width is only 32 bits wide. Any Java method is limited to 32 KB in size because of the limitations of a 16-bit offset for branching and jumping instructions. The number of local variables per stack frame is 256 because the index is only 8 bits. Also, the number of constant pool entries is limited by its 16-bit index to 32 thousand per method.

To call these limitations is being quite futurist. Because most machines only have 16 to 32 MB of memory anyway, 4 GB is still some years in the future. The 32 KB limit for a method is restrictive in some sense—but remember, this is a single method. If you need methods larger than 32 KB, then chances are you should rethink your object-oriented strategy.

Of course, most people didn't think Bill Gates was ridiculous in predicting that 640 KB was all we would ever need back at the birth of the personal computer. Technology has an amazing capability to catch up, and surpass, our own imaginations. There may be a time in the near future when Java will need to be expanded to take into account larger program memory needs. However, for today's needs—and the next decade's Internet— Java has all the storage needed to tie up all available bandwidth.

Summary

We have covered what are perhaps the most complicated topics in Java—the run-time environment and the Java Virtual Machine. By now you should have some understanding of how these systems work and how the execution of code works in general. The art of compiler and interpreter writing is an arcane and ephemeral subject. In today's Visual C++ and Visual Basic development environments, the idea of assembler code is enough to frighten most people away. What was considered a necessary talent for code writing even four years ago has now been placed to the side for more high-level languages. Of course, Java is one of those languages, and it is for the exact reason of making the distribution of dynamic content easier that it was developed. It is important, however, to appreciate the low-level functions of a system that allow the high-level languages to run.

Hopefully, this chapter has provided the necessary information about low-level function in the Java environment to finish your picture of the entire Java canvas. The Java specification is one that stretches from the run-time developer to the end user, and every stage in between. It is important to be able to view whatever your goals for Java are within this framework.

Appendix

Further Information

This listing includes books and Internet addresses you might find useful for finding out more about Java, and programming in general.

Internet Addresses

➤ `http://java.sun.com/` is the home page of Java. It directs you to the latest releases and information on Java.

➤ `http://www.sun.com/` is the Sun Online Magazine, which presents interesting articles on what is going on at Sun, including information and behind the scenes looks at the development of Java.

➤ Sun provides many Java related lists that you can subscribe to. You can subscribe to these by sending a message with SUBSCRIBE as the text to *listName*-`request@java.sun.com`, where listName is the name of the specific list you want to join.

➤ **java-announce:** This list sends out information on new releases and ports of the Java language.

➤ **java-interest:** This list is for those interested in the Java language.

➤ **java-interest-digest:** This list sends out a digest of the day's list traffic for java-interest.

➤ **java-porting:** This list is for those interested in porting Java to additional architectures.

➤ **java-porting-digest:** This list sends out a digest of the day's list traffic for java-porting.

➤ **hotjava-interest:** This list is for those interested in the HotJava browser.

➤ **hotjava-interest-digest:** This list sends out a digest of the day's hotjava-interest traffic.

➤ `http://vrml.wired.com/` is the home page of the Virtual Reality Modelling Language. Check it out for more information on VRML and where it is going.

Index

PLUG YOURSELF INTO...

THE MACMILLAN INFORMATION SUPERLIBRARY™

Free information and vast computer resources from the world's leading computer book publisher—online!

FIND THE BOOKS THAT ARE RIGHT FOR YOU!

A complete online catalog, plus sample chapters and tables of contents give you an in-depth look at *all* of our books, including hard-to-find titles. It's the best way to find the books you need!

- ● STAY INFORMED with the latest computer industry news through our online newsletter, press releases, and customized Information SuperLibrary Reports.

- ● GET FAST ANSWERS to your questions about MCP books and software.

- ● VISIT our online bookstore for the latest information and editions!

- ● COMMUNICATE with our expert authors through e-mail and conferences.

- ● DOWNLOAD SOFTWARE from the immense MCP library:
    - Source code and files from MCP books
    - The best shareware, freeware, and demos

- ● DISCOVER HOT SPOTS on other parts of the Internet.

- ● WIN BOOKS in ongoing contests and giveaways!

TO PLUG INTO MCP: ➤

GOPHER: gopher.mcp.com

FTP: ftp.mcp.com

WORLD WIDE WEB: **http://www.mcp.com**

WANT MORE INFORMATION?

CHECK OUT THESE RELATED TOPICS OR SEE YOUR LOCAL BOOKSTORE

CAD and 3D Studio

As the number one CAD publisher in the world, and as a Registered Publisher of Autodesk, New Riders Publishing provides unequaled content on this complex topic. Industry-leading products include AutoCAD and 3D Studio.

Networking

As the leading Novell NetWare publisher, New Riders Publishing delivers cutting-edge products for network professionals. We publish books for all levels of users, from those wanting to gain NetWare Certification, to those administering or installing a network. Leading books in this category include *Inside NetWare 3.12*, *CNE Training Guide: Managing NetWare Systems*, *Inside TCP/IP*, and *NetWare: The Professional Reference*.

Graphics

New Riders provides readers with the most comprehensive product tutorials and references available for the graphics market. Best-sellers include *Inside CorelDRAW! 5*, *Inside Photoshop 3*, and *Adobe Photoshop NOW!*

Internet and Communications

As one of the fastest growing publishers in the communications market, New Riders provides unparalleled information and detail on this ever-changing topic area. We publish international best-sellers such as *New Riders' Official Internet Yellow Pages, 2nd Edition*, a directory of over 10,000 listings of Internet sites and resources from around the world, and *Riding the Internet Highway, Deluxe Edition*.

Operating Systems

Expanding off our expertise in technical markets, and driven by the needs of the computing and business professional, New Riders offers comprehensive references for experienced and advanced users of today's most popular operating systems, including *Understanding Windows 95*, *Inside Unix*, *Inside Windows 3.11 Platinum Edition*, *Inside OS/2 Warp Version 3*, and *Inside MS-DOS 6.22*.

Other Markets

Professionals looking to increase productivity and maximize the potential of their software and hardware should spend time discovering our line of products for Word, Excel, and Lotus 1-2-3. These titles include *Inside Word 6 for Windows*, *Inside Excel 5 for Windows*, *Inside 1-2-3 Release 5*, and *Inside WordPerfect for Windows*.

Orders/Customer Service **1-800-653-6156**   Source Code **NRP95**

New Riders Publishing   201 West 103rd Street ◆ Indianapolis, Indiana 46290 USA

Name _____ Title _____

Company _____ Type of business _____

Address _____

City/State/ZIP _____

Have you used these types of books before?   ☐ yes   ☐ no

If yes, which ones? _____
_____

How many computer books do you purchase each year?   ☐ 1–5   ☐ 6 or more

How did you learn about this book? _____

Where did you purchase this book? _____

Which applications do you currently use? _____
_____

Which computer magazines do you subscribe to? _____
_____

What trade shows do you attend? _____
_____

Comments: _____
_____
_____

Would you like to be placed on our preferred mailing list?   ☐ yes   ☐ no

☐ **I would like to see my name in print!** You may use my name and quote me in future New Riders products and promotions. My daytime phone number is: _____

New Riders Publishing   201 West 103rd Street ◆ Indianapolis, Indiana 46290 USA

Fax to **317-581-4670**   Orders/Customer Service **1-800-653-6156**   Source Code **NRP95**

Fold Here

BUSINESS REPLY MAIL
FIRST-CLASS MAIL PERMIT NO. 9918 INDIANAPOLIS IN

POSTAGE WILL BE PAID BY THE ADDRESSEE

**NEW RIDERS PUBLISHING
201 W 103RD ST
INDIANAPOLIS IN 46290-9058**